The Vatican
and Homosexuality

THE VATICAN
AND HOMOSEXUALITY

Reactions to the "Letter to the Bishops of
the Catholic Church on the
Pastoral Care of Homosexual Persons"

Edited by
Jeannine Gramick
and
Pat Furey

CROSSROAD · NEW YORK

1988

The Crossroad Publishing Company
370 Lexington Avenue, New York, N.Y. 10017

Printed in the United States of America

Library of Congress Cataloging-in-Publication Data

The Vatican and homosexuality : reactions to the "Letter to the
bishops of the Catholic Church on the pastoral care of homosexual
persons" / edited by Jeannine Gramick and Pat Furey.
    p.   cm.
ISBN 0-8245-0864-5
    1. Homosexuality—Religious aspects—Catholic Church. 2. Gay
—Pastoral counseling of. 3. Catholic Church—Doctrines.
I. Gramick, Jeannine. II. Furey, Pat
BX1795.H66V38   1988
259'.0880664—dc19   87

Acknowledgments

"The Vatican Can Slight Scripture for Its Purpose," by Dan Grippo, has been
reprinted by permission of the *National Catholic Reporter*, P.O. Box 419281,
Kansas City, MO 64141.

"Toward an Understanding of the Letter 'On the Pastoral Care of Homosexual
Persons,'" by Archbishop John R. Quinn," has been reprinted by permission
of America Press, Inc., 106 W. 56th St., New York, NY 10019. All rights
reserved. © 1987.

To lesbian and gay Catholics throughout the world and to the people who minister with them, that they may know that other members of the Body of Christ experience their pain from the family of faith, stand with them in their struggles to speak their truth, and celebrate their unwavering hope that all may recognize that where Love is, there is God.

"We cannot fulfill our task simply by an uncritical application of solutions designed in past ages for problems which have qualitatively changed, or which did not exist in the past."

> Archbishop John R. Quinn
> Address to the Pope
> San Francisco, 16 September 1987

"I know the Church is not a democracy ruled by popular vote, but I expect to be treated as a mature, educated, responsible adult. Not to question, not to challenge, not to have the authorities involve me in the understanding is to deny my dignity as a person. . . . In my cultural experience, questioning is neither rebellion nor dissent. Rather, it is a desire to participate and is a sign of both love and maturity."

> Mrs. Donna Hanson
> Address to the Pope
> San Francisco, 18 September 1987

"The faithful are more inclined to look at the intrinsic worth of an argument proposed by teachers in the Church, than to accept it on the basis of authority itself. Since so often that teaching touches on areas where many of the faithful have professional competency . . . they wish to be able to contribute through their own professional skills to solving the issues. This demands a new kind of collaboration and a wider range of consultation on the part of the teaching office of the Church."

> Archbishop Rembert Weakland
> Address to the Pope
> San Francisco, 16 September 1987

"When the ordained ministry exercises its teaching role, it needs to listen to the Spirit who speaks through the laity in virtue of their baptism."

> Cardinal George Basil Hume
> Intervention at the Synod of the Laity
> Rome, October 1987

"[W]e recognize that our experience is a place where God speaks and where God reveals God's self. We desire, for ourselves and for all believing women, complete incorporation in the Church. In its critical decision-making responsibility, the Church needs the fulness of women's gifts and the strength of women's commitments. Women, in the company of all God's people who experience the blessings of our Church . . . also contend with sinfulness in our Church. . . . Acknowledging the essential holiness of the Church, nevertheless, we contend with the reality of sin in the Church when we encounter the inability to dialogue with an openness born of love."

Helen Maher Garvey, BVM
Address to the Pope
San Francisco, 17 September 1987

Contents

Contents   · xi

Part III · The Future: Debate and Developments

Introduction

On 31 October 1986, the Vatican released a "Letter to the Bishops of the Catholic Church on the Pastoral Care of Homosexual Persons." The letter itself was dated 1 October and signed by two officials of the Congregation for the Doctrine of the Faith. The full text of the letter is printed in this volume, and the reader is urged to consider that document carefully before proceeding to the other contributions which critique, analyze, and discuss the implications of the Vatican letter.

The appearance of the document did not come as a surprise to those who were aware of rumors, which had been circulating for at least a year, that the Vatican was working on a statement on homosexuality. In fact, it was supposed to have appeared sooner. Apparently the version that had been drawn up did not go much beyond *Persona Humana,* the 1975 "Declaration on Certain Questions Concerning Sexual Ethics," and so it was decided to postpone publication.

In the meantime the Vatican had already issued the document on liberation theology (1984) and was also preparing one on the moral aspects of certain technologies for procreation. The latter appeared in 1987 less than four months after the document on homosexuality. The same Congregation has also been working on another document, one dealing with principles of fundamental moral theology.

Since 1975 the issue of homosexuality has grown slowly in the consciousness of the Church as one of the issues requiring a more adequate response than that given in the declaration on sexual ethics of that year. The recent letter on pastoral care acknowledges that the declaration, and its interpretation in some quarters, was a catalyst for a more expanded treatment of the subject. There were other factors that prompted the writing of the Vatican letter, such as theological and pastoral initiatives being undertaken in various parts of the world. In several countries, but especially in the United States, there was a good deal of ferment in Catholic circles between 1975 and 1985 around the issue of homosexuality. Not only individual theologians and educators but also individual bishops and state conferences of bishops were writing on the subject. In 1976 Bishop Francis Mugavero issued a pastoral letter on sexuality which, while upholding the norm of heterosexuality, judged other orientations rather mildly in stating that they respected "less adequately" the full spectrum of human relationships. In the same year the U.S. bishops in a pastoral letter on moral values adopted a strong stance in favor of civil rights for homosexual people, encouraged them to have an "active role" in the Christian community, and urged the Christian community to provide homosexual people with a "special degree of pastoral understanding and care."

In 1976 the Catholic community also saw the publication of John McNeill's *The Church and the Homosexual,* a book that signaled the opening of a period of lively and vigorous discussion and debate on the topic. Although McNeill had waited for several years for permission to publish the work, the intense interest it stirred in all quarters led to his eventual silencing for ten years. In 1987 he was expelled from the Jesuits when he broke the ban on speaking and writing by denouncing the CDF letter and announcing his intention to challenge once again the magisterial position on homosexuality.

One year later in 1977 two important theological works appeared in the United States both of which broke new ground in the theological and pastoral approaches to homosexuality. The first of these was a report from the Committee on the Study of Human Sexuality of the Catholic Theological Society of America, which argued for support of committed homosexual relationships as consonant with the book's criteria for genital expression of "creative growth towards integration." Philip Keane's *Sexual Morality: A Catholic Perspective* also argued for the acceptance of homogenital expression based on the principles of proportionalism. Although both works were criticized by church authorities and academic peers, their conclusions were widely received and affirmed by the majority of mainline contemporary theologians. On a more popular level, Richard Woods's *Another Kind of Love* began to explore the relationship between homosexuality and spirituality.

In 1979 the Catholic Council for Church and Society, an agency of the bishops of the Netherlands, published *Homosexual People in Society* as a discussion guide for grass-roots Catholics. The work dealt mostly with societal discrimination and biblical texts, but also wondered aloud whether there were any valid reasons for the condemnation of all homogenital expression.

Also in 1979 the Catholic Social Welfare Commission of the bishops of

England and Wales published *An Introduction to the Pastoral Care of Homosexual People,* containing balanced and reasonable guidelines for ministry with homosexual people. In this document pastors are counseled to distinguish between "irresponsible indiscriminate sexual activity and the permanent association between two homosexual persons who feel incapable of enduring a solitary life devoid of sexual expression." It also stated that in questions of sacramental absolution and holy communion the pastor can be guided by the general principles of fundamental moral theology. These principles recognize that in the face of an invincible doubt of law or fact one is permitted to follow a true and solidly probable opinion in favor of a more liberal interpretation. The Vatican was not happy with this document. Since its publication continued pressure has been put on the English hierarchy to issue a revised and much less lenient version more in keeping with the tone and direction of the CDF letter. A new and more stringent draft has already been drawn up but was withdrawn from the agenda of the national meeting of bishops after it received strong criticisms from people who were consulted privately about its content.

The year 1980 brought the publication of *Christianity, Social Tolerance, and Homosexuality* by a young medieval historian at Yale University, Dr. John Boswell. Boswell argues that church attitudes and policies about homosexuality have not always been harsh and rigid, that the classical scriptural texts used for the traditional condemnation of homosexuality will not bear the weight put upon them, and that religious life has always provided a comfortable and accepting environment for homosexual people.

In 1981 the Archdiocese of Baltimore established one of the first official diocesan ministries for lesbian and gay Catholics after issuing a theological rationale for such a ministry. The statement said that the homosexual orientation is "in no way held to be a sinful condition" and that like heterosexuality it represents the starting point for one's response to Christ. In the same year New Ways Ministry, a national Catholic gay and lesbian ministry group established in 1977, sponsored the first national symposium on homosexuality and the Catholic Church in Washington, D.C. The papers from this event appeared in 1983 in a book titled *Homosexuality and the Catholic Church.*

Also in 1983 the Archdiocese of San Francisco issued the first comprehensive pastoral plan for ministry with homosexual people. For the first time in an official Catholic document the homosexual orientation was judged not to be in all cases "truncated sexual development." The same statement declared that it is important "to carefully interpret the meaning of [homo]sexual activity in this person's life; that is, to understand the pattern of life in which sexual activity takes place and to take into consideration the meaning that these sexual acts have for different people."

Again in 1983 the Washington State Catholic Conference, consisting of the bishops of three dioceses of Washington State, published *Prejudice against Homosexuals and the Ministry of the Church*. In this far-reaching work on discrimination, the bishops suggested that Catholic teaching on homosexuality needs "rethinking and development." They also urged the Church to undertake "ongoing theological research and criticism, with regard to its own theological tradition on homosexuality, none of which is infallibly taught." Archbishop Raymond Hunthausen, one of the Washington bishops, also welcomed Dignity, the organization for Catholic homosexual people and friends, to celebrate its biannual convention mass in the Seattle cathedral that same year. When Hunthausen was later relieved of some of his authority in certain areas of diocesan life, this decision was used by Roman authorities as a reason, among others, for appointing an auxiliary to oversee ministry to homosexual people.

In 1983 there also appeared an anthology of theological and pastoral articles on homosexuality titled *A Challenge to Love: Gay and Lesbian Catholics in the Church*. Although the work received favorable reviews and contained an introduction by the ordinary of an East Coast diocese, the Vatican tried unsuccessfully to prevent the work from being reprinted after the first printing. It did succeed, however, in forcing the bishop to have his name removed from the book's jacket.

In 1985 the Archdiocesan Gay and Lesbian Outreach of the Archdiocese of Baltimore published *Homosexuality: A Positive Catholic Perspective*. The booklet's question-and-answer format presented succinct and current information from several related fields in such a way as to promote a positive attitude toward homosexual people. Although the work did not deny magisterial teaching on homogenital expression, its positive approach aroused the concern of some church authorities and subsequently the booklet was withdrawn from publication by the archbishop of Baltimore, though it was never officially repudiated.

In the meantime support groups and organizations of Catholic homosexual women and men were springing up in many countries. Dignity, the largest such organization, was established in 1969 and grew to some five thousand members with a hundred or more chapters in the United States, many of which were holding services in Catholic facilities. In Australia, Affirmation was performing a similar function though on a much smaller scale. In Great Britain an organization called Quest managed to maintain a workable and friendly relationship with the hierarchy there and to avoid any semblance of a confrontational stance. In Italy groups like Il Guado, David e Gionata, and Omosessuali Credenti stressed religious and theological concerns not addressed by the many political and social groups there. In France David and Jonathan spread quickly throughout the country to serve the needs of gay and lesbian Christians, most of whom were Catholic. In Holland such groups have long existed although always of an ecumenical character and including gay clergy and those engaged in theological research or pastoral ministry.

Other organizations were also mushrooming in the United States. Some of these like Dignity and the Conference for Catholic Lesbians offered direct support to gay and lesbian Catholics. Others such as Communications Ministry, Inc., Christian Community Association, and Rest, Renewal and Re-Creation aided gay clergy and religious. Still other groups such as New Ways Ministry, SIGMA (Sisters in Gay Ministry Associated), and the Consultation on Homosexuality, Social Justice, and Roman Catholic Theology promoted dialogue and offered resources to the heterosexual as well as homosexual communities.

Reactions to the Vatican letter in the United States were, as might have been expected, swift and strong. One prominent Catholic and former Trappist monk writing for the *Washington Post* dismissed the document as "homophobic rantings." A more dispassionate and scholarly response contained in this volume came from the archbishop of San Francisco. Very few U. S. bishops commented on the letter, and at their annual meeting in November of 1986 the National Conference of Catholic Bishops, preoccupied as they were with the Hunthausen affair, scarcely had the time or inclination to deal with another explosive topic.

Few diocesan newspapers carried the complete text of the document other than Philadelphia and Washington, D.C., where such would have been expected. Most were satisfied with running a news story and comments from individuals and groups supporting or criticizing the letter. A coalition of Catholic groups representing gay and lesbian people or those involved in ministry with them called a press conference outside the residence of the papal pronuncio in Washington to issue statements on the letter. Other mainline groups like the Association for the Rights of Catholics in the Church also issued statements critiquing the letter.

In 1987 more detailed commentaries on the letter appeared in Catholic journals, and the letters-to-the-editor columns of the major Catholic papers were filled for weeks with letters, many from gay and lesbian Catholics. In some cities prayers services, candlelight ceremonies, liturgies, and demonstrations were held, mostly by gay and lesbian Catholics to give some outlet to the feelings of pain and rejection that the letter had generated. Plans were laid for gay and lesbian demonstrations during the papal visit. One series of prepapal-visit protests, focusing on women's issues and sponsored by a coalition of Catholic women's groups, at Archbishop Laghi's residence in Washington, D.C., included a day devoted to the concerns of lesbian and gay Catholics. Jeannine Gramick details some of the reactions in her contribution in this work.

Since the publication of the letter Dignity chapters in more than a dozen cities have been expelled from Catholic facilities. In all cases these actions have been taken by bishops as a direct result of the Vatican letter, which instructs bishops to determine for themselves in light of the letter what "interventions" should be taken in their own dioceses. In a few cases negotiations between the chapters and the local bishop have resulted in the chapter's being allowed to continue to meet on Catholic premises. In other cases such as in Chicago, Milwaukee, and San Francisco the chapters have not been expelled nor have they been asked to take an orthodoxy test. The full story of Dignity and the U.S. bishops will be told eventually when a project on that topic that has been undertaken by Catholics Speak Out is completed.

In the meantime, although the dust has settled somewhat on the controversies generated by the letter, the dialogue is by no means ended. The purpose of this work is to make another contribution to the discussion of which the Vatican letter is a crucial component. This is not to imply that the letter is simply one more opinion or another voice in the discussion. As Patrick Granfield points out in *The Limits of the Papacy*, "the teaching of the Church enjoys the presumption of truth; it is not simply one opinion among many, but the authentic voice of the Church guided by the Spirit. . . . A refusal to accept the ordinary noninfallible teaching of the Church should be an exception." Benedict Ashley's contribution in this volume represents an attempt to affirm the Vatican letter in its doctrinal positions and to encourage compassionate pastoral care based on the truth of church teaching.

However, as John Quinn points out in his opening contribution, which models a form of dialogue that this work follows, there are doctrinal affirmations in the Vatican letter and there are affirmations that pertain more or less to the realm of social commentary. Many of the chapters in this book deal with the latter, and some object vigorously to judgments in the letter about civil rights, the nature of pastoral care, and the sources and logic employed to support the letter's contentions. Dan Grippo and Lillanna Kopp discuss the biblical and empirical data respectively, while Robert Nugent explores the Vatican's understanding of the scientific meaning of sexual orientation. Ann Patrick Ware outlines several presuppositions that underlie the letter's approach and which she suggests militate against its reception. John Coleman wonders whether we have adequately clarified the relationship between principles of morality and the responsibility of ecclesial bodies in the area of civil rights. Peter van Gennip develops an understanding of pastoral care that has as its main concern the good of the person rather than the authority of the Church, and from a feminist perspective, Mary Segers questions whether public law ought to reflect the moral theology of the Church. Next, Carolyn Osiek discusses the concept of the common good in the classical Roman law tradition and in the American democratic experience and shows how they differ in their application to the issue of homosexuality.

Other contributors suggest, either directly or indirectly, that even the doctrinal affirmations are not immune from dissent and development. Underlying some of the contributions is the issue of the nature of the teaching authority of the Church and how it is exercised. Again, Granfield offers a pertinent insight: "every Church teaching . . . can be further understood and developed. The entire Church—hierarchy, theologians, and laity—share in the task of grasping more fully and accurately the truth of what the Church teaches."

That there has been development in the Church's teachings on sexuality, though not always in a positive way, is commonly accepted. That there is gradual development even in the teachings on homosexuality is evidenced by James Pollock's article and its implication that this development could go even further. But can this development result in the kind of acceptance that Robert Francoeur, Rosemary Haughton, and John Giles Milhaven suggest from their analyses of differing models of human sexuality and the experiences of lesbian and gay individuals?

There are those who would be satisfied with nothing less than a reversal of the condemnation of homogenital activity. John Quinn suggests that these people are soaring into "realms of fantasy." Such a reversal would surely entail a radically different understanding of human sexuality and of the human person. André Guindon in his analysis of human sexuality as language offers new anthropological and ethical models for dealing with human sexual gestures that could move us in a new direction for understanding both the human person and human sexual language.

Apart from the philosophical and theological issues, several contributors focus on the letter's pastoral implications. Margaret Thompson and Sarah Sherman discuss the impact of the letter on lay people and women religious respectively, while Margaret Traxler reminds us of a group of people affected indirectly but no less negatively because of their hidden status. Peter Hebblethwaite faces head on the crux of the heterosexual norm, but offers practical advice to gay and lesbian Catholics in their efforts to change church teachings. He advises them to cultivate a certain holiness and resist responding to the letter with anger and hatred.

It makes little sense to place full responsibility for the letter on Cardinal Ratzinger. According to an American priest who works in the Vatican, Ratzinger "is doing only what the pope himself wants done. He does not operate in a vacuum." This is apparently confirmed by Ronald Modras's careful analyses of the thought of John Paul II in the area of sexuality which shows up so clearly in the Vatican letter.

Peter Harris stresses the personal response of gay and lesbian Catholics to the letter and urges homosexual people to understand what real liberation means for them and for the Church as well. Joan Timmerman attempts to situate the letter in its proper framework and reminds us that chastity as a virtue has never been identified with abstinence from all sexual activity. Timmerman also discusses the relationship between sexuality and sacramentality and the need for the Church to overcome false dualities.

The opening paragraph of the Vatican letter refers to the current public debate about homosexuality that is occurring "even in Catholic circles." But is the Vatican willing to enter at all into this debate or dialogue beyond its present contribution? By her brief account of nineteenth- and twentieth-century theological development, Mary Jo Weaver contends that the Vatican would prefer to close the debate, although it states that the complexity of the issue calls for "attentive study, active concern and honest, theologically well-balanced counsel." William Shannon congratulates Quinn for speaking aloud his concerns about the Vatican letter. We congratulate Shannon in his courage in raising the crucial issue of the relationships among the teaching authority of Rome, the teaching authority of individual bishops, and that of regional or national conferences. These questions underlie not only the letter on homosexuality but also the recent statement on AIDS by the Administrative Board of the United States Catholic Conference. A forthcoming document from Rome on the status of bishops' conferences will provide more material for a continuing discussion of this important ecclesial issue.

These articles are meant to be a contribution to the lively debate about homosexuality that has been taking place in Catholic circles for many years and that shows no signs of abating. It is our hope that the discussion will always proceed with full respect for persons and for the nature and mission of the Church and its ministry of teaching.

Homosexuality is a complex human reality not easily admitting of simplistic analyses either pastoral or theological. Fundamentally it has to do with the meaning of human sexuality and personhood. For those of us in the Christian and Catholic traditions, the accepted wisdom exerts a strong and powerful influence. A questioning of this wisdom can serve both to clarify and to reinforce the tradition but also to modify and to develop it. The current discussion and debate is but one point on a long historical continuum. Its final outcome lies far beyond the horizon of the participants of the discourse. May our modest efforts be a positive part of that story.

Jeannine Gramick
Pat Furey

Congregation for the Doctrine of the Faith

Letter to the Bishops of the Catholic Church on the Pastoral Care of Homosexual Persons

1. The issue of homosexuality and the moral evaluation of homosexual acts have increasingly become a matter of public debate, even in Catholic circles. Since this debate often advances arguments and makes assertions inconsistent with the teaching of the Catholic Church, it is quite rightly a cause for concern to all engaged in the pastoral ministry, and this Congregation has judged it to be of sufficiently grave and widespread importance to address to the Bishops of the Catholic Church this Letter on the Pastoral Care of Homosexual Persons.

2. Naturally, an exhaustive treatment of this complex issue cannot be attempted here, but we will focus our reflection within the distinctive context of the Catholic moral perspective. It is a perspective which finds support in the more secure findings of the natural sciences, which have their own legitimate and proper methodology and field of inquiry.

However, the Catholic moral viewpoint is founded on human reason illumined by faith and is consciously motivated by the desire to do the will of God our Father. The Church is thus in a position to learn from scientific discovery but also to transcend the horizons of science and to be confident that her more global vision does greater justice to the rich reality of the human person in his spiritual and physical dimensions, created by God and heir, by grace, to eternal life.

It is within this context, then, that it can be clearly seen that the phenomenon of homosexuality, complex as it is, and with its many consequences for society and ecclesial life, is a proper focus for the

Church's pastoral care. It thus requires of her ministers attentive study, active concern and honest, theologically well-balanced counsel.

3. Explicit treatment of the problem was given in this Congregation's "Declaration on Certain Questions Concerning Sexual Ethics" of December 29, 1975. That document stressed the duty of trying to understand the homosexual condition and noted that culpability for homosexual acts should only be judged with prudence. At the same time the Congregation took note of the distinction commonly drawn between the homosexual condition or tendency and individual homosexual actions. These were described as deprived of their essential and indispensable finality, as being "intrinsically disordered", and able in no case to be approved of (cf. n. 8, § 4).

In the discussion which followed the publication of the Declaration, however, an overly benign interpretation was given to the homosexual condition itself, some going so far as to call it neutral, or even good. Although the particular inclination of the homosexual person is not a sin, it is a more or less strong tendency ordered toward an intrinsic moral evil; and thus the inclination itself must be seen as an objective disorder.

Therefore special concern and pastoral attention should be directed toward those who have this condition, lest they be led to believe that the living out of this orientation in homosexual activity is a morally acceptable option. It is not.

4. An essential dimension of authentic pastoral care is the identification of causes of confusion regarding the Church's teaching. One is a new exegesis of Sacred Scripture which claims variously that Scripture has nothing to say on the subject of homosexuality, or that it somehow tacitly approves of it, or that all of its moral injunctions are so culture-bound that they are no longer applicable to contemporary life. These views are gravely erroneous and call for particular attention here.

5. It is quite true that the Biblical literature owes to the different epochs in which it was written a good deal of its varied patterns of thought and expression (*Dei Verbum* 12). The Church today addresses the Gospel to a world which differs in many ways from ancient days. But the world in which the New Testament was written was already quite diverse from the situation in which the Sacred Scriptures of the Hebrew People had been written or compiled, for example.

What should be noticed is that, in the presence of such remarkable diversity, there is nevertheless a clear consistency within the Scriptures themselves on the moral issue of homosexual behaviour. The Church's doctrine regarding this issue is thus based, not on isolated phrases for facile theological argument, but on the solid foundation of a constant Biblical testimony. The community of faith today, in unbroken continuity with the Jewish and Christian communities within which the ancient Scriptures were written, continues to be nourished by those same Scriptures and by the Spirit of Truth whose Word they are. It is likewise essential to recognize that the Scriptures are not properly understood when they are interpreted in a way which contradicts the Church's living Tradition. To be correct, the interpretation of Scripture must be in substantial accord with that Tradition.

The Vatican Council II in *Dei Verbum* 10, put it this way: "It is clear, therefore, that in the supremely wise arrangement of God, sacred Tradition, sacred Scripture, and the Magisterium of the Church are so connected and associated that one of them cannot stand without the others. Working together, each in its own way under the action of the one Holy Spirit, they all contribute effectively to the salvation of souls". In that spirit we wish to outline briefly the Biblical teaching here.

6. Providing a basic plan for understanding this entire discussion of homosexuality is the theology of creation we find in Genesis. God, in his infinite wisdom and love, brings into existence all of reality as a reflection of his goodness. He fashions mankind, male and female, in his own image and likeness. Human beings, therefore, are nothing less than the work of God himself; and in the complementarity of the sexes, they are called to reflect the inner unity of the Creator. They do this in a striking way in their cooperation with him in the transmission of life by a mutual donation of the self to the other.

In Genesis 3, we find that this truth about persons being an image of God has been obscured by original sin. There inevitably follows a loss of awareness of the covenantal character of the union these persons had with God and with each other. The human body retains its "spousal significance" but this is now clouded by sin. Thus, in Genesis 19:1–11, the deterioration due to sin continues in the story of the men of Sodom. There can be no doubt of the moral judgement made there against homosexual relations. In Leviticus 18:22 and 20:13, in the course of describing the conditions necessary for belonging to the Chosen People, the author excludes from the People of God those who behave in a homosexual fashion.

Against the background of this exposition of theocratic law, an eschatological perspective is developed by St. Paul when, in 1 Cor. 6:9, he proposes the same doctrine and lists those who behave in a homosexual fashion among those who shall not enter the Kingdom of God.

In Romans 1:18–32, still building on the moral traditions of his forebears, but in the new context of the confrontation between Christianity and the pagan society of his day, Paul uses homosexual behaviour as an example of the blindness which has overcome humankind. Instead of the original harmony between Creator and creatures, the acute distortion of idolatry has led to all kinds of moral excess. Paul is at a loss to find a clearer example of this disharmony than homosexual relations. Finally, 1 Tim. 1, in full continuity with the Biblical position, singles out those who spread wrong doctrine and in v. 10 explicitly names as sinners those who engage in homosexual acts.

7. The Church, obedient to the Lord who founded her and gave to her the sacramental life, celebrates the divine plan of the loving and live-giving union of men and women in the sacrament of marriage. It is only in the marital relationship that the use of the sexual faculty can be morally good. A person engaging in homosexual behaviour therefore acts immorally.

To chose someone of the same sex for one's sexual activity is to annul the rich symbolism and meaning, not to mention the goals, of the Creator's sexual design. Homosexual activity is not a complementary union, able to transmit life; and so it thwarts the call to a life of that form of self-giving which the Gospel says is the essence of Christian living. This does not mean that homosexual persons are not often generous and giving of themselves; but when they engage in homosexual activity they confirm within themselves a disordered sexual inclination which is essentially self-indulgent.

As in every moral disorder, homosexual activity prevents one's own fulfillment and happiness by acting contrary to the creative wisdom of God. The Church, in rejecting erroneous opinions regarding homosexuality, does not limit but rather defends personal freedom and dignity realistically and authentically understood.

8. Thus, the Church's teaching today is in organic continuity with the Scriptural perspective and with her own constant Tradition. Though today's world is in many ways quite new, the Christian community senses the profound and lasting bonds which join us to those generations who have gone before us, "marked with the sign of faith".

Nevertheless, increasing numbers of people today, even within the Church, are bringing enormous pressure to bear on the Church to accept the homosexual condition as though it were not disordered and to condone homosexual activity. Those within the Church who argue in this fashion often have close ties with those with similar views outside it. These latter groups are guided by a vision opposed to the truth about the human person, which is fully disclosed in the mystery of Christ. They reflect, even if not entirely consciously, a materialistic ideology which denies the transcendent nature of the human person as well as the supernatural vocation of every individual.

The Church's ministers must ensure that homosexual persons in their care will not be misled by this point of view, so profoundly opposed to the teaching of the Church. But the risk is great and there are many who seek to create confusion regarding the Church's position, and then to use that confusion to their own advantage.

9. The movement within the Church, which takes the form of pressure groups of various names and sizes, attempts to give the impression that it represents all homosexual persons who are Catholics. As a matter of fact, its membership is by and large restricted to those who either ignore the teaching of the Church or seek somehow to undermine it. It brings together under the aegis of Catholicism homosexual persons who have no intention of abandoning their homosexual behaviour. One tactic used is to protest that any and all criticism of or reservations about homosexual people, their activity and lifestyle, are simply diverse forms of unjust discrimination.

There is an effort in some countries to manipulate the Church by gaining the often well-intentioned support of her pastors with a view to changing civil-statutes and laws. This is done in order to conform to these pressure groups' concept that homosexuality is at least a completely harmless, if not an entirely good, thing. Even when the practice of homosexuality may seriously threaten the lives and well-being of a large number of people, its advocates remain undeterred and refuse to consider the magnitude of the risks involved.

The Church can never be so callous. It is true that her clear position cannot be revised by pressure from civil legislation or the trend of the moment. But she is really concerned about the many who are not represented by the pro-homosexual movement and about those who may have been tempted to believe its deceitful propaganda. She is also aware that the view that homosexual activity is equivalent to, or as acceptable as, the sexual expression of conjugal love has a direct impact on society's understanding of the nature and rights of the family and puts them in jeopardy.

10. It is deplorable that homosexual persons have been and are the object of violent malice in speech or in action. Such treatment deserves condemnation from the Church's pastors wherever it occurs. It reveals a kind

of disregard for others which endangers the most fundamental principles of a healthy society. The intrinsic dignity of each person must always be respected in word, in action and in law.

But the proper reaction to crimes committed against homosexual persons should not be to claim that the homosexual condition is not disordered. When such a claim is made and when homosexual activity is consequently condoned, or when civil legislation is introduced to protect behavior to which no one has any conceivable right, neither the Church nor society at large should be surprised when other distorted notions and practices gain ground, and irrational and violent reactions increase.

11. It has been argued that the homosexual orientation in certain cases is not the result of deliberate choice; and so the homosexual person would then have no choice but to behave in a homosexual fashion. Lacking freedom, such a person, even if engaged in homosexual activity, would not be culpable.

Here, the Church's wise moral tradition is necessary since it warns against generalizations in judging individual cases. In fact, circumstances may exist, or may have existed in the past, which would reduce or remove the culpability of the individual in a given instance; or other circumstances may increase it. What is at all costs to be avoided is the unfounded and demeaning assumption that the sexual behaviour of homosexual persons is always and totally compulsive and therefore inculpable. What is essential is that the fundamental liberty which characterizes the human person and gives him his dignity be recognized as belonging to the homosexual person as well. As in every conversion from evil, the abandonment of homosexual activity will require a profound collaboration of the individual with God's liberating grace.

12. What, then, are homosexual persons to do who seek to follow the Lord? Fundamentally, they are called to enact the will of God in their life by joining whatever sufferings and difficulties they experience in virtue of their condition to the sacrifice of the Lord's Cross. That Cross, for the believer, is a fruitful sacrifice since from that death come life and redemption. While any call to carry the cross or to understand a Christian's suffering in this way will predictably be met with bitter ridicule by some, it should be remembered that this is the way to eternal life for *all* who follow Christ.

It is, in effect, none other than the teaching of Paul the Apostle to the Galatians when he says that the Spirit produces in the lives of the faithful "love, joy, peace, patience, kindness, goodness, trustfulness, gentleness and self-control" (5:22) and further (v. 24), "You cannot belong to Christ unless you crucify all self-indulgent passions and desires."

It is easily misunderstood, however, if it is merely seen as a pointless effort at self-denial. The Cross *is* a denial of self, but in service to the will of God himself who makes life come from death and empowers those who trust in him to practise virtue in place of vice.

To celebrate the Paschal Mystery, it is necessary to let that Mystery become imprinted in the fabric of daily life. To refuse to sacrifice one's own will in obedience to the will of the Lord is effectively to prevent salvation. Just as the Cross was central to the expression of God's redemptive love for us in Jesus, so the conformity of the self-denial of homosexual men and women with the sacrifice of the Lord will constitute for them a source of self-giving which will save them from a way of life which constantly threatens to destroy them.

Christians who are homosexual are called, as all of us are, to a chaste life. As they dedicate their lives to understanding the nature of God's personal call to them, they will be able to celebrate the Sacrament of Penance more faithfully and receive the Lord's grace so freely offered there in order to convert their lives more fully to his Way.

13. We recognize, of course, that in great measure the clear and successful communication of the Church's teaching to all the faithful, and to society at large, depends on the correct instruction and fidelity of her pastoral ministers. The Bishops have the particularly grave responsibility to see to it that their assistants in the ministry, above all the priests, are rightly informed and personally disposed to bring the teaching of the Church in its integrity to everyone.

The characteristic concern and good will exhibited by many clergy and religious in their pastoral care for homosexual persons is admirable, and, we hope, will not diminish. Such devoted ministers should have the confidence that they are faithfully following the will of the Lord by encouraging the homosexual person to lead a chaste life and by affirming that person's God-given dignity and worth.

14. With this in mind, this Congregation wishes to ask the Bishops to be especially cautious of any programmes which may seek to pressure the Church to change her teaching, even while claiming not to do so. A careful examination of their public statements and the activities they promote reveals a studied ambiguity by which they attempt to mislead the pastors and the faithful. For example, they may present the teaching of the Magisterium, but only as if it were an optional source for the formation of

one's conscience. Its specific authority is not recognized. Some of these groups will use the word "Catholic" to describe either the organization or its intended members, yet they do not defend and promote the teaching of the Magisterium; indeed, they even openly attack it. While their members may claim a desire to conform their lives to the teaching of Jesus, in fact they abandon the teaching of his Church. This contradictory action should not have the support of the Bishops in any way.

15. We encourage the Bishops, then, to provide pastoral care in full accord with the teaching of the Church for homosexual persons of their dioceses. No authentic pastoral programme will include organizations in which homosexual persons associate with each other without clearly stating that homosexual activity is immoral. A truly pastoral approach will appreciate the need for homosexual persons to avoid the near occasions of sin.

We would heartily encourage programmes where these dangers are avoided. But we wish to make it clear that departure from the Church's teaching, or silence about it, in an effort to provide pastoral care is neither caring nor pastoral. Only what is true can ultimately be pastoral. The neglect of the Church's position prevents homosexual men and women from receiving the care they need and deserve.

An authentic pastoral programme will assist homosexual persons at all levels of the spiritual life: through the sacraments, and in particular through the frequent and sincere use of the sacrament of Reconciliation, through prayer, witness, counsel and individual care. In such a way, the entire Christian community can come to recognize its own call to assist its brothers and sisters, without deluding them or isolating them.

16. From this multi-faceted approach there are numerous advantages to be gained, not the least of which is the realization that a homosexual person, as every human being, deeply needs to be nourished at many different levels simultaneously.

The human person, made in the image and likeness of God, can hardly be adequately described by a reductionist reference to his or her sexual orientation. Every one living on the face of the earth has personal problems and difficulties, but challenges to growth, strengths, talents and gifts as well. Today, the Church provides a badly needed context for the care of the human person when she refuses to consider the person as a "heterosexual" or a "homosexual" and insists that every person has a fundamental identity: the creature of God, and by grace, his child and heir to eternal life.

17. In bringing this entire matter to the Bishops' attention, this Congregation wishes to support their efforts to assure that the teaching of the Lord and his Church on this important question be communicated fully to all the faithful.

In light of the points made above, they should decide for their own dioceses the extent to which an intervention on their part is indicated. In addition, should they consider it helpful, further coordinated action at the level of their National Bishops' Conference may be envisioned.

In a particular way, we would ask the Bishops to support, with the means at their disposal, the development of appropriate forms of pastoral care for homosexual persons. These would include the assistance of the psychological, sociological and medical sciences, in full accord with the teaching of the Church.

They are encouraged to call on the assistance of all Catholic theologians who, by teaching what the Church teaches, and by deepening their reflections on the true meaning of human sexuality and Christian marriage with the virtues it engenders, will make an important contribution in this particular area of pastoral care.

The Bishops are asked to exercise special care in the selection of pastoral ministers so that by their own high degree of spiritual and personal maturity and by their fidelity to the Magisterium, they may be of real service to homosexual persons, promoting their health and well-being in the fullest sense. Such ministers will reject theological opinions which dissent from the teaching of the Church and which, therefore, cannot be used as guidelines for pastoral care.

We encourage the Bishops to promote appropriate catechetical programmes based on the truth about human sexuality in its relationship to the family as taught by the Church. Such programmes should provide a good context within which to deal with the question of homosexuality.

This catechesis would also assist those families of homosexual persons to deal with this problem which affects them so deeply.

All support should be withdrawn from any organizations which seek to undermine the teaching of the Church, which are ambiguous about it, or which neglect it entirely. Such support, or even the semblance of such support, can be gravely misinterpreted. Special attention should be given to the practice of scheduling religious services and to the use of Church buildings by these groups, including the facilities of Catholic schools and colleges. To some, such permission to use Church property may seem only just and charitable; but in reality it is contradictory to the purpose for which these institutions were founded, it is misleading and often scandalous.

In assessing proposed legislation, the Bishops should keep as their uppermost concern the responsibility to defend and promote family life.

18. The Lord Jesus promised, "You shall know the truth and the truth shall set you free" (Jn. 8:32). Scripture bids us speak the truth in love (cf. Eph. 4:15). The God who is at once truth and love calls the Church to minister to every man, woman and child with the pastoral solicitude of our compassionate Lord. It is in this spirit that we have addressed this Letter to the Bishops of the Church, with the hope that it will be of some help as they care for those whose suffering can only be intensified by error and lightened by truth.

During an audience granted to the undersigned Prefect, His Holiness, Pope John Paul II, approved this Letter, adopted in an ordinary session of the Congregation for the Doctrine of the Faith, and ordered it to be published.

Given at Rome, 1 October 1986.

JOSEPH CARDINAL RATZINGER
Prefect

ALBERTO BOVONE
Titular Archbishop of Caesarea in Numidia
Secretary

Part I
THE DOCUMENT:
ANALYSES AND CRITIQUES

1
Toward an Understanding of the Letter "On the Pastoral Care of Homosexual Persons"

John R. Quinn

Widespread attention was given recently to a document from the Congregation for the Doctrine of the Faith entitled "Letter to the Bishops of the Catholic Church on the Pastoral Care of Homosexual Persons" (1986). A good deal of comment was negative, especially on the part of those who read the document as condemnatory of homosexual persons.

At the outset, it should be noted that the document is in the form of a letter and is addressed to the bishops of the Catholic Church. It is not addressed to the general public and, consequently, is not written in popular, everyday language but in technical, precise language. On the one hand, this contributes to the clarity of the document, yet, paradoxically, it also contributes to its obscurity. Clear, technical language is not likely to be understood correctly by those who are not familiar with it.

In assessing the letter, we should note that it has been approved, as theologians say, *in forma communi*. This means that although Pope John Paul II has approved the document, it is not a document of the pope but a document of the Congregation for the Doctrine of the Faith. Nevertheless, it is an authentic teaching of the Holy See, and for this reason it carries weight apart from the merit of its intrinsic arguments precisely by reason of the formal authority of the Apostolic See. It is an act of the teaching Church and cannot be regarded simply as just another theological opinion.

Having an objective understanding of such a document according to the mind of the Church is important. Hence it is appropriate to ask: What kind of assent does such a document require? An examination of the letter reveals that it contains affirmations of different kinds. For instance, some affirmations are of a doctrinal nature and represent the constant teaching of the Church. An example of this kind of affirmation would be the statement: "It is only in the marital relationship that the use of the sexual faculty can be morally good. A person engaging in homosexual behavior therefore acts immorally" (no. 7).

On the other hand, there are affirmations that are not of a doctrinal nature but pertain more or less to the realm of social commentary. An example of this kind of affirmation would be that "[When] homosexual activity is consequently condoned, or when civil legislation is introduced to protect behavior to which no one has any conceivable right, neither the church nor society at large should be surprised when other distorted notions and practices gain ground, and irrational and violent reactions increase" (no. 10). Clearly these are different kinds of affirmation that do not call for the same measure of assent. The former is a witness to the constant moral teaching of the Church. The latter is a judgment about the social effects of certain ways of thinking or acting.

Given this necessary distinction, the document as such does not claim to be *de fide*. It is not a dogmatic definition. Still, as an authentic teaching of the magisterium it does lay claim to internal and respectful assent, particularly in those matters that are doctrinal in character and witness to the constant teaching of the Church.

Central moral affirmations. The central moral affirmation of the letter is: "It is only in the marital relationship that the use of the sexual faculty can be morally good. A person engaging in homosexual behavior therefore acts immorally" (no. 7). Of course, in virtue of this principle, those who commit adultery or who engage in heterosexual behavior before marriage also act immorally.

This principle is based on two biblical foundations. The first is the creation narrative in Genesis in which man and woman are created as complementary, each destined for the other. This reveals God's plan for creation. The differentiation of the sexes is meant for the union of the two in the service of life and love. The second foundation of the letter's teaching is found in three Old Testament and three New Testament texts that explicitly condemn homosexual acts. The understanding of these texts has been a constant in the moral tradition of the Church. The most recent biblical scholarship also supports this understanding. For instance, Richard B. Hays, writing in the *Journal of Religious Ethics* (Spring 1986), makes a detailed analysis of the first chapter of Romans. He concludes that the condemnation of homosexual acts is here beyond question and that this is the consistent stance of the Scriptures.

Consequently, the Church cannot be faulted for its teaching on the grounds that such teaching is in conflict with Scripture or with the best contemporary exegesis. It should be clear from these indications that those who entertain the hope that the Church will alter its moral teaching on homosexuality or that it can be forced to do so through various forms of pressure are soaring into the realms of fantasy.

Scope of the letter. Given the clarity of its moral teaching, what is the scope of the letter? Its second paragraph begins: "Naturally, an exhaustive treatment of this complex issue cannot be attempted here." Hence the letter itself indicates that its scope is limited; some things are left unsaid.

Furthermore, the word *complex* is used twice in the same paragraph, indicating that the subject is not dealt with easily. For this reason, it states that the Church requires of its ministers "attentive study, active concern and honest, theologically well-balanced counsel." It further states that "the Church is thus in a position to learn from scientific discovery." In other words, there is more to be learned at the empirical level. Nevertheless, the moral teaching of the Church, based in the Scriptures, must be the basis of understanding "the phenomenon of homosexuality, complex as it is."

Positive affirmations. Because the letter was reported in such a negative way and created such a bitter reaction in some areas, I believe it will be helpful to point out some of its many positive aspects. Among the positive affirmations found in the letter are these:

"The particular inclination of the homosexual person is not a sin" (no. 3).

"Homosexual persons are often generous and giving of themselves" (no. 3).

"It is deplorable that homosexual persons have been and are the object of violent malice in speech or in action. Such treatment deserves condemnation from the Church's pastors wherever it occurs . . . [and] the intrinsic dignity of each person must always be respected in word, in action and in law" (no. 10).

"What is essential is that the fundamental liberty that characterizes the human person and gives him his dignity be recognized as belonging to the homosexual person as well" (no. 11).

"The characteristic concern and good will exhibited by many clergy and religious in their pastoral care for homosexual persons is admirable and, we hope, will not diminish" (no. 13).

"A homosexual person, as every human being, deeply needs to be nourished at many different levels simultaneously. . . . The human person, made in the image and likeness of God, can hardly be adequately described by a reductionist reference to his or her sexual orientation. . . .

Today the Church provides a badly needed context for the care of the human person when [it] refuses to consider the person as a 'heterosexual' or a 'homosexual' and insists that every person has a fundamental identity: the creature of God and, by grace, His child and heir to eternal life" (no. 16).

The letter and pastoral practice. The letter's doctrinal and biblical analysis is complemented by its treatment of pastoral practice. Having ruled out homosexual acts as contrary to the teaching of Scripture and of God's plan for creation, the letter quotes a 1976 document on sexual ethics: "Culpability for homosexual acts should only be judged with prudence" (no. 3).

Then for the first time in a magisterial document, the letter admits the possibility that the homosexual *orientation* may not be "the result of deliberate choice" (no. 11). And having noted this, it continues: "Here, the Church's wise moral tradition is necessary since it warns against generalizations in judging individual cases."

The reason for avoiding generalizations is: "In fact, circumstances may exist, or may have existed in the past, that would reduce or remove the culpability of the individual in a given instance; or other circumstances may increase it" (no. 11).

What is to be avoided is "the unfounded and demeaning assumption that the sexual behavior of homosexual persons is always and totally compulsive and therefore inculpable."

The pastoral stance, then, is to uphold the Church's teaching and, within that framework, to be cautious in judging culpability—avoiding the extremes of saying that there is always culpability or that there is never culpability.

The homosexual orientation. The section of the letter dealing with the homosexual orientation has created one of the most negative reactions. It states; "Although the particular inclination of the homosexual person is not a sin, it is a more or less strong tendency ordered toward an intrinsic moral evil; and thus the inclination itself must be seen as an objective disorder" (no. 3).

This is philosophical language. The inclination is a disorder because it is directed to an object that is disordered. The inclination and the object are in the same order philosphically. But "the particular inclination of the homosexual person is not a sin" (no. 3).

In trying to understand this affirmation, we should advert to two things. First, every person has disordered inclinations. For instance, the inclination to rash judgment is disordered, the inclination to cowardice, the inclination to hypocrisy—these are all disordered inclinations. Consequently, homosexual persons are not the only ones who have disordered inclinations. Second, the letter does not say that the homosexual person is disordered. The inclination, not the person, is described as disordered. Speaking of the homosexual person, the letter states that the Church "refuses to consider the person as a 'heterosexual' or a 'homosexual' and insists that every person has a fundamental identity: the creature of God and, by grace, His child and heir to eternal life" (no. 16). Consequently, the document affirms the spiritual and human dignity of the homosexual *person* while placing a negative moral judgment on homosexual *acts* and a negative philosophical judgment on the homosexual *inclination* or orientation, which it clearly states is not a sin or moral evil.

Why was the letter written? A variety of concerns lay behind and led to the writing of the letter. The letter itself mentions some of them. The increasing public debate about homosexuality, the enunciation of positions that are incompatible with the teaching of the Church, the increasingly positive appraisal of the homosexual orientation used as a basis for a positive appraisal of homosexual acts. But still another source of concern for the Church is that certain militant elements appear to be posing a threat to family life. The Church is fearful of the trivialization of sex and of the trivialization of its relationship to marriage and the family. While the Church does not place all homosexuals in one category, it does want to diminish the harmful effects of some homosexual groups and individuals.

How should homosexual persons be treated? We may find an answer to this question in several documents of the magisterium. I would begin by applying the words of Pope Paul VI in *Humanae Vitae* to homosexual persons. He said: "To diminish in no way the saving teaching of Christ constitutes an eminent form of charity for souls. But this must ever be accompanied by patience and goodness, such as the Lord Himself gave example of in dealing with men. Having come not to condemn but to save, He was indeed intransigent with evil, but merciful toward individuals. In their difficulties, may [homosexual persons] always find, in the words and in the heart of a priest, the echo of the voice and the love of the Redeemer" (no. 29).

Pope John Paul II, addressing a group of bishops from the United States during their ad limina visit (5 September 1983), said:

> In particular, the bishop is a sign of the love of Jesus Christ: He expresses to all individuals and groups of whatever tendency—with a universal charity—the love of the Good Shepherd. His love embraces sinners with an easiness and naturalness that mirrors the redeeming

love of the Savior. To those in need, in trouble and in pain, he offers the love of understanding and consolation. . . .

As a sign of Christ's love, the bishop is also a sign of Christ's compassion, since he represents Jesus the High Priest who is able to sympathize with human weakness, the one who was tempted in every way we are, yet never sinned. The consciousness on the part of the bishop of personal sin, coupled with repentance and with the forgiveness received from the Lord, makes his human expression of compassion even more authentic and credible. . . .

The bishop, precisely because he is compassionate and understands the weakness of humanity and the fact that its needs and aspirations can only be satisfied by the full truth of creation and redemption, will proclaim without fear or ambiguity the many controverted truths of our age. He will proclaim them with pastoral love, in terms that will never unnecessarily offend or alienate his hearers.

And the bishops of the United States wrote in their 1976 pastoral letter "To Live in Christ Jesus": "Some persons find themselves through no fault of their own to have a homosexual orientation. Homosexuals, like everyone else, should not suffer from prejudice against their basic human rights. They have a right to respect, friendship and justice. They should have an active role in the Christian community. Homosexual activity, however, as distinguished from homosexual orientation, is morally wrong. Like heterosexual persons, homosexuals are called to give witness to chastity, avoiding, with God's grace, behavior that is wrong for them, just as nonmarital sexual relations are wrong for heterosexuals. Nonetheless, because heterosexuals can usually look forward to marriage, and homosexuals, while their orientation continues, might not, the Christian community should provide them a special degree of pastoral understanding and care" (no. 52).

Conclusion. Moral norms provide vectors for human behavior and development. Some people reach the minimum and stop. Others move on toward the heights. Others plod along and find it a slow and tedious journey marked by setbacks. Not all measure up perfectly to these norms at all times. But without moral norms it would be a darksome journey. It would be a chaotic journey if the Church's moral teaching were so fluid as to change with every change of viewpoint in secular society.

Pope Paul VI's words, addressed to an international congress in 1970, apply equally well to the struggles of the homosexual person:

It is only little by little that the human being is able to order and integrate his multiple tendencies, to the point of arranging them harmoniously in that virtue of conjugal chastity wherein the couple finds its full human and Christian development. . . . Their conscience demands to be respected, educated and formed in an atmosphere of confidence and not of anguish. The moral laws, far from being inhumanly cold in an abstract objectivity, are there to guide the spouses in their progress. When they truly strive to live the profound demands of holy love, patiently and humbly, without becoming discouraged by failures, then the moral laws . . . are no longer rejected as a hindrance, but recognized as a powerful help.

The final portion of Richard Hays's article, to which I made reference earlier, is most useful. He says: "Certainly any discussion of the normative application of Romans 1 must not neglect the powerful impact of Paul's rhetorical reversal in Rom. 2:1—all of us stand 'without excuse' before God, Jews and Gentiles alike, heterosexuals and homosexuals alike. Thus, Romans 1 should decisively undercut any self-righteous condemnation of homosexual behavior. Those who follow the church's tradition by upholding the authority of Paul's teaching against the morality of homosexual acts must do so with due humility."

2

A Response to
Archbishop Quinn

William H. Shannon

It was with a feeling of hope that I read Archbishop John R. Quinn's comments (first printed in the 7 February 1987 issue of *America*) on the "Letter to the Bishops of the Catholic Church on the Pastoral Care of Homosexual Persons" from the Congregation for the Doctrine of the Faith. My hope stemmed not from the fact that I agreed with everything he said in his article, but from the more important fact that he, as a bishop of the Church, was willing to open a public dialogue about a document that has pained and distressed many people in the Church. It is true that he did not say explicitly that he was inviting dialogue; but the modest, tentative character of his title "Toward an Understanding of the Letter 'On the Pastoral Care of Homosexual Persons' " seemed, to me at least, an implicit call to others in the Church to speak aloud to one another about this letter and even to respond to his remarks about it. It may well be that I am reading into his article something that was not there, but which I found because of the strong feelings I have that dialogue, not just on this issue but on so many issues, is desperately needed in the Church today and yet is so obviously and conspicuously absent. So I do accept with gratitude the call to respond to his article, if indeed he was extending such an invitation. And if this was not his intention, I can only ask his pardon for presuming to make a response that he did not ask for.

The purpose of the archbishop's article, as I read it, was to say all the positive things that could be said about the CDF letter. He wanted to make clear that people should not read the document as "condemnatory of homosexual persons." I honestly respect the efforts he made to point out the affirmations which the document makes, for instance, its insistence on the individual worth and the intrinsic dignity of every person and the need that that dignity "always be respected in word, in action and in law" (no. 10). Yet I feel it necessary to say that, when all the positive

20

affirmations have been given their due, the impression that finally comes through to me from his article is not an enthusiastic endorsement of the CDF letter but an effort to deal with it because it is there. The sense I get is not that he is welcoming a document that might be helpful in the Church's effort to minister to homosexual persons, but attempting to justify one that might well be harmful to ministries that already exist. I ask his pardon if I am misinterpreting his words, but what I seem to hear— perhaps subliminally and perhaps because this is what I choose to hear— is a plea for understanding; "The letter is not really as bad as it sounds. It says some worthwhile things. It's not going to hurt as much as you think."

What was very telling to me is the fact that when he discusses the question "How should homosexual persons be treated?" he makes use of three magisterial statements (two papal and one episcopal), but he quotes absolutely nothing from the CDF letter. Thus he makes use of that marvelously sensitive plea of Pope Paul VI, in *Humanae Vitae,* that God's people may "always find, in the words and in the heart of a priest, the echo of the voice and the love of the Redeemer." He also quotes the moving words of Pope John Paul II, addressed in 1983, to a group of American bishops telling them that as bishops they must be "the sign of Christ's compassion," representing the High Priest "who is able to sympathize with human weakness." Finally, he turns to the pastoral letter of the American bishops "To Live in Christ Jesus" and the call in that document to the Christian community to provide "a special degree of pastoral understanding and care" to homosexual persons. These statements make clear the Church's desire to deal compassionately with homosexual persons. But what is striking is the conspicuous absence from this section of his article of any statement from the CDF letter. Is it not puzzling that there seems to be no "quotable statement" about the pastoral care of homosexual persons in a document which by its title claims explicitly to be dealing with that very subject?

While I can understand his desire to present the CDF letter in as favorable a a light as possible because he would not want it to be divisive in the Church, I must say that I am confused by some aspects of the ecclesiology that seem to emerge. Thus the archbishop claims to see as a significant breakthrough in the understanding of homosexuality—indeed, a "first" in magisterial pronouncements—the concession in the CDF letter that the homosexual condition may be a "given" in some people, and not something they have chosen. He states that "for the first time in a magisterial document, the letter admits the possibility that the homosexual *orientation* may not be 'the result of deliberate choice.'" Yet a number of paragraphs later he quotes from a magisterial statement of the American bishops which said the same thing and was published some ten years earlier. In their 1976 pastoral letter "To Live in Christ Jesus," the American bishops said: "Some persons find themselves through no fault of their own to have a homosexual orientation." It seems to me that "through no fault of their own" (the bishops' pastoral) and "not the result of deliberate choice" (the CDF letter) mean the same thing. And if they do, then it would seem clear that ten years prior to the CDF letter there was a magisterial statement indicating that the homosexual person does not "choose," but rather "discovers" his or her homosexual orientation. And that magisterial statement came from the American bishops.

This brings me to what I believe is the radical ecclesiological question which the archbishop's article seems to bring to light, yet fails to deal with—namely, what is the relationship between the ordinary magisterium of the papal office and the ordinary magisterium of the bishops of the Catholic Church? At the very beginning of his article, he noted that the letter is addressed not to the general public but to the bishops of the Catholic Church. For this reason he points out that one should expect that the language of a letter to bishops will have a different tone from one addressed to a more general audience. I must say that I nodded my head when I read that and presumed he was going to say that a letter written to bishops is written in collegial converse with them. Instead, he tells us that it is written in "technical, precise language" that is "not likely to be understood correctly by those who are not familiar with it." I must say that, if by "technical, precise language" the archbishop means "theological language" and is saying that only bishops are able to understand such language, his judgment seems uninformed and, if I may be excused for saying so, extremely condescending. If, on the other hand, he is suggesting that there is a special kind of knowledge and speech that only bishops are privy to, this seems dangerously close to the kind of gnosticism (a special knowledge unrooted in and transcending human experience and possessed only by a select few) that the Church has had to struggle against almost from the very beginning.

Deeper than the problem of whether or not bishops possess a "special language" which they alone understand is the ecclesial question: What happens when "magisterium" meets "magisterium"? Granted, as the archbishop makes clear in his article, that this letter is "an act of the teaching church and cannot be regarded simply as just another theological opinion," and granted further that such an act of the teaching Church calls for the *"obsequium religiosum"* (religious "submission" or "respect," depending on the way one translates *obsequium*) which Vatican II says all the faithful must give to the teachings of the papal magisterium, the question still needs to be asked: What does such a statement call for from bishops who also exercise "ordinary magisterium" in the Church? While one would surely hope that the bishops are to be counted among the "faithful," they nonetheless possess in virtue of their own episcopal ordination a special relationship to the bishop of Rome. They are not his "delegates." According to *Lumen Gentium* (no. 22) "the order of bishops is the successor to the college of the apostles in teaching authority and pastoral rule." Together with their head, the bishop of Rome, and never without that head, the college of bishops is the subject of supreme and full power over the universal Church. *Lumen Gentium* (no. 23) speaks of the ordinary magisterium of the bishops in the dioceses entrusted to their care by the Holy Spirit. They exercise, we are told, "pastoral government over the portion of the people of God entrusted to their care." While their primary care is their own dioceses, they are, because of their membership in the episcopal college and as successors of the apostles, obliged by Christ's command to be "solicitous for the whole Church."

Should not one expect that the ordinary magisterium of the papal office—especially when it is exercised through subordinates (such as a Roman congregation), even though with the approval of the pope—would, on a matter that is a sensitive issue for the whole Church, have consulted those who also exercise the ordinary magisterium in the Church, namely, the bishops of the various local churches and also the conferences of bishops of various areas of the world?

Such consultation would seem particularly appropriate with regard to the subject matter of the present letter: the care of homosexual persons. It would be reasonable to think that the Congregation for the Doctrine of the Faith, whose members would necessarily be limited in the amount of pastoral care they would have been able to offer to homosexual persons, could have profited greatly by consulting the ordinary magisterium of the bishops in various parts of the world to ascertain the "pastoral practice" that obtained in the various local churches spread throughout the Catholic world. Thirteen years previous to this present letter, the American bishops distributed a fifteen-page booklet "Principles to Guide Confessors in Questions of Homosexuality." Many dioceses in the United States have had for some time ministries that serve the homosexual community. One would expect that in thirteen years a good deal of experience could have been gained about homosexual people and how to minister to them. This experience could have been helpful to those in the Congregation who wrote this letter.

The CDF letter gives no indication that any such consultation of the American bishops—or any other group of bishops—took place as a preliminary step toward its writing. One cannot help but feel that to bypass collegiality on an issue of such grave concern to many people was an omission that is as difficult to understand as it is to justify.

One is forced to ask the question: Why was such consultation of the bishops omitted? Did the Congregation feel that the bishops had nothing to contribute on this issue? Did they feel no need to learn about the pastoral practices already going on in many local churches? Did they believe that they possessed a priori all the truth necessary to address the topic of the letter? Do we not have to face the fact that many Catholics of good faith are going to ask the question: How much credibility can be given to a document that ignores the ongoing experience of the many local churches?

Must we not also ask the question: Would not Archbishop Quinn, as well as the rest of the American bishops, have been more comfortable if they had received a preliminary letter from the Congregation asking them what the pastoral practices for the care of homosexual persons actually were in their local churches? If the Congregation had gathered the facts of this experience and then written a second letter drawing on the experiences of the many local churches, they might well have come up with the same doctrinal stance that is set forth in the present letter. But there would be the sense that the stance, whatever it might be, had grown out of the experience of God's people. There is a good bit of wisdom in the statement that concludes the letters to each of the seven churches in the Book of Revelation: "Let the one who has ears heed the Spirit's word to the churches" (Rev. 2:7). It is good ecclesiology to say that what the Spirit speaks to each of the churches can be important for all of the churches.

If the CDF letter highlights an ecclesial problem that remains unaddressed in the archbishop's article, there is also the hermeneutical problem that haunts any biblical research into those texts that are commonly adduced as condemning homosexuality. Archbishop Quinn is satisfied in his article to accept the interpretation of the Congregation, backed up by references to an article in the *Journal of Religious Ethics* that deals with chapter 1 of Romans. I would like to look briefly at the hermeneutical principle cited in the letter and then at the application of that principle. The principle set forth in number 5 would delight any biblical scholar, for it states clearly that thought patterns and modes of expression in the Bible differ from one period of biblical history to another and also between the biblical period and contemporary times. One could find ample illustrations of this principle by browsing through any of the ten volumes of Kittel's *Theological Dictionary of the New Testament*. (A simple example would be the word *presbyteroi*, which originally meant "the elders" in the community, then was used to designate office-bearers—not always advanced in age—and has come to mean leaders of cult, priests, in our contemporary usage of the term. This would be but one instance of how thought patterns and modes of expression are affected by time, history, culture, etc.).

One would expect that the enunciation of this principle of biblical interpretation would be followed by a "therefore"; instead, it is followed by a "nevertheless." What I mean is that what one might expect is that the letter, after stating this hermeneutical principle, would go on to say: "*Therefore* one cannot assume that a consistent understanding of the meaning of "homosexuality" and a univocal use of the word *homosexual* would have persisted through the various periods of the writing of the Bible and the different ages of the Church's history. What we actually read, however, is: "nevertheless, in the presence of such remarkable diversity, there is a clear consistency within the Scriptures themselves on the moral issue of homosexual behavior" (no. 5).

One feels compelled to say that such a statement misses the point of the very principle previously enunciated. The biblical writers saw homosexuality at times in the context of male temple prostitution, at other times (Gen. 19, perhaps?) in the context of gang rape, at still other times as *unnatural* behavior on the part of *heterosexuals*. Thus it seems quite plausible to suggest that the homosexual behavior that Paul so clearly condemns in Romans 1:27 involved men who were heterosexual or at least thought to be so by Paul. For the biblical authors knew nothing of a homosexual condition that was not "chosen," but "given." They certainly would have had no notion of homosexuality as a way of relating humanly to another person in the context of love, fidelity, and mutuality. I am not in any sense addressing the question as to whether such a way of relating is morally justifiable or not. I simply intend to say that this is what homosexual people mean today when they speak of responsible homosexual behavior, and, further, to say that this way of understanding homosexuality would have been beyond the ken of the biblical writers. We may judge that what some people call "responsible homosexual behavior" is not responsible at all and needs to be condemned. But our condemnation would have to be based on our particular understanding of sexuality, not on a hermeneutic that would ask biblical writers to condemn something they could never even have thought of.

I find it necessary to disagree with the archbishop on the question: What is the central moral affirmation of the CDF letter? He says it is the statement: "It is only in the marital relationship that the use of the sexual faculty can be morally good. A person engaging in homosexual behavior therefore acts immorally" (no. 7). I would claim that, while the statement he has chosen is certainly central to official Roman Catholic teaching on sexuality, the affirmation that is at the heart of this letter—the affirmation that homosexual persons find most painful—is the declaration that the homosexual orientation is itself "an objective disorder."

This letter clearly attaches great importance to this declaration. Indeed, it would not be unfair to say that the letter was written primarily in order that this declaration might be made. My reason for saying this is that number 3 of the letter makes it clear that a principal intent of the letter was to clarify a position stated in the Congregation's *Persona Humana*, or "Declaration on Certain Questions Concerning Sexual Ethics" (29 December 1975). This declaration noted the difference between the homosexual condition and homosexual behavior and described only the latter as "intrinsically disordered." Declaring that since the publication of the 1975 statement "an overly benign interpretation was given to the homosexual condition itself," the CDF letter makes clear its intent to correct such misunderstandings. It says:

> Although the particular inclination of the homosexual person is not a sin, it is a more or less strong tendency ordered toward an intrinsic moral evil; and thus the inclination itself must be seen as an objective disorder. [no. 3]

What this statement is saying is *that a person who is not heterosexual is a person whose sexuality is an "objective disorder."* Since our sexuality is part of what constitutes us as persons, the letter is really saying that part of what constitutes the homosexual person as a person is an "objective disorder." Further it is said—and this would follow logically from the "objective disorder" evaluation—that the condition of being a homosexual person is itself "a more or less strong tendency ordered toward an intrinsic moral evil." Whether one agrees with this position or does not, it is not difficult to see the psychological damage that could be done to a person by telling him or her that his or her very person was ordered toward intrinsic moral evil. It would be like telling someone that he or she is carrying a moral time bomb. It would be to say that such a person is a constant proximate occasion of sin to himself or herself.

I can only express the hope that this brief response to Archbishop Quinn may be seen as part of the ongoing debate on the issue of homosexuality which the CDF letter refers to in its first paragraph. The letter speaks of the debate, though it refuses to become party to it. In fact, one gets the impression that it is not entering the debate but seeking to close it.

For it says that the "debate often advances arguments and makes assertions inconsistent with the teaching of the Catholic Church." While we are never told what these "arguments" and "assertions" are, we are left with no doubt that it is clearly the assumption of the Congregation that the teaching of the Church is known clearly, and in all its concreteness, anterior to the debate and without any regard for the "arguments" and "assertions" made in the debate. Such a position would seem to foreclose the possibility that new knowledge might emerge from the debate that could further clarify Catholic teaching and perhaps even lead to a modification of past teaching.

Almost two decades ago (30 August 1968) Pope Paul VI wrote to a congress of German Catholics about a debate. It was the debate that at the time was swirling around his (then) recently published encyclical *Humanae Vitae*. This is what he said: "May the *lively debate* aroused by our encyclical lead to a better knowledge of God's will." In a book that I published in 1970 that bore the title *The Lively Debate,* I pointed out that Pope Paul made the "debate" aroused by the encyclical, and not the encyclical itself, the basis for his hope that people might be led to a better knowledge of God's will. Is it possible to hope that the debate on the issue of homosexuality, which the CDF letter has aroused, will be able to lead us to a deeper knowledge of God's will concerning the very subject of that letter: the pastoral care of homosexual persons?

3

The Vatican Letter:
Presuppositions and Objections

Ann Patrick Ware

Like other documents which reiterate teachings which are at present under challenge from theologians and non-theologians alike within the Roman Catholic Church, the recent "Letter to the Bishops of the Roman Catholic Church on the Pastoral Care of Homosexual Persons" proceeds from certain presuppositions which are themselves outmoded, contradicted by other Vatican documents, or themselves theologically unsound. I would like to discuss four of these presuppositions and then go on to cite some specific objections.

The first of these is a docetic understanding of the Church. Docetism was an early heresy which held that Christ had no human body and only appeared to die on the cross. Contemporary docetists have a way of presenting the Church as a disembodied concept, speaking an eternal truth arrived at in some mysterious and infallible way. Though no women have any voice whatsoever in formulating doctrine, the Church is made to appear feminine. "She" is always correct in "her" teaching, despite the sad lessons of history which show some teachings to have been gravely in error. "She" knows in some unfathomable way the certainties of God's truth and God's will, certainties which are removed from human scrutiny because *above* human critique.

A second presupposition of the writers of this document is that all Catholics clearly understand and accept that the few who make up the magisterium can decide what the teaching of the whole Church should be and propagate it as though it were of divine origin in every detail. But developments in ecclesiology and in the theology of revelation which were such a promising and enlivening factor in the Second Vatican Council have now become a part of the common understanding of the faith which "ordinary" Catholics now espouse. The Catholic folk do believe that they

28

are the People of God (*Lumen Gentium*, no. 9), that the laity have particular competencies not proper to clerics (no. 37), and that pastors, "aided by the experience of the laity can more clearly and more suitably come to decisions regarding spiritual and temporal matters" (no. 37). They believe that "all the faithful of Christ of whatever rank or status are called to the fullness of the Christian life and to the perfection of charity" (no. 40), and believing too that "the Spirit produces and urges love among the believers" (no. 7), they do not understand or agree that their experience should have no weight or consideration in the life and teaching of the Church. This is especially true in matters of sexuality, where the laity have experience from which clerics by their vow of celibacy are, or should be, excluded.

Women, too, have their own challenge to the "teaching authority." Swept up by both male language and male thinking into the generic "he" (women have to think of themselves as "man," "sons of God," "brothers of Christ"), they reemerge amazingly as "Holy Mother Church" when it comes to teaching what they have had no part in producing and, worse, when it comes to judging the lives of others.

A third presupposition which undergirds this document, as it does other recent pronouncements on controverted issues, is that mere repetition makes a weak argument strong or a false statement true. Wrapped in the mantle of tradition, such repetition seems to proceed on the assumption that the people have not really heard what authorities are saying, and that if the Catholic folk really heard, they would obey. Not so. The more compassionate and gospel-centered understanding of what it means to be in the community of faith, which was the heritage of Vatican II, has fired the self-consciousness and commitment of Catholics. They perceive hierarchical high-handedness in a way no longer acceptable to them as it once was; and they expect to be regarded with consideration and even consulted in matters where only they have experience.

A fourth overriding assumption (perhaps stance would better describe it) is that the "Church's" motives in promulgating doctrine are always pure and good; others' in questioning it are faulty if not downright bad. Having enumerated four assumptions underlying the Vatican letter, and most other Vatican pronouncements, I now wish to point out a number of specific objections.

Despite its title, the letter is not pastoral. One might expect pastoral concern to be about the distress of homosexual persons, homophobia in society, injustice (up to and including murder) to a sizable segment of the human family. Instead, the opening words of the letter make it clear that the cause for concern is the presence of arguments and assertions inconsistent with Catholic teaching. It is not that living human beings are struggling with problems of how to love; it is that magisterial authority is suffering a diminishment.

One might expect some words of comfort, understanding, acknowledgment of a problem, some attribution at least of honesty and integrity to homosexuals who have elected to stay within the Church. Instead, the letter does not hesitate to declare, in opposition to a solid body of opinion within the scientific community, that even the inclination to homosexuality is an intrinsic disorder. It thus relegates thousands of people (indeed, we do not even know how many) to a state of sickness, of pathological debility. These "intrinsically disordered" are to be a special object of the Church's concern lest they think that acting according to their inclination is morally acceptable.

There is no attempt to reconcile the conflicting theological opinions which stand side by side within the framework of this Vatican theology: namely, (1) that the "disordered inclination," which even the document dares not call voluntary, must, if not chosen, be God-given and thus good; and (2) that not to act on the inclination during a lifetime demands celibacy, which is also not a matter of pure choice but clearly defined as a gift (*Optatam Totius*, no. 10). The letter fudges when it says that "homosexuals are called as all Christians are to a chaste life" (no 12). Other Christians can be chaste within their sexual activity. Homosexuals, by the Church's definition, cannot. They are obliged, under threat of their destruction (no. 12), to what is impossible without a special gift, and even this document dares not imply that all homosexuals have the "gift" of celibacy.

There is a curious emphasis in this letter on promoting and upholding the institution of marriage and the family (nos. 7, 9, 17), almost as though homosexuals were responsible for the fact that in this country one out of two marriages will end in divorce. In fact, the text seems to make marriage "the essence of Christian living" with its form of self-giving (no. 7)! (This is somewhat astounding in a Church which has a long history of glorifying virginity.) Yet it persists in denying to homosexuals its blessing on a union that cannot "transmit life," which it readily grants to heterosexuals, many of whom also cannot transmit life because of the sterility of one partner or both. Indeed, this Church which boldly claims that it does not consider a person as a "heterosexual" or a "homosexual" (no. 16) denies to its homosexual members any assistance or encouragement in establishing a loving, faithful, committed, and permanent union. Further, in the context of homosexual persons associating with one another (no. 15) the document seems to say that even such association should not be encouraged since it entails "the near occasions of sin." Pastoral, indeed!

The authors of this letter obviously felt that it was important to refute the considerable body of scholarly research which interprets texts, earlier understood as condemnatory of homosexuality, to be instead judgments on those who refused the neighbor or even the stranger hospitality. But it is well to remember what Scripture says of itself, that it is a two-edged sword. It seems particularly insensitive, if not foolish, to choose for a supporting text against homosexuality the story of Lot who reproved the men of Sodom for wanting to have their way with his male guests but readily turned over to them his virgin daughters for their pleasure! Pity the minister engaged in "pastoral care" who has to explain that the one part of the story means what it says but the other part does not. The handling of Scripture in this document is simply another instance of mechanical repetition instead of courteous and reasoned response to those scholars who hold a different opinion.

The authors may claim that the Church cannot be as callous as the "pressure groups" who hold that homosexuality is harmless, yet the Congregation for the Doctrine of the Faith does not hesitate to take a number of cheap shots. One is at activist groups who work to change laws inimical to the civil rights of gay and lesbian people (no. 9). Another is at homosexuals themselves with the implication that only they are self-indulgent in their sexual activity (no. 7). Still another is that homosexuals should find their "self-giving" in participating in the Sacrifice of the Cross—while others, not disordered, may find it in the ecstasy of sex (no. 12).

It is my view that this document is not pastoral, not theologically sound, but harsh and unfeeling. It is also dangerous. No longer, I believe, can responsible people get away with deploring violence and acts of malice while at the same time fueling the fires that cause such acts. In declaring homosexuals to be intrinsically disordered, these Vatican officials all but sanction the acts of those who wish to bring everything into "order" by ridding society, violently if need be, of troublemakers. What does it mean, after all, to be "disordered" or "out of order"? The "disordered" are askew, impaired, sick, "psychos." If a thing is "out of order," it doesn't work; it is useless until someone "fixes" it. If it can't be fixed, it should be discarded. That this kind of language should be used about the same people who are "children of God," as the letter insists, is shocking. That it should appear in a letter which purports to be pastoral is a scandal. Further, making the case, as it is made in number 10, that those who claim or support civil rights for homosexuals are virtually promoting "other distorted notions and practices" is an unbelievable departure from sane discourse.

Once again, the victim is blamed for the malice and irrationality of the evildoer. What has any of this to do with the gospel or with pastoral care?

References

Lumen Gentium, "Dogmatic Constitution on the Church." In *The Documents of Vatican II*, edited by Walter M. Abbott. New York: America Press, 1966.

Optatam Totius, "Decree on Priestly Formation." In *The Documents of Vatican II*, edited by Walter M. Abbott. New York: America Press, 1966.

4

The Vatican Can Slight
Scripture for Its Purpose

Dan Grippo

The authors of the recent Vatican statement on homosexuality claim, early in the document, that there is "a clear consistency within the Scriptures themselves on the moral issue of homosexual behavior . . . a constant biblical testimony."

Nothing could be further from the truth. The six scripture passages cited by the Vatican authors are interpreted in a distorted and woefully inadequate fashion that will only serve to perpetuate time-honored prejudices. The fact is that the Bible says very little about homosexual behavior, and nothing at all about persons with a homosexual orientation.

The Vatican authors begin with the Sodom story (Gen. 19:1–11) and limit their remarks to the following: "There can be no doubt of the moral judgment made there against homosexual relations."

The meaning of the story, and the way in which it came to be seen as a judgment against homosexual practices, requires more explanation. Scholars, beginning with Derrick Sherwin Bailey in 1955 *(Homosexuality and the Western Christian Tradition)*, have pointed out that none of the many biblical references to Sodom mentions homosexual practices as the cause of the city's downfall.

These later passages depict Sodom as a symbol of utter destruction and its sin as one of great magnitude, but "pride," "complacency," "arrogance," and "barbarity" are more typical descriptions of the sin (Ezek. 16:49, Is. 3:9). The biblical authors held strong and varying opinions on the sin of Sodom, but none of them equated that sin with homosexual practices.

John McNeill *(The Church and the Homosexual)* highlights this point from a different angle. He points out that none of the biblical passages that are traditionally understood as condemning homosexual practices mentions the Sodom story. Yet, such a reference would have been obvious

33

if the sin had been understood in biblical times as involving such practices.

Bailey and McNeill conclude that the sin of Sodom is primarily one of inhospitality, a very serious sin in the Jewish tradition. Other commentators see a sexual theme in the story but argue that the story condemns the kind of decadence, violence, and callous disregard for human dignity that is epitomized in the gang rape of innocent visitors.

The gender of the victims is of less importance than the violent nature of the crime, according to this argument. Scholars point to the parallel, and probably derivative, story of gang rape in Judges 19, the so-called Outrage of Gibeah. The story begins, like Sodom, with an attempt at homosexual rape but ends up with a violent heterosexual gang rape that leads to a woman's death. "The sin of Gibeah was worse than the sin of Sodom. It was not only the sin of intent to commit rape, homosexual or heterosexual, but the commission of the rape—plus murder," says Tom Horner (*Jonathan Loved David: Homosexuality in Biblical Times*).

By the end of the first century A.D., however, the sin of Sodom had become widely identified among Jews and early Christians with homosexual practices. If biblical authors were not responsible for this identification, what factors brought it about? Two sources have been postulated: Jewish apocrypha, a body of pseudonymous and anonymous writings from 200 B.C. to A.D. 200; and Jewish scholars such as Philo and Josephus, who had considerable contact with, and found displeasure in, the sexual practices of the Hellenistic world they lived in.

In the apocrypha, the phrase "changing the order of nature" was first used in connection with Sodom. The phrase in this context, however, did not refer to men having sex with other men, but rather to the desire of the men of Sodom to have sex with angels. (The influence of this addition to the Sodom tradition can be seen in the two New Testament passages, Jude 6–7 and 2 Pet. 2:6–8.) Later references to Sodom in the apocrypha become quite distorted: 2 Enoch 10:4, for example, speaks of "child corruption after the Sodomitic fashion."

Philo expressly associated Sodom with homosexual practices in the treatise *De Abrahamo,* allowing his imagination full reign in a lurid description that owes more to the seamy underworld of first-century Alexandria than it does to Genesis. Josephus, like the author of 2 Enoch, equates the sin of Sodom with the sexual abuse of children. Thus, by the time we come to Clement of Alexandria, who died about A.D. 215, pederasty was fully a part of the conception of the sin of Sodom.

Bailey summarizes the development of the Sodom tradition this way: "Despite occasional allusions to (Sodom's) arrogance and inhospitality, and to the wealth and plenty which were supposed to have led to its fall, the Sodom of the Old Testament . . . clearly had no place in the thought of the early church, but only the Sodom of Philo and Josephus, in which homosexual vice and especially that associated with the 'love of boys' was believed to have been rampant."

The Vatican authors turn next to Leviticus 18:22 and 20:13, of which they say, "In the course of describing the conditions necessary for belonging to the chosen people, the author excludes from the people of God those who behave in a homosexual fashion."

A key to understanding the Holiness Code (Lev. 17–26) is the use of the word *abomination*. It does not usually signify something intrinsically evil, like the crimes of rape or theft discussed elsewhere in Leviticus, but rather something that is ritually unclean, like the eating of pork discussed in the same chapter as homosexual activity. Its dominant note is that of idolatry.

Johannes Pedersen *(Israel)* contends that homosexual practices were accepted and widely practiced in the ancient Near East and thus were associated with Israel's greatest fear: cultural and religious assimilation. It is helpful to refer to the beginning of Leviticus 18, where the link is made between the things being condemned and the objectionable practices of the Egyptians and Canaanites: "Yahweh spoke to Moses; he said, 'Speak to the sons of Israel and say to them: I am Yahweh your God. You must not behave as they do in Egypt where once you lived; you must not behave as they do in Canaan where I am taking you. You must not follow their laws. You must follow my customs and keep my laws; by them you must lead your life' " (Lev. 18:1–4).

The Levitical proscription against homosexual acts may have been added to the Holiness Code at a relatively late date, during the period of Persian dominance over Israel (539–333 B.C.), when Judaism was influenced by Persian Zoroastrianism, a rationalist and dualist philosophical system that saw no purpose in sexual activity save the absolute necessity of procreation. Sex for any other purpose was considered not only unnecessary, but detrimental to the soul. Obviously, homosexual activity would be viewed with hostility in such a system.

A passage from the *Venidad*, a book of ritual purity that is part of the *Zend-Avesta*, the holy book of Zoroastrians, bears a striking resemblance to the Levitical passages in question: "The man that lies with mankind as man lies with womankind . . . is a *Daeva* (Devil)."

The cultic roots of early condemnations of homosexuality are attested to by Edward Westermarck *(Christianity and Morals)*: "The excessive sinfulness which was attached to homosexual love by Zoroastrianism, Hebraism and Christianity had quite a special foundation. It cannot be sufficiently accounted for either by utilitarian considerations or instinctive disgust. . . . The fact is that homosexual practices were intimately associated with the greatest sins: unbelief, idolatry or heresy."

Three other factors influencing Jewish attitudes toward homosexual behavior need to be mentioned: the place of family and progeny in ancient cultures, the stance patriarchal cultures take toward homosexuality, and the use of sodomy as a form of conquest and punishment among ancient military peoples.

Family and progeny were vital to the survival of tribal peoples. Children were an absolute necessity when there was no other form of economic security. Beyond this consideration, for the Jewish people, children were also the fulfillment of the promise God made to Abraham (Gen. 12:1–3). They were the hope of the future embodied, the everlasting nation brought into being—ultimately, they were the Jewish expression of the universal hope for immortality. Homosexual behavior within such a culture would not be looked upon with favor.

Coupled with this was the almost sacred aura with which the male seed was looked upon. Most ancient civilizations considered semen to be the source of all life. It was thought that the woman's contribution was merely to act as incubator within which this precious fluid could develop and come to term. Any nonreproductive spilling of the "life fluid" was seen as sacrilege.

Psychologist and historian G. Rattray Taylor (Sex in History) contends that patriarchal societies in general are hostile to homosexual behavior among men, deploring the idea that any man would take the "lesser feminine" role in sex. He contrasts what he calls "patrist" societies— which have been authoritarian, conservative, strongly subordinationist in their views on women and horrified by homosexual practices—with "matrist" societies, which have been tolerant, inquiring, democratic, inclined to enhance the status of women and accepting of homosexual practices.

Matrist societies seem to have predated patrist ones and only slowly gave way to them. Robert Graves (The White Goddess: A Historical Grammar of Poetic Myth) claims that early Israel was influenced by the matrilineal (descent reckoned through the mother's family) Philistines, cultural ancestors of the Greeks. Biblical traces of this influence may exist in the account of Samson going to the home of his bride to live, rather than the reverse, and in the ancient biblical statement in Genesis 2:24: "Therefore, a man leaves his father and his mother and cleaves to his wife."

A final factor that may have shaped the Jewish aversion to homosexual activity was the common practice of using sodomy as an expression of scorn and domination among warring peoples. The Egyptians and many others commonly subjected defeated male enemies to sodomy as a way of punishing them, and although there is no evidence that the Jews were ever subjected to this treatment, certainly a small tribe among powerful ones would have reason to fear it.

Thus, while it is clear that Leviticus 18:22 and 20:13 do condemn homosexual activity among males, it is also clear that such behavior was condemned because of its perceived association with peoples and practices the Jews found reprehensible and threatening. It was most particularly associated with idolatry and cultic impurity. It was also behavior that made no sense to an underpopulated people that depended on high fertility for their very survival.

In 1 Corinthians 6:9, St. Paul, following Leviticus, "lists those who behave in a homosexual fashion among those who shall not enter the kingdom of God," say the Vatican authors.

Paul's list of groups that will be excluded from the kingdom includes two Greek words, *malakoi* and *arsenokoitai* which are often translated "homosexuals" or "sodomites." *Malakoi* literally means "soft," and in a moral context is used to signify loose, morally weak, or lacking in self-control. Yale scholar John Boswell *(Christianity, Social Tolerance and Homosexuality)*, among others, thinks there is no justification for connecting it with homosexual behavior.

The exact meaning of *arsenokoitai* is disputed. Boswell argues that Greek authors carefully distinguished *arsenokoitai* from *arrenokoitai*, the latter meaning "ones (m.) who 'go to bed' with men," the former (used by Paul) meaning simply "males who 'go to bed,'" that is, male prostitutes servicing females.

Boswell supports his argument by pointing out that none of the early Greek fathers, even St. John Chrysostom, who detested homosexual behavior and used 125 different words to describe it, ever used *arsenokoitai* to describe homosexual persons. The word was used, however, by Chrysostom and others to describe heterosexual male prostitutes.

McNeill is also uncomfortable with translating *arsenokoitai* as "homosexual." He points out that Paul would have had a number of other, more specific Greek words at his disposal had he wished to specify such behavior. He also finds "male prostitute" a more accurate translation.

The Vatican authors say that in Romans 1:18–32 "Paul uses homosexual behavior as an example of the blindness which has overcome humankind." Here again we are dealing with a passage that concerns itself with idolatry. In verses 22–25, Paul attributes the behavior he is about to condemn to false worship.

Paul's use of the phrase *para physin* is often translated as "unnatural" or "against nature." Boswell notes, "The modern reader is apt to read into that phrase a wealth of associations derived from later philosophical developments, scholastic theology, Freudian psychology, social taboos as well as personal misgivings."

Paul's meaning, however, is not clear. He uses the phrase in a variety of contexts in his letters, at one point expressing the idea that God himself had acted *para physin* in grafting a wild olive branch (the gentiles) onto a cultivated tree (the inheritance of the Jews) (Romans 11:24). Thus the phrase does not necessarily imply a moral judgment on an action as wrong.

Rather, scholars argue, the phrase for Paul is always linked to religious and cultural heritage. There are two senses of the passage that can be brought out. First, there is the notion of the person who has gone beyond his or her "natural," that is, heterosexual, appetite in order to indulge in new sexual pleasures. There is no sense of a *condition* of homosexuality, but only of heterosexuals engaging in a perversion of their natural sexuality.

Second, *physis* can be seen as referring to the "nature" of the chosen people, who were forbidden by Levitical law to have homosexual relations. Paul seems to be implying that the gentiles, having rejected the true God, as a result also reject their true sexual nature and go beyond what is "natural" and what is legal for the Jews.

Thus Romans 1:18–32 can only be seen as condemning all homosexual behavior if one rejects the notion that some people have a more or less fixed homosexual orientation or condition.

Because the term "homosexual condition" is used frequently in both the Vatican's 1975 "Declaration on Certain Questions Concerning Sexual Ethics" and the current document, one would assume that the Vatican does believe that such a fixed condition or orientation exists.

Finally, the Vatican authors say that 1 Timothy 1, "in full continuity with the biblical position, singles out those who spread wrong doctrine, and in verse 10 explicitly names as sinners those who engage in homosexual acts."

Here, as in 1 Corinthians, we find *arsenokoitai* appearing among a list of vices, this time without *malakoi*. Instead, it follows *pornio,* a word indicating general sexual corruption. The reasons scholars contest the association of *arsenokoitai* with homosexual behavior were given in the discussion of the passage from Corinthians.

The Vatican authors say nothing about biblical passages that portray same-sex relationships in highly positive terms. Two examples are the relationships of Jonathan and David (1 Sam. 18:1–4, 20:30, 20:40–41, 2

Sam. 1:26) and Ruth and Naomi (Ru. 1:16–17). A physical relationship does not have to be postulated (though the possibility cannot be ruled out) for these relationships to give witness to the bonding and depth that can exist between members of the same sex.

Nor do the Vatican authors quote any Gospel passages in the text. It is not that Jesus avoided talking about sex. Rather, he spoke of attitudes of mind and heart more than of actual deeds (Mt. 5:27–28, 15:18–19). The authors do not quote the Gospels, central to Christian faith, because they cannot—none of the terms used in biblical times to refer to homosexual activity appears anywhere in the Gospels, though the Gospel writers and Jesus himself were certainly aware of such practices.

Approval cannot be posited from silence, but neither can disapproval, much less outright condemnation. And although Jesus supported the indissolubility of marriage, he did not believe that marriage was for everyone; he himself was single. He was clearly comfortable with and emotionally close to both men and women and did not mind being physically close to either (Jn. 11:3, 5, 36; 13:23, 19:26, 21:20). It should also be noted that Jesus did not hesitate to associate with those judged to be most sinful by his society (Lk. 7:39).

What has been offered here is but a brief overview of the kind of scholarship that has been going on for the past thirty years with regard to the biblical passages cited by the Vatican authors.

In condemning this scholarship, the Vatican authors say that the views put forth are "gravely erroneous and call for particular attention" in their pastoral.

The six passages selected, and the Vatican interpretations, then follow in three paragraphs. Whether one finds the overview offered in this article convincing, it seems reasonable to contend that the passages are complex enough to warrant more than a couple of paragraphs. If the recent scholarship is going to be called "gravely erroneous," then it ought to be at least addressed. Further, it should be refuted if possible by better scholarship.

Dismissing it out of hand and interpreting Scripture by way of conclusionary statements is intellectually dishonest and pastorally unjust. The injustice is more than an academic one when the "solid foundation of a constant biblical testimony" becomes the basis for the grave and sweeping conclusions reached in the pastoral letter, namely, that homosexual Catholics have no faithful option but to live celibate lives and that Catholic organizations unwilling to accept and espouse the official church teaching on this issue, to the exclusion of any other possible understandings, should be barred from the use of church facilities and the benefits of pastoral care.

5

A Problem of
Manipulated Data

Lillanna Kopp

In the fall of 1986, some White House basement staffers busied themselves promoting their own unique brand of American foreign policy, presumably bypassing input and consent from the president, secretary of state, the CIA, and Congress. At the same time, Cardinal Joseph Ratzinger was busy in the Congregation for the Doctrine of the Faith office preparing a seemingly undocumented letter to Catholic bishops of the world on the proper pastoral care of homosexuals. The letter's contents, now widely disseminated by mass media, is calling worldwide attention to the problematic teaching authority currently being exercised in that ancient and once academically distinguished institution.

Eighty percent of all the scientists who have ever lived are reportedly alive in the world today. Thousands of them on every continent have intense cross-disciplinary interest and research investment in the complex, multifaceted phenomenon of homosexuality. The Vatican document, however, bypasses the world's academic, scientific, and religious communities whose research and collegial dialogue could have updated its views and tempered its astounding claim that deductive human reasoning enlightened by faith can allow church authorities to "transcend the horizons of science" to a "more global vision" that "does greater justice to the rich reality of the human person" (no. 2). Such appearance of disdain for interdisciplinary and interdenominational teamwork and of reliance on prescientific data is a scandal in the magisterium, not just because it is the epitome of conservative fundamentalism—a diversity the Church can countenance—but also because the letter fails thereby to acknowledge that, over and above Scripture and tradition, the Spirit of Wisdom continues to enlighten and direct humankind through the scientific mode of revelation and the *sensus fidelium*. The letter repudiates, in effect, Vatican II's Pastoral Constitution on the Church in the Modern World where

40

bishops of the Church affirmed that "in pastoral care, appropriate use must be made not only of theological principles, but also the findings of the secular sciences, especially psychology and sociology," in order to "blend modern science and its theories and understanding of the most recent discoveries with Christian morality and doctrine" (*Gaudium et Spes*, no. 62).

To impose selective, problematic, demonstrably untrue and incompletely researched opinions on world Catholics, masked in the guise of magisterial certitude, is to invite the designation "academic fraud" from world scholars. Most importantly, however, in a religion that gives priority to love and compassion, readers may be surprised to discern homophobic righteousness and misinformation used as tools of doctrinal manipulation, and violation of the biblical injunction to "speak the truth in love" (Eph. 4:5).

The scientific community has been professionally and humanistically cautious in publishing prematurely conclusions relative to the nature and etiology of homophilia (same-sex love); the Vatican letter rushed into press with irresponsible and unfounded conclusions that have to be refuted, in justice, by professionals in the field. If the modus operandi is perceived to involve specious, fundamentalist biblical interpretation and the willful exclusion of relevant specialized research data from the above mentioned disciplines, then the image of the professionalism and integrity which should characterize church administrators will be severely tarnished.

It is already known from extensive media coverage that in the years immediately preceding the publication of the letter on homosexuality there have been concentrated attempts to silence or discredit internal church dissent by bishops, theologians, scripture scholars, and feminist nuns by threatening their jobs, their academic freedom to teach, publish, or question, and even their membership in religious congregations. It is presumed that many of these will nevertheless risk retaliative wrath and set about denouncing the misinformation and manipulation of historic facts in the Vatican letter.

The goal of this chapter is not to usurp the prerogatives of moral theologians, nor to anticipate their growing consensus on the morality of homosexual activity in a committed relationship. It is rather to contend that the Vatican letter is flawed irremediably by content and methodology because it uses as its basic source material: (1) fundamentalist biblical exegesis, (2) prescientific church tradition, and (3) seriously inexact historical data.

Fundamentalist Biblical Exegesis

The claim that Scripture contains a "clear consistency" (no. 5) on homosexuality is among the weakest and most easily contested assertions. "The Church's doctrine regarding this issue," the letter asserts, "rests on the solid foundation of a constant biblical tradition" (no. 5). Contemporary scripture scholars using cross-disciplinary research tools will provide detailed critiques of the problematic exegesis. Here, however, only the briefest distillation of some few fragments of their research is necessary.

In the original language of the Bible the terms *homosexual* and *homosexuality* are never used, thus leaving homophobic fundamentalists much room for creativity. Moreover, the Gospels never mention sexual acts between two men or two women. In Paul, Timothy, and some few Old Testament texts where sexual acts between males are mentioned, they are set within three contexts: (1) as acts of violence, (2) as acts of lust, and (3) as acts of sacred ritual in fertility cults. They are never mentioned as acts of love. Nevertheless, fundamentalists persist in calling the major crime of Sodom (Gen. 19:1–11) homosexuality, not recognizing the fact that the entire city's population of heterosexual men were attempting to gang-rape Lot's guests for whom Hebrew law demanded hospitality. Furthermore, psychologically and sociologically defined, rape is NOT a sexual act but an extreme act of violence exercised to humiliate another and to assert one's dominance or power over that other. In step with fundamentalist interpretation, the letter calls the above exegesis "gravely erroneous" and insists, "There can be no doubt of the moral judgment made there against homosexual relations" (no. 6).

Jesus apparently interpreted the Sodom story, like modern exegetes, in a way quite contrary to later church tradition. Speaking to his friends this ancient exegete said, "When you enter a town and they do not make you welcome . . . , I tell you, it will be more bearable for Sodom on that great day than for that town" (Lk. 10: 10–13). Here, Jesus seemingly indicated that inhospitality and lack of love was the sin of Sodom, and not homophilic love.

Homophilia or constitutional homosexuality, defined in the scientific community as a fixed, unalterable orientation toward same-sex love, was never mentioned in either Scripture or early church tradition for the simple reason that it was an unknown, unnamed phenomenon in prescientific times. Homosexuality, a seemingly natural variation of approximately 13 percent of male populations and 7 percent of female populations is only partially understood today within the pooled research finds of the biologic and behavioral sciences. Its nature and etiology appear even more opaque to those who purport to make an ethical issue of a constitutional variation.

Prescientific Church Tradition

There is an inherent danger in the contention that church tradition has always been scripturally on-track. The Vatican letter states, "It is essential to recognize that the Scriptures are not properly understood when they are interpreted in a way that contradicts the living tradition of the Church. To be correct, the interpretation of the Scripture must be in substantial accord with that tradition" (no. 5).

To suggest that church doctrine is outside the realm of reform or more perfect development through a deeper understanding of the Scriptures, made possible through the contemporary tools of scientific research, is sheer fundamentalism. Jesus' use of the Sodom story was certainly not in accord with later tradition but Jesus could hardly be accused of not having "properly understood" it.

Many traditions of the Church have been less than Christian from their inception. Paramount among these are the authoritative church teachings promoting anti-Semitism, racism, sexism, heterosexism, and patriarchal authoritarianism, all seriously antithetical to the teachings of Jesus. What has been called the constant, consistent, unchanging teachings of the Church on human nature and human sexuality have been seriously flawed for almost two thousand years because the thinking of the church fathers and later scholars was influenced by the following: (1) erroneous and opposing anthropologies; (2) an inadequate understanding of human biology and psychology; (3) a philosophy of dualism that precluded a holistic view of personhood; (4) a distorted view of sex as evil and unclean, a view in diametric opposition to Jewish Scripture where it is written, "God saw everything [s]he had made, and behold, it was very good" (Gen. 1:3); (5) a misogynous view of women as "misbegotten males," inferior to men "in body, in mind, and morally" (Aquinas, *Summa Theologica*, pt. 1, ques. 92, art.1).

The combination of these errors has so seriously deformed heterosexual relations, even up to the present moment, that a corrective is being developed through the systematic research of Christian feminists and other scholars. Their critique charges church doctrine with accountability for two problems church leaders evasively credit to secularism and sin: (1) a worldwide increase in divorce initiated by women who are no longer forced by economic and educational deprivation to submit to patriarchal dominance, whether ecclesial, familial, or societal; and (2) a worldwide increase in lesbianism and lesbian communities whose members are making more of a politico-religious statement protesting male control than expressing any basic homophile orientation.

Adrienne Rich (1980), a feminist researcher and author, offers historical data illustrating the contention that the patriarchal model of Christianity has short-circuited all varieties of same-sex love and friendship by imputing to them the suspicion of sin and genital activity. Attempting to counteract the Church's denigration of same-sex love, some feminists are proposing that women begin to perceive themselves on just one affinity continuum which includes no dichotomy into straights and lesbians, but where all women, single and married, are represented as celebrating together the goodness, dignity, and reality of same-sex friendships (Bunch, 1975). This would follow the model of Scripture which spotlighted without suspicion or condemnation the unusual love between David and Jonathan, and between Jesus and his beloved John.

I do not believe that a combination of Scripture, tradition, and magisterial insight allows one to "transcend . . . science" relative to the etiology and nature of homosexuality. It is imperative to recall Vatican II's explanation of the content and meaning of divine revelation: "The Scripture contains revelation . . . but not all Scripture is revelation. All Scripture is inspired, but not all is revealed. Similarly, tradition comes to include much that is only of human origin, however, venerable and valuable . . . a written record is a dead letter, needing constant interpretation and commentary in succeeding ages" (MacKenzie, 1966: 108–9).

Inexact Historical Data

The letter contradicts the historic records of Western civilization when it states, "The Church, obedient to the Lord who founded her and gave her the sacramental life, celebrates the divine plan of the loving and life-giving union of men and women in the sacrament of marriage. It is only in the marital relationship that the use of the faculty can be morally good. A person engaging in homosexual behavior therefore acts immorally" (no. 7).

Only in the sixteenth century did the sacrament of matrimony emerge as we now know it; only in the most recent part of the twentieth has the Church through the Vatican document "Educational Guidance in Human Love" required marriage to include the twofold values of mutual love and openness to procreation. The Church has not always promoted the mutual love of spouses "in organic continuity with the scriptural perspective and her own constant tradition" (no. 8). On the contrary, through its constant denigration of women as evil and inferior, the Catholic hierarchy through the ages has made a mockery of any claim that it promoted heterosexual love and the equality requisite for true mutuality. Recall that Cyril of Alexandria, called one of the greatest Fathers of the Church, affirmed God's continuing curse on women. Clement of Alexandria stated emphatically that every woman ought to be overcome with shame at the very thought that she is a woman. Augustine taught that sexuality is wholly animal, not properly human at all, and that even the marital embrace of one's wife is at least a venial sin. Eleven hundred years after Paul denied that woman was created in the image and likeness of God (1 Cor. 11:7), Gratian made the first codification of canon law continue the Church's demand, not for love and mutuality between spouses, but that women be subject to their husbands "as woman was not made to God's image" (Gratian, c. 12, 13, 133, q. 5).

Historically, the Church did not believe that women were called by marriage to mutual love with their husbands. Aquinas claimed that woman not only is inferior in body, mind, and morally but also "is less capable of restraint and self-control" (*Summa Theologica*, pt. 1, ques. 92), that original sin did deepen all these problems but that she was inferior to man even before the fall. Aquinas continued, "Therefore woman is meant to be servile and under male domination." She is a defective person whom God created as a perambulating incubator for the precious male seed. Aquinas disagreed with the earliest creation account in Genesis 2 in which the Yahwist tradition affirmed that God created Eve for mutual love and companionship and to dispel Adam's loneliness. Aquinas asserts that woman is acceptable for raising a man's children but that for the male's companionship, comfort, and spiritual help "Man is best served by man."

In juxtaposition to the false claim that the Church has persistently elevated marriage to a sacred union, a small sample of contrasting historical evidence from *The Woman's Encyclopedia* (Walker, 1983) needs to be placed. Paul (1 Cor. 7:9) contended that it was better not to marry at all, but that for the release of sexual tension it was better to marry than to burn. Origen held that matrimony is impure and unholy, a means of sexual passion. Saint Jerome wrote that the purpose of a man was to cut down with the ax of virginity the wood of marriage. Saint Ambrose claimed that marriage was a crime against God because it changed the state of virginity that God gave every man and woman at birth and that marriage was a prostitution of a member of Christ. Married people ought to blush, he said, at the state in which they were living. Tertullian called marriage a moral crime more dreadful than any punishment or death. It was *spurcitiae,* "obscenity or filth." Augustine stated flatly that marriage is a sin, that birth is demonstrably accursed because every child emerges between feces and urine. Tatian called marriage a corruption, a polluted and foul way of life. Under his influence the Syrian Church ruled that no person could become Christian except celibate men and that no man who had ever married could be baptized. Saint Bernard claimed that it was easier for a man to bring the dead back to life than to live with a woman without endangering his soul.

The Council of Trent decreed that a person who even hinted that the state of matrimony might be more blessed than celibacy would be declared anathema, accursed and excommunicated. Informal common-law marriages were the norm in Christendom for at least its first twelve hundred years. Even as late as the Middle Ages there was no ecclesiastical definition of a valid marriage. Bastardy was commonplace in all social classes. The earliest form of Christian marriage was a simple blessing of the newly wedded pair, *in facie ecclesiae,* outside the closed doors of the Church to keep pollution and lust out of God's house. This blessing was a technical violation of canon law but it became popular and gradually won acceptance. In 1215 the Fourth Lateran Council granted it legal status.

Contemporary research by women scholars and others has documented massive evidence that might have been used in a lengthier critique of the Vatican letter. The few examples cited above suffice to illustrate how the letter glosses over or distorts historical evidence. Also from the above historical selections, constitutional homosexuals and lesbians can draw some faint hope when they observe that women and even heterosexual marriages were once degraded in much the same manner as they themselves and for roughly the same interrelated reasons.

The Church has transcended many of its past errors and may be expected to continue doing so at an accelerated pace as feminist research in all fields continues to unmask the deeply deforming impact of patriarchy on Christianity.

References

Bunch, C., and N. Myron, eds. *Lesbianism and the Women's Movement.* Baltimore: Diana Press, 1975.
MacKenzie, R. A. F. "Introduction to the Dogmatic Constitution on Divine

Revelation." In *The Documents of Vatican II,* edited by W. M. Abbott. New York: America Press, 1966.

Rich, A. "Compulsory Heterosexuality and the Lesbian Experience." *Signs 5,* no. 4 (Summer 1980): 631–60.

Walker, B. *The Woman's Encyclopedia of Myths and Secrets.* New York: Harper and Row, 1983, pp. 585–97.

6

Sexual Orientation
in Vatican Thinking

Robert Nugent

At the 1980 Synod of Bishops, "On the Family," Cardinal Joseph Bernardin, speaking for the U.S. bishops, pleaded for a more positive theology of human sexuality. He noted that in many parts of the world there is a significant gap between church teachings on sexual matters and the ideas of both laity and clergy on the same subject. Bernardin also suggested that the Church's credibility in sexual ethics is undermined when magisterial teaching is simply ignored by a large number of Catholics.

He told the participants that the Church's moral teachings are seldom accepted solely on the argument from authority, but rather when they are perceived as "reasonable, persuasive and related to the actual experience."[1] He was not calling for any substantial change in current teaching on human sexuality, but he was suggesting that a renewed and more positive theology of sexuality would help people see more clearly why the Catholic tradition takes the positions it does. Once this renewed theology was in place, he thought that it would be much easier to situate within it the traditional sexual teachings such as that on homosexuality.

One of the elements which the cardinal suggested ought to be a part of a more positive approach to sexuality was the conviction that sexuality is a relational power and not merely a capacity for performing specific acts. Speaking of sexuality in 1984, he said that "sexuality is also intrinsically relational—it draws people together. This is true, incidentially, not only in a narrow genital sense but in a broader sense. Sexuality, broadly conceived, might be understood as a capacity for entering into relationships with others."[2]

Whatever might be said of the Vatican letter on the pastoral care of homosexual persons, it is quite clear that Bernardin's plea for a more positive exposition of human sexuality fell upon deaf ears in Rome. Unlike most other Vatican statements, the original version of the letter on homosexuality was written in English. This is not surprising since it is generally thought that the target audience for the letter was the U.S. Catholic Church. It is this Church which more than any other has devoted a significant amount of energy to developing both the pastoral and the theological aspects of the topic of homosexuality. According to some observers familiar with Roman documents, the Vatican letter evidences a style and phraseology which distinguish it from previous Roman documents. Some commentators have also suggested that the letter or an initial draft might have originated in the United States (the St. Ignatius Institute in San Francisco has been mentioned) or at least been the work of a North American member of the Roman Curia.

For at least a year rumors had been circulating that a statement on homosexuality was in preparation and at least one such report found its way into print in the British Catholic press. No announcement was made concerning what consultation, if any, took place in drafting the letter. This is a rather standard criticism of Roman documents and one which apparently has had some effect. In a story following the publication of the document on procreation, a Vatican official stated that the Congregation had consulted sixty moralists and theologians, more than twenty scientists and even mothers in preparing the statement. These consultants were not named because it was thought that by doing so it would appear to place the document's weight on the consultors' authority rather than on the Church's magisterium.

According to one source in the United States, the Vatican did consult Cardinals Bernardin, Law, and O'Connor, as well as Archbishop Quinn of San Francisco, prior to the document's publication. If this is true, then one can safely assume that at least Quinn's input did not find its way into the final version of the Vatican letter which stands in marked contrast both in spirit and language to Quinn's pastoral plan for ministry for homosexual people in the archdiocese of San Francisco.[3] Perhaps this is what prompted Quinn to make the only substantial comment on the Vatican letter from the U.S. Catholic hierarchy.[4] Most of the U.S. bishops chose silence and very few had the full text published in their diocesan papers. Many were reported to have been personally disturbed by the document but none chose to make this public. The archbishop of Cincinnati, Daniel Pilarczk, who was elected in 1986 as vice-president of the National Conference of Catholic Bishops, characterized some of the document's wording as "less than felicitous," but accepted its basic teaching. Archbishop Quinn is reported to have registered a protest with the papal pronuncio, and many bishops were disturbed that they were caught unaware by the publication of the document, which they had not yet seen when it was released in Rome, and the media descended on them with questions and requests for explanations. The Conference of Bishops of England and Wales was also reported to have registered a formal protest with the Vatican as to the manner of the document's release which left them unprepared for the strong reactions which the letter generated among diverse segments of the Catholic community.

A close reading of the Vatican letter reveals an approach much closer to that of the more orthodox-minded bishops in the United States. Chief among these is the 1984 letter by Archbishop James Hickey of Washington, DC. Two prominent national Catholic organizations dealing with homosexuality, New Ways Ministry and Dignity, have their headquarters in Hickey's archdiocese. Several years ago Hickey conducted an extensive inquiry on Dignity and forwarded to Rome a thick dossier on the group's policies and programs. Since 1981, Hickey has also attempted to discredit among his fellow bishops the work of New Ways Ministry and to impede many of its educational programs. Hickey accused the group of "ambiguity" in its presentation of magisterial teaching on homosexuality by seeming to equate magisterial teaching with dissenting theological teaching and by giving the impression that people had some options in their moral decison-making. The Vatican letter likewise warns bishops about groups whose public statements and activities reveal a "studied ambiguity" by presenting magisterial teaching but "only as if it were an optional source for the formation of one's conscience" (no. 11). There is no doubt that Hickey was a persistent and formidable presence in Rome calling for a clear and strong stand against certain pastoral and theological trends in the United States.

This chapter will contrast the understanding and use of the concept of "sexual orientation" found in the Vatican letter and other official Catholic statements from the United States in the past ten years and then reflect on some of the pastoral and theological implications of these different evaluations of the homosexual identity.

Sexual Orientation

Official U.S. Catholic statements have accepted the distinction which is commonly made between homosexual orientation and homosexual—or, more precisely, homogenital—behavior. The U.S. bishops first made this distinction in their 1976 pastoral letter "To Live in Christ Jesus," and it was confirmed by John Paul II when he referred to their section of the letter on homosexuality in his 1979 Chicago address to them. Since that time every official Catholic statement on the subject has taken great pains to point out the importance of the distinction in discussing homosexuality.

In exploring the meaning of sexual orientation, theologians, pastors, and human sexuality experts have tried to develop the components of sexual orientation and to avoid equating orientation with behavior. The San Francisco pastoral plan, for example, defines homosexual people as individuals who sustain "a psychic constitution that orients them toward a same-sex psychological, emotional and erotic structure."[5] Homogenital behavior as such is not even mentioned in the definition. Neither does Archbishop Hickey allude to homogenital behavior when he defines homosexuality as a "predominant, persistent and exclusive psychological attraction toward persons of the same sex."[6]

The growing trend among U.S. Catholic theologians, pastors, educators, and counselors, is to affirm the homosexual person *as a person* and to explore the concept of sexual orientation especially as it relates to other areas of an individual's life. The impetus for this has come from two sources. Human sexuality studies indicate that sexual orientation has several components including—but not limited to—genital behavior. The other components are sexual fantasies such as day and night dreams, erotic attraction, and romantic feelings. Sexual orientation is also related to intimacy needs, interpersonal communication, and relationships involving companionship and mutual support. The *homogenital* component of sexual orientation is more directly related to orgasmic pleasure, relief for sexual tensions, ecstacy, and pair-bonding. On the popular level the distinciton is made between the one whom an individual "falls in love" with and the one with whom one "has sex." The former, especially for older people and over an extended period of time, is a more authentic indicator of sexual orientation than the latter.

A second impetus for exploring and utilizing the fuller meaning of sexual orientation, especially in its affective components, is a pastoral concern in helping gay and lesbian Christians to integrate church teaching that human sexuality is a crucial component of human identity that has important implications for our relationships with the self, others, and even with God. If human sexuality has a profound influence on the way we experience life, and if one's sexual orientation is a part of that human sexuality, then the sexual orientation of homosexual people and the positive values associated with it—even apart from homogenital expression—need to be embraced and affirmed by the individual and by the community. This growing insight into a more positive evaluation of the homosexual orientation in the U.S. Catholic community is directly related to a reconsideration of the assertion that the homosexual orientation is morally neutral.

The controversial 1973 change by the American Psychiatric Association has also been incorporated as part of Catholic thinking in *Ministry and Homosexuality in the Archdiocese of San Francisco.* By and large the majority of counselors, theologians, and pastors, much like their counterparts in the therapeutic professions, have accepted the declassification of homosexual orientation as a mental illness or emotional disorder in and of itself, although not all psychologists and psychiatrists accept the change by the APA's Committee on Nomenclature. The general trend, however, is away from change of orientation therapy, and more toward therapy which helps promote self-acceptance, affirmation, and the learning of coping skills for inter- and intrapersonal relationships in an often hostile social environment. While some opponents of the change still claim that politics played a major role in the declassification, it is generally recognized that the change was based on solid empirical evidence involving both patient and nonpatient samples.[7]

Let us look now at the Vatican letter to see how it understands and utilizes the concept of sexual orientation and what kind of psychological and moral judgments it makes about the homosexual orientation. The letter refers to an earlier document, *Persona Humana,* or "Declaration on Some Questions Concerning Sexual Ethics," issued by the Congregation for the Doctrine of the Faith in 1975. That document, we are told, "took note of the distinction commonly drawn between the homosexual condition or tendency and individual homosexual actions" (no. 3). *Persona Humana* actually never uses the word *orientation,* but speaks only of a homosexual "tendency." The most significant distinction that *Persona Humana* made was *not* that between orientation/tendency and behavior, but between homosexual tendency (orientation?) that is *transitory* and not incurable, and one that makes a person *definitively* homosexual because of an innate instinct or a constitution which is pathological and incurable.

This distinction is important insofar as the magisterium publicly commits itself to a recognition of people who are constitutionally or definitely homosexually oriented. It is this constitutional homosexual identity which theologians and others have built upon in their attempts to affirm homosexual individuals in their personhood and in their sexuality as an integral and central part of that personhood, even apart from homogenital expressions.

While the Vatican letter theoretically acknowledges the orientation and behavior distinction, however, it consistently equates "homosexuality" with homogenital behavior. All other facets of the homosexual identity are disregarded or acknowledged only indirectly and as if they had no real usefulness. Only once is there any awareness that homosexual people are more than their sexual expression when the letter states that "a homosexual person, as every human being, deeply needs to be nourished at many different levels simultaneously" (no. 16). In the context of the statement, however, it is clear that such nourishment is spiritual (sacraments, counseling, etc.) and hardly the emotional and affective, let alone erotic, nourishment of same-sex relationships.

The letter uses the word *orientation* only in three places and invariably equates it with homogenital behavior. In place of the word *orientation* the letter refers to the homosexual "condition," "tendency," and "inclination" (no. 3). There is no clear indication that any of these terms refer to what we know of sexual orientation as a clinical term from human sexuality studies. This general use of the word *orientation* is both deliberate and conscious.

Gabriel Moran has pointed out the confusion of the letter's terminology when he wrote that the Vatican has not really condemned the homosexual orientation simply because the document has not really engaged the issue. Moran noted that the letter "tosses about 'inclination,' 'tendency,' 'condition,' and other words whose meanings are not clear. But whether these words appeal to an assumed common sense or whether they are rooted in medieval theories of the person, they are not equivalent to what the contemporary world means by 'sexual orientation'."[8]

When the word *orientation* is employed in the letter, it always seems to refer to sexual behavior. Thus, for example, in number 11 the letter alludes to a line of reasoning which argues that since people seem to have no personal choice in their sexual orientation, allowance ought to be made for particular exceptions in which some manifestations of homogenital expression could be judged ethically moral. The Vatican letter distorts this argument by claiming that some people say that since the "homosexual orientation" is not in certain cases the result of deliberate choice, the homosexual individual "would then have no choice but to behave in a homosexual fashion" (no. 11).

Feigning horror that anyone would thus reduce homosexual behavior to that which is "always and totally compulsive" (no. 11)—which no one does—the letter nobly recognizes and defends for the homosexual person "the fundamental liberty which characterizes the human person and gives him [or her] dignity" (no. 11). This liberty, says the letter, must be recognized as belonging to the homosexual person as well. While no one will contest this, it is obvious that the letter does not intend that this liberty could include the liberty to express one's homosexual orientation in responsible genital modes.

In number 10 there seems to be a similar identification of "condition" with "activity." While decrying any violence against homosexual people, the letter argues that an inappropriate response to violence is to claim that the homosexual condition is not disordered. When this claim is made and when "homosexual activity is consequently condoned," or when legislation is introduced "to protect behavior," we should not be surprised at the increase of violence (no. 10).

In number 16 the very valid point is made that the human person can hardly be described adequately by a reductionist reference to "sexual orientation." This advice seems well placed especially since some church leaders see lesbian and gay people only in terms of their sexual orientation which is often identified solely with genital behavior. But the comment which immediately follows this warning reveals the writer's bias against the concept of sexual orientation as a valid psychological reality. Everyone, we are told, has "personal problems and difficulties" (no. 16). The homosexual condition/tendency/inclination or orientation is simply another kind of human problem or difficulty. Bolstering its argument against the validation of the scientific reality of sexual orientation, the letter states that the Church provides a badly needed context for pastoral care "when she refuses to consider the person a 'heterosexual' or a 'homosexual' " (no. 16). We all have a fundamental identity as creatures of God and, by God's grace, children and heirs to eternal life. Certainly no one will dispute this identity. But some children of God also have a black or a Hispanic identity and the Church takes these identities seriously in educational programs against racism and in pastoral outreaches to these groups. So, while the warning against reductionism is admirable in itself, the refusal to consider a person a *homosexual,* in practice, amounts to a denial of the psychosexual identity of the gay male and lesbian woman. This would not be true, however, in the case of considering people as *heterosexual* because, the letter argues, this sexual identity is a part of the creator's "sexual design" (no. 7).

Theological and Pastoral Implications

It is to the Vatican's distinct advantage in arguing its case against any psychological or moral acceptance of homosexuality to link as closely as possible—even at times to collapse—homosexual behavior with the homosexual condition. In this way *both* may be included in the one inclusive moral judgment of "disordered." This judgment has aroused the strongest opposition and the greatest discussion despite Quinn's attempt to soften the blow by describing the judgment as belonging to the philosophical order. Since the inclination is "a more or less strong tendency ordered toward an intrinsic moral evil . . . the inclination itself must be seen as an objective disorder" (no. 3). Thus a neat closure to the discussion is put into place: homogenital acts are lacking "finality" and are *objectively* disordered though not always *subjectively* sinful; the tendency toward these "acts" is also *objectively* disordered although not necessarily *subjectively* sinful. In this way the Vatican can even retain the "morally neutral" judgment on the orientation insofar as the individual is not necessarily held subjectively accountable for having an objectively disordered sexuality.

But once again the document betrays a serious misunderstanding of homosexuality as an orientation. Sexual orientation is not fundamentally or even primarily a tendency toward *acts,* but a psychosexual attraction (erotic, emotional, and affective) toward particular individual *persons.* The strategy of the letter to identify and link orientation and behavior is designed to counter another strategy which distinguishes the two in order to make separate moral and psychological judgments. The document is quite aware of this trend when it says that since 1975 some interpreters have given an overly benign evaluation to the homosexual condition going so far as to call it morally neutral or even good. One might also wonder if this warning applies to Archbishop Hickey's statement that a homosexual orientation "is not morally wrong in and of itself."[9]

To affirm the concept of a homosexual orientation in all of its psychological, sociological, and anthropological implications is to pave the way for a positive affirmation of the homosexual identity even apart from any overt genital expression. For most people a positive judgment on the orientation coupled with a negative evaluation of embodied genital expressions is an inadequate solution to the tensions many feel between the lived experience of their sexuality and their church membership. But the Vatican is not willing to concede any positive value to homosexuality even in its nongenital manifestations. Strangely enough, even one of earliest and most traditional treatments of homosexuality recognizes the deeper need of gay and lesbian people for friendship and intimacy. In *Principles to Guide Confessors in Questions of Homosexuality,* the author recognizes that the "deeper need of any human being is for friendship rather than genital expression, although this is usually an element in heterosexual relationships."[10] The same document advises the formation of stable friendships with at least one person, even another homosexual person. Despite what some might call an "occasion of sin," this is justified "considering his [or her] need for deep human relationships, and the good which will come from them in the future."[11]

The pastoral plan from San Francisco echoes similar sentiments when it says that it is a need for "closeness and intimacy that leads the homosexual person to seek stable relationships with another person."[12] And a moral theologian attempting to spell out the implications of affirming homosexual persons in their affective needs goes even further, stating that homosexual people have a "right and responsibility to actualize [their] human capacity for intimacy and relationships and to integrate [their] sexuality in those relationships. In other words, the homosexual has a right to establish stable, healthy, committed relationships of love—that is what it is to be a human person."[13] This is in sharp contrast to the advice of the Vatican letter that homosexual people have to follow Paul's injunction to crucify their "self-indulgent passions and desires" (no. 12) and warning that organizations for them might be "near occasions of sin" (no. 15). This attitude again betrays a strong tendency to identify homosexual orientation with uncontrollable sexual impulses and genital behavior.

Ironically, what has transpired in the U.S. Catholic community in the past ten years is exactly what the Vatican letter advises. Theologians and pastors have taken into serious consideration the assistance of the "psychological, sociological and medical sciences" (no. 17) in their approach to homosexual persons. Yet it is these very sciences which would support a more favorable interpretation of the homosexual orientation as one psychologically healthy form of human sexual identity. The San Francisco plan suggests that homosexuality be considered a "building block"[14] rather than a stumbling block in the ongoing search for unity and harmony, and urges church ministers to take seriously the feelings of homosexual people including their deep feelings about the "rightness"[15] of their sexuality. Sensitive pastoral expertise can help homosexual people "respect his or her own individual 'secret core.' "[16]

If the homosexual orientation is not psychologically disordered and if sexuality (including homosexuality) is central to human personhood, could we not affirm the homosexual orientation apart from gential expression as an avenue for some people to other human goods and values? This is the direction in which some U.S. Catholic thinkers are moving. The Vatican letter on homosexuality is an attempt to distance the magisterium from the implications of these more positive and affirming psychological, theological, and pastoral approaches.

While the letter acknowledges the legitimate and proper methodology of the natural sciences and even acknowledges that the Church can "learn from scientific discovery" (no. 2), there is the added caution that the Church can also transcend the limited horizons of science and do greater justice to the rich reality of the human person. For the magisterium the full and authentic reality of the human person of necessity requires heterosexuality. Any other manifestations of sexuality must be explained as a distortion of the creator's design. Among the explanations which have been put forth to explain the presence of homosexuality are psychological immaturity, impaired psychosexual development, and the effects of original sin which have affected the man-woman relationship.[17] From the magisterial perspective, human sexuality has its morally proper meaning only in heterosexual, married and procreative love.

Although the Vatican letter confuses terminology and is reluctant to validate or incorporate current data from the natural sciences which in any way might challenge or compromise its essentialist approach to human nature and assumptions about human sexuality, it does raise some crucial questions which might contribute to the formulation of the kind of sexual theology called for by Cardinal Bernardin and even go far beyond his original challenge. The cogency of a position which describes the homosexual identity as "objectively disordered" and all homosexual expression as lacking in "finality" stands or falls with the cogency of theological and biblical teachings about a timeless human nature. Theologically the question can be asked: Is there anything about Christian faith and life, or about the disclosures of God to which they are a response, that oblige us in all self-consistency to claim that heterosexuality is a timelessly unchanging structure of human nature which the creator intends as part of human fulfillment? Many would answer this with an unqualified yes. Others might argue that a Christian understanding of what is "normative" or "natural" for humanity should be grounded not in a doctrine of unchangeable creation, but in a Christian witness to a life to which we are summoned as future promise rather than past accomplishment.

Is the homosexual orientation and expression contradictory to humanity? Does the Christian faith have any stake in defending the view that human nature is an unchanging essense, a structure God-given and unchanging cross-culturally in all historical periods? And does faith have any stake in claiming that heterosexuality is an essential component of that structure? The Vatican letter urges "attentive study, active concern and honest, theologically well-balanced counsel" (no. 2) be given to the phenomenon of homosexuality because of its consequences for society and ecclesial life. In urging this study, the letter acknowledges, albeit

implicitly, that the issues involved are not necessarily closed once and for all, although it surely never envisions the kinds of questions just posed.[18]
If we are willing to engage the real and deeper issues and questions which any discussion of the topic of homosexuality begins to uncover, we might be able to halt the damage to the Church's credibility noted by Cardinal Bernardin at the beginning of this chapter. We might also be able to begin to lay some of the groundwork for a more positive approach to human sexuality and an articulation of magisterial teachings which will be accepted because they are reasonable, persuasive, and related to actual human experience.

Notes

1. J. Grootaers and J. Selling, *The 1980 Synod of Bishops "On the Family"* (Leuven, Belgium: Leuven University Press, 1983), p. 61.
2. D. Lehman, "Archdiocese Says Gay Love Acceptable, Sex Acts Not," *Chicago Sun-Times,* 20 July 1980, p. 5.
3. Senate of Priests, "Ministry and Homosexuality in the Archdiocese of San Francisco" (San Francisco: Senate of Priests, 1983).
4. J. R. Quinn, "Toward an Understanding of the Letter 'On the Pastoral Care of Homosexual Persons,' " *America* 156, no. 5 (7 February 1987), pp. 92–95, 116; reprinted in this volume.
5. Senate of Priests, "Ministry and Homosexuality," p. 10.
6. J. A. Hickey, "Letter on Homosexuality," in *Homosexuality and the Magisterium,* edited by J. Gallagher (Mt. Rainier, MD: New Ways Ministry, 1983), p. 94.
7. A good account of the APA change is found in R. Bayer, *Homosexuality and American Psychiatry* (New York: Basic Books, 1981).
8. G. Moran, "Gays: The Rome Way," *National Catholic Reporter,* 26 December 1986, p. 13.
9. Hickey, "Letter on Homosexuality," p. 95.
10. National Conference of Catholic Bishops, *Principles to Guide Confessors in Questions of Homosexuality* (Washington, DC: United States Catholic Conference, 1973), p. 11.
11. Ibid.
12. Senate of Priests, "Ministry and Homosexuality," pp. 16–17.
13. Lehman, "Archdiocese Says," p. 5.
14. Senate of Priests, "Ministry and Homosexuality," p. 9.
15. Ibid., p. 8.
16. Ibid., p. 20.
17. See Sacred Congregation for Catholic Education, "Educational Guidance in Human Love," in *Homosexuality and the Magisterium,* p. 89.
18. The author is indebted to Professor David Kelsey of the faculty of the Yale Divinity School for the formulation of the theological issues.

7

Two Unanswered Questions

John Coleman

The 1986 letter on the pastoral care of homosexual persons from the Congregation for the Doctrine of the Faith leaves unanswered completely two rather fundamental questions. The document itself admits that "an exhaustive treatment of this complex issue [i.e., homosexuality] cannot be attempted here" (no. 2). The first question then is this: What is the inner relationship between Catholic moral theology and applied pastoral theology? The second is: What is the Catholic position on laws protecting the civil liberties of homosexual persons in society, that is, their right to nondiscrimination policies and practices in housing, jobs, health care, citizens rights, and so on?

Morality and Pastoral Care

Catholic theology tends to make a distinction—not an absolute dichotomy—between the moral ideal enunciated in norms and principles and the pastoral care of those who can not yet fully embody the ideal. Its canon law recognizes *internal* and *external* forum solutions. Its pastoral practice toward the divorced, without compromising the Catholic ideal of indissolubility, moves compassionately. Respect for persons and their often slow growth into virtue and moral integrity serves as a counterweight to fidelity to abstract ideals and truth. Compassion counterbalances a legitimate concern for upholding the moral ideal.

Pope Paul VI, speaking to an international congress in 1970, enunciated this classic Catholic tension as it relates to his moral ideal of conjugal chastity promulgated in *Humanae Vitae* and its pastoral application:

> It is only little by little that the human being is able to order and integrate his multiple tendencies to the point of arranging them harmoniously in that virtue of conjugal chastity wherein the couple finds its full human and Christian development . . . their conscience

demands to be respected, educated and formed in an atmosphere of confidence and not anguish. The moral laws, far from being inhumanly cold in an abstract objectivity, are there to guide the spouses in their progress. When they truly strive to live the profound demands of holy love, patiently and humbly, without becoming discouraged by failures, then the moral laws . . . are no longer rejected as a hindrance, but recognized as a powerful help."[1]

Moral theology and pastoral application exist in a certain tension.

The moral theology of the so-called Roman school, especially, notoriously does not theoretically bridge the distance between the moral norm and pastoral applications. Thus, Jan Visser, one of the principal authors of the earlier document from the Congregation in 1975, "Declaration on Certain Questions Concerning Sexual Ethics," said in a printed interview that despite the clear moral condemnations of homosexual activity in that declaration, pastoral care might accept what the abstract principle rejects: "When one is dealing with people who are so deeply homosexual that they will be in serious personal and, perhaps, social trouble, unless they attain a steady partnership within their homosexual lives, one can recommend them to seek such a partnership and one accepts this relationship as the best they can do in their present situation."[2] Yet one would never have guessed from a reading of the declaration that its principal author held such pastoral opinions. Moral and pastoral theology remain, in his mind, two separate domains which do not, truly, interpenetrate. The teaching uncompromisingly adheres to a moral ideal; pastoral application allows for flexibility and compassion.

Classic Catholic moral theology looked to four elements in evaluating moral decisions, intentions and acts: (1) the moral norm, (2) the person's character (Karl Rahner remarks that a venial sin means something quite different in a person going from vice to virtue than vice versa), (3) consequences of actions, and (4) the situation. Thus some Catholic moral theologians have always felt uncomfortable with the sharp chasm in the Roman school between moral and pastoral theology. They desire greater congruence between the two realities. In the school which seeks to integrate the two more closely one finds Charles Curran, Louis Jannsens, and Bernard Häring.

The issue of the relationship of moral and pastoral theology remains unresolved by the CDF letter. Clearly it articulates one position on the question: no confusion between the two domains. But no authoritative Catholic position on the question exists. Moreover, the letter itself is not consistent on the question. A number of issues which it raises involve pastoral applications rather than moral norms as such. Among these are

Two Unanswered Questions · 61

the use of Catholic facilities by groups such as Dignity (no. 17) and support for civil laws guaranteeing protection from discrimination for homosexual people (no. 19). One wonders if those who support Visser's pastoral applications are included in the strictures against support for those who are "ambiguous" about church teaching on homosexuality (no. 17).

Conspicuously absent from the CDF letter is the kind of compassion, a sense of the moral life as a growth process and attention to persons and situations as well as ideal norms that one finds at least some glimpses of in the 1975 declaration on sexual ethics. Thus the latter document urged "prudence in judging the subjective seriousness or particular sinful acts"[3] and stated that "in the pastoral field, those homosexuals must certainly be treated with understanding and sustained in the hope of overcoming their personal difficulties and their inability to fit into society. Their culpability will be judged with prudence."[4] In place of this persistent pastoral tone the 1986 letter suggests that homosexual persons are callous in the face of the AIDS crisis (no. 19) and somehow responsible for violence perpetrated against them. Along with many others I was shocked by this rhetorical tone and asked, "Where is the mother in Mother Church, the pastoral nurturer, the one who does not trample on the broken reed?"

But the larger question of method has, in no way, really been answered by the document. What, precisely, *is* the relationship between moral and pastoral theology? One theory sharply divides the two yet allows a pastoral application which takes into account the subjective state, growth, and movement to moral integrity of the person. This is Visser's position. Another tries to achieve some deeper integration of the two as exemplified by Curran and Häring. The 1986 CDF letter mixes the two genres, subsumes some pastoral applications under the moral rubric, but studiously avoids any statement of pastoral compassion for the struggles of homosexual Christians. The larger theological question of application of moral principles to concrete pastoral situations and the relation of moral to pastoral theology as methods and praxis can not be settled by a fiat. Until that question is raised and answered—not finessed by ukase—we still do not really know what the "pastoral care" of homosexual persons in the Church should look like.

Civil Legislation on Homosexual Rights

The Vatican letter also does some finessing of hard questions when it deals with laws regulating discrimination against homosexual citizens. I was pleased when I read Archbishop John R. Quinn's commentary on the letter printed elsewhere in this collection. Quinn distinguishes between doctrinal affirmations and those which pertain more or less to "social commentary," and which have no doctrinal weight. He cites the statement of the letter about civil legislation as an example of the latter. Numbers 10 and 17 of the CDF letter seem to suggest that bishops should oppose civil laws which propose nondiscrimination for homosexual people out of a duty to protect family values. This position of the Congregation is a novelty in Catholic teaching and a dangerous simplification of a complex issue. Classically, beginning with Aquinas, Catholic thought has distinguished between the morality of certain acts and laws regulating those acts. The tradition has never been of one mind whether the law has to condemn contraception or divorce, for example. Indeed, the classic position of Aquinas in discussing the question of prostitution held that a moral evil could be tolerated by law to avoid even greater evils. One of the glories of classic Catholic moral teaching—its casuistry—was its nuanced positions, its sense of the real world of moral choices as complex, sometimes murky, and involving a balance of multiple human goods which are sometimes in conflict with one another.

I was shocked by the easy way in which the letter delicately manipulates some of these traditional Catholic distinctions. Its cavalier remark about "civil legislation . . . to protect behavior to which no one has any conceivable right" (no. 10) should be contrasted with Cardinal Joseph Bernardin's more traditional and careful position on gay rights legislation: "in the case of gay rights legislation I seek to balance two values: (1) the fact that no person should be discriminated against because of his or her sexual orientation; (2) the normativeness of heterosexual marital intimacy as the proper context for intimate genital encounters."[5] The CDF letter never addressed Bernardin's first value. Even the cardinal himself is forced to admit, "I have learned how difficult it is in our legal system for legislators who agree with my position to draft appropriate legislation."[6] Law and morality in the traditional Catholic theory should never be simply conflated as the CDF letter seems to do.

Number 10 of the letter has the feel of the older Catholic teaching that "error has no rights." I would have thought that the Vatican II Declaration on Religious Freedom would have helped to clarify this previous mistake. Error has no rights, but persons—who may or may not be in what Catholics feel to be partial error—retain their full range of human and civil rights because of their inherent dignity as human persons. They are, in fact, obliged morally to follow their conscience, even if it is erroneous.

Many homosexual people see the right to express their sexual orientation in actions and life choices as a matter of fundamental dignity and religious seriousness. They see this as a question of integrity of conscience and truth. In this sense the comments of Vatican II's Declaration on Religious Freedom would seem to apply to them: "No one is to be forced in a manner contrary to his own beliefs, whether privately or publicly, whether alone or in association with others."[7] "In consequence, the right to immunity (from civil coercion) continues to exist, even in those who do not live up to their obligation of seeking the truth and adhering to it and the exercise of this right is not to be impeded, provided that just public order be observed."[8] "Government is to see to it that equality of citizens before the law, which is itself an element of the common good, is never violated, whether openly or covertly. . . . Nor is there to be discrimination among citizens."[9] For many homosexual citizens, being true to their orientation is central, religiously core, to their integrity of conscience. Even if Catholics think that conscience erroneous, argues the Declaration on Religious Freedom, the law should respect their freedom of conscience in these matters.

I have long held that a classic Catholic case can and should be made for support of civil liberties for homosexual people grounded on their human dignity as persons and that this case *need not,* in principle, in any way compromise the affirmation made in the CDF letter that "It is only in the marital relationship that the use of the sexual faculty can be morally good. A person engaging in homosexual behavior therefore acts immorally" (no. 7). No logic demands that acceptance of this maxim include a program to deny civil liberties to homosexual citizens. Catholic logic might argue, indeed, the very opposite. Even Catholics who view homosexual behavior as a moral error cannot deny that homosexual persons continue to have and deserve all their basic human rights. It has been my understanding of the Declaration on Religious Freedom that Catholic teaching should support these rights—not necessarily laws which recognize homosexuality as such as a social alternative (e.g., domestic partners' laws), but certainly all ordinary civil liberties against discrimination in housing, employment, job opportunities, and so on.

My dilemma when told that an authentic teaching of the magisterium such as the 1986 CDF letter demands internal and respectful assent is how I am to square this assent with what seems to be a contradiction between various teachings of the magisterium. Vatican II affirms that those in error who, nevertheless, follow their conscience have a right and a duty to seek human dignity as they see it and that the civil law should respect this freedom of conscience. The document from the Congregation seems to deny this conciliar teaching. The Congregation would have been better served by being more traditionally Catholic, less innovative, and by reasserting the traditional Catholic distinction between moral goods and evils and the laws which protect moral goods and proscribe moral evils. Not all moral evils can or should be proscribed by law precisely to avoid a greater evil. Laws which discriminate against homosexual people strike me as perpetrating such great moral evil that they should be resisted on traditional Catholic grounds. In *We Hold These Truths*, John Courtney Murray argued that laws against contraception would involve a greater evil of state intrusiveness into bedrooms. A similar logic would apply to the private acts of consenting homosexual adults. It is clear, to me at least, that a classic and traditional case can be made for Catholic support for civil liberties for homosexual people. In this, I find the recent CDF letter quite untraditional. For this reason, I think the U.S. Catholic bishops were much closer to the mark when they taught that "Homosexuals, like everyone else, should not suffer from prejudice against their basic human rights. They have a right to respect, friendship and justice. They should have an active role in the Christian community."[10]

A friend of mine told me that in a conversation with a U.S. bishop known to be relatively conservative theologically the bishop said to him that he found the CDF letter an embarrassment pastorally. Its tone and rhetoric lacked compassion. In his justly famous *colloquium morale* in Rome in the fall of 1986, Joseph Fuchs, professor emeritus of moral theology at the Gregorian University, asked whether the scripture argument in the document grounds the conclusions drawn and answered in the negative. One certainly has to wonder what such a document might have looked like if it had been written by a genuine pastor such as Pope John XXIII. But the burden of my own response to the letter lies more in a different argument. It has not answered for us two telling questions in Catholic moral theology. How are we to relate moral norms to pastoral applications? What is the relation of law and morality and, in particular, the status of a Catholic case for supporting, in law, the civil rights of homosexual persons? Until these two questions are explicitly posed and adequately answered, not only is the CDF letter not "exhaustive," but it is also very confusing.

Notes

1. Paul VI, "Christian Witness in Married Life," *The Pope Speaks* 15, no. 2 (1970): 126.

2. J. McManus, "The Declaration on Certain Questions Concerning Sexual Ethics," *Clergy Review* 61, no. 6 (June 1976): 233.

3. J. Gallagher, ed., *Homosexuality and the Magisterium* (Mt. Rainier, MD: New Ways Ministry, 1986), p. 5.

4. Ibid.

5. J. Bernardin, "I Too Struggle," *Commonweal*, 26 December 1986, p. 683.

6. Ibid., p. 684.

7. In J. Gremillion, ed., *The Gospel of Justice and Peace* (New York: Orbis Books, 1976), p. 339.

8. Ibid.

9. In Gremillion, p. 342.

10. National Conference of Catholic Bishops, "To Live in Christ Jesus" (Washington, DC, 11 November 1976), quoted in Gallagher, p. 9.

8

Pastoral Care and Homosexual Persons: Whose Definitions?

P. A. van Gennip

The following reflections reveal a deep disappointment with the Vatican letter on homosexuality, and provide the motives for the final judgment on the adequacy of the document. The letter falls short because it doesn't do justice to the seriousness and the nuances of the problems at stake. Another reason for this negative judgment is the fact that since the Congregation for the Doctrine of the Faith has a particular role in the teaching office of the Church, one should expect quality arguments and explanations from such a work.

In view of this expectation it is really less important whether or not one holds the same opinion as the Congregation. In matters of controversy, especially, even though one might be reluctant to accept strict points of view, we can be challenged by the document's argumentation to come to a new way of thinking about the issues. It seems to me, however, that three main objections prevent this letter from having this kind of effect: (1) in several places it is marred by inferior and suggestive remarks; (2) its tone is such, that even in its structure, it suggests a kind of hypocrisy; (3) it is intellectually inconsistent in several areas.

If these basic objections are correct (and this chapter will attempt to illustrate them from the document itself), then two things are at stake in this letter. The first is a responsible approach to homosexuality. And the second is the credibility of the Congregation for the Doctrine of the Faith as one of the most important locales of support for the teaching office as well as the teaching authority of the office itself.

As an aside, the latter problem cannot be avoided by simply demanding blind obedience from the faithful. The document is a form of speaking wisely in concrete matters or a way of speaking prudentially. The degrees of theological certainty of this kind of teaching need to be carefully distinguished.[1] The letter's continual appeal to the authentic teaching of the Church seems to be used more to fill in the gaps in the reasoning process than to affirm the document's doctrinal status. Therefore, until further notice the letter may be considered to be a working paper, that is, a collection of pastoral suggestions and their underlying motivations written for bishops and pastors.

Elements of Rhetoric

The letter makes some allusions to recent events and offers certain qualifications to developments that are much in the news. In itself this could be considered progress in that the Congregation has tried to make the usual degree of abstraction more concrete and to break from a more formal and official style. But this attempt presupposes, however, a clear presentation based on a nuanced view of the facts. In point of fact, however, there is quite a lot to find fault with in the document itself.

The fact that homosexuality itself is presented as a "problem" and therefore as an object of special pastoral care will be seen by some as an example of a too theoretical and tendentious approach to the topic. It should be remarked, however, that this perspective may not be judged negatively beforehand. Homosexual people, for instance, who do not view themselves as "problems" can live with the fact that there are other approaches, traditions, and ways of thinking that raise questions about the "problem" point of view. They are ready to answer these questions openly and honestly. The problem is not that certain ecclesiastical circles have objections to homosexuality. The problem lies in the way they approach these objections. The following are some examples.

In number 8 the text seems to imply that those in the Church who insist on a correction of the teaching about homosexuality are in close affiliation with similar movements outside the Church (the gay liberation movement) and therefore, consciously or unconsciously, support a materialistic ideology. In number 7 homosexual acts are always and *in se* a reinforcement of a disorderly sexual drive which has to be reduced to pure self-indulgence, regardless of the intentions of the individual person. In number 9 it is said that certain pressure groups want to give the impression that they represent all homosexual persons who are Catholic, but in reality they ignore the teaching of the Church or undermine it; and if the remarks about homosexual practices that are a threat to the "lives and well-being of a large number of people" is a reference to the AIDS crisis, then it has to be rejected as in very bad taste. In number 10 does the text mean that the legal protection that the civil authorities give to homosexual people is too much and a source of understandable violence in society? In number 14 we are warned of wolves in sheep's clothing who in their calculated ambiguity want to bring pressure on the Church and attack its authority in view of changing the one, true teaching.

Such rhetorical qualifications do not occur very often in recent official church documents. As a member of the faithful I think that they should not appear here either. It is especially deplorable that they reoccur with a subject matter such as this. These approaches appeal more readily to prejudices both positive and negative than to clear insights and well-balanced judgments. Therefore one assumes a much more serious responsibility in speaking or writing in this way.

The Concept of Pastoral Care

The letter defines itself explicitly as a pastoral letter. There are several definitions of pastoral care.[2] Therefore it is not easy to discern whether this definition offered is correct. It might be helpful, then, to summarize how the letter itself understands the word *pastoral*.

The document assumes that there is only one teaching on the question of homosexuality—one which throughout the ages has come from the inscrutable ordinances of God. Everyone who does not give full consent to this teaching must be mistrusted, and suggestions that the teaching needs to be adapted or changed are an assault on truth itself. Homosexual people who are or want to be Catholic should not do anything but put this theory into practice unchanged. The Church helps them to do this and that is its pastoral ministry. All disciplinary measures have to be employed to avoid anything else being done other than helping put church teaching into practice. Help from "outside sources," such as science or politics, is welcomed but only acceptable insofar as they begin from these principles.

On the positive side of this understanding of pastoral is the fact that it is unambiguous. But it is also very clear that by its very lack of ambiguity it does not fulfill a central condition for a concept of pastoral: the concrete situation of people with all their possibilities and problems is not taken into account. It looks at the teaching but does not in the least listen to the people involved. Neither their questions seem to be heard nor their experiences, expectations, possibilities, failures given any consideration.

The letter thereby at least seems to be somewhat hypocritical. A number of times it is stated that the Church tries to enhance the real salvation of homosexual people. But immediately it is said that this has to be done within the Church's doctrinal and disciplinary framework. That is the only guarantee for salvation. The question is not asked whether the human reality offers any proof for this kind of identification. It is clear, however, that in the view of the Congregation it is in the best interest of the Church to assert this identification of salvation with church doctrine. But whose interest is really being served in such an understanding of pastoral: the interest of homosexual people or the interest of the Church?

A large majority of the priests and pastoral assistants of the city of 's Hertogenbosch in the Netherlands have let their bishop know that in the event that he would take any disciplinary measures against homosexual people as a result of the Vatican letter, they would refuse any cooperation. One of them, a well-known conservative priest-theologian, was very instrumental in initiating this response of refusal to cooperate. The Vatican letter obviously takes its starting point in the assumption that homosexual people by very definition are hedonists lacking any discipline. In pastoral experience, however, one is clearly confronted with homosexual people who are genuinely concerned with finding for themselves a responsible way of living. Therefore the letter's starting point is unacceptable for directives for pastoral care.

However, even for homosexual people for whom this is not or at least not that obviously true, the best pastoral approach of the Church would be not to confront them with harsh doctrine. At least the question should be raised why there is such a large gap between doctrine and practice. The contrast between the Church's demand for sexual continence and various gradations of promiscuity is very sharp and, humanly speaking, even a caricature. Is there really always such debauchery and limitless hedonism among homosexual people? Isn't there in many cases a structural and/or personal *force majeur*, an attempt to stay more or less mentally healthy and even an expression of compassion in relation to others?

It is very important in this context to draw attention to the fact that the problem under discussion here is not typically homosexual morality. It is a matter of sexual morality in general. In the heterosexual community all kinds of sexual behaviors can be found that are not in accordance with church teaching. Here, again, the Church's pastoral ministry is confronted with the major question whether homosexual people are to be identified with infidelity, debauchery, or a lack of moral discipline. Many times certain other factors play a role. And this raises the question whether homosexual people are helped by simply enunciating those principles which, if observed, are supposed to help them attain their eventual salvation even though the observation is sometimes impossible.

We know that the possibilities of staying in touch with the ideal are easily destroyed if the distance between realities (for which often no other alternative is available) and an ideal is too great.[3] The plea for chastity as a way of life has to stay attuned to peoples' actual circumstances and opportunities. It should not conflict with real life in such a way that it would more easily provoke licentiousness than limit it. Once again, by proposing the harsh alternatives of either complete abstinence or moral condemnation, this approach to homosexuality is very sharp edged.

How should the Church approach this matter? From a need to defend an objective world order deduced from a specific interpretation of the belief that God is the creator of heaven and earth and all its fullness? Or from the evangelical mission to be neighbor, to confirm the brother and sister and to be compassionate, and in so doing keep the adventure of the love of God and others alive in all aspects of human life?

Circular Reasoning and Inner Contradictions

This is the third level on which the Vatican letter can be critiqued. Because of the questions and emphases provided by the document itself, it is also the most essential area. It has to do with the doctrine's motivation and cogency.[4]

We are not speaking about the doctrine itself now. Not because it is presented as the only truth and therefore cannot be questioned without losing one's Catholicity. It has already been indicated that the letter does not have such a strong dogmatic status either in its content or its form. The fact that in places it suggests that it does have this status can be seen as another rhetorical device. It is also possible to view this as a way of concealing an inner lack of cogency.

Whether one accepts the doctrine of the letter or not, there seem to be some gaps in its line of reasoning. For those who adhere to the letter's viewpoint, a reflection on these questions can solidify their position of agreement. For others who do not follow the document's views or do so only partially, a reflection on the gaps can be the way to continue to plead for a more responsible adaptation of the letter's positions.

The importance of this discussion for all parties requires that all reject any approach which tries to render ambiguous either the Church's teaching on the matter or its authority.[5] In the Catholic Church the importance of reason in the unfolding of revelation was always acknowledged. Since this matter is so closely linked up with a discussion of the natural order, this reflection ought not be closed prematurely by an appeal to supernatural authority.

At the same time, the right of the Congregation to give various directives to the bishops for various kinds of pastoral care is not to be denied. It can also be said in favor of the Congregation that it tried to base these directives in an understanding of the content of the issue at hand. It is certainly possible that either the bishops because of internal discipline or other political considerations do not want to involve themselves in a discussion about these directives or that they are quite motivated to follow them completely. The point being made is that the view behind the directives does not therefore have to be right. And so, for example, because of the impact of all these factors the real questions that can be addressed to the document's views are not yet answered.

From the standpoint of theology and from a need for intellectually consistent reasoning in general, it is necessary to examine more closely the five following aspects: the evaluation of the homosexual orientation; the evaluation of homosexual behavior; the Christian demand for self denial; the interfacing of different legal systems; the problem of historical and local limitedness.

The evaluation of the homosexual orientation

In the booklet *Homosexual People in Society*[6] the Dutch Council for Church and Society says that if one accepts the special character of the homosexual orientation, then there is a need for a more convincing account for the condemnation of homosexual behavior than is usually found in church documents. These latter usually say that the orientation must be judged as "deficient" because it leads to homosexual behavior.[7]

Two remarks can be made here. The first is related to a statement of Professor T. Beemer[8]: this view embodies a more harsh condemnation of homosexual people than was usually found up until now. In the past only certain kinds of behavior used to be condemned. Now the orientation is condemned and, accordingly, the person also in a very vital but not all-decisive aspect of his or her being.

This condemnation goes further than the teaching of the Church that all people are naturally sinful but able to do good by cooperating with grace. Heterosexual people, however, are even more able, while cooperating with grace (which seems to be their sexual orientation itself), to give an expression to the rich symbolism which the creator has laid into creation.[9] Homosexual people, however, cannot go any further than avoiding the near occasion of sin that is actually already present in their own sexual orientation as an "objective disorder."

The second remark concerns the question: What exactly is meant by the concept "objective disorder"? It is a totally new concept. Human imperfection, up until recently, found a more specific expression in the two basic concepts of illness and sin. Illness is a catch-all for human imperfection in the *natural* order; sin is the same thing in the *moral* order. It seems that the term, "objective disorder" is deliberately chosen to avoid both these terms.

That is understandable. If "illness" were chosen, the possibility of affirming free will in order to choose continence would have become very minimal. After all, one cannot put the moral duty on a blind person to see better! If "sin" were chosen, the possibility of speaking of free will wouldn't even have been necessary. The burden of guilt would have been increased beforehand in such a way that each motive to decrease it would have been undermined by a kind of predestination. Therefore the choice of "objective disorder" is quite understandable. A concept was needed that expresses the evil of the orientation and at the same time allows for some sensible motivation for continence as a way to keep to a minimum the damage that has already been done.

These suppositions do not make the concept clear, by the way. It seems to me that the attempt to resolve the dilemma was not really successful. This is especially so because it has unexpected repercussions for those homosexual people who, convinced in the deepest part of themselves that they are "that way," chose the royal route of continence as a lay person, monk, or minister. Now they are confronted with the fact that their choice to avoid the "near occasion of sin" doesn't resolve very much. For the real problem is not in the avoidable near occasion somewhere else, but structurally inside of themselves as an "objective disorder." They are their own "near occasion" of sin!

The evaluation of homosexual behavior

That the homosexual orientation is an "objective disorder" is proved by the fact that homosexual individuals have a natural access to the objective evil of homosexual behavior. This shift of the burden of proof makes one curious as to the reasons why and how homosexual behavior is an objective evil.

The letter is concise in this point: homosexual behavior is objectively evil because Scripture and the teaching office say so. It has to be said to be evil because it is not heterosexual behavior. The linking of the original order of creation with the "nuptial meaning" of the body and sexuality[10] indicates that for the Christian marriage is the only morally responsible way of living sexuality. Only marital sexuality does justice to the objectives and the rich symbolism put into the natural order by the creator. This is further developed in three criteria of heterosexuality: (1) complementarity is expressed that (2) brings forth life and (3) therein gives existence the form of self-giving. These three criteria are valid in relation to one another.

It is clear that they can only be valid criteria in this context because the point of departure is a biological one. Only in a strict biological perspective can it be concluded that homosexual relationships are never able to live up to these criteria. It cannot be excluded beforehand, however, that a homosexual relationship in a more metaphorical, personal, or spiritual sense will meet these criteria; that is, a mutually complementary union of persons that is fecund for themselves and their environment and that inspires and enables them to deep forms of self-giving which, according to the gospel, is the very essence of the Christian life.[11]

It should be questioned whether the same amount of complementarity, fecundity, and self-giving can be reached through the practice of continence. This is particularly a question in the case of those who haven't received the grace of virginity for the sake of the reign of God, but who are only burdened with the "objective disorder" of a homosexual orientation. To pose the question seems at the very same time to answer it.

The question whether homosexual behavior could not also be an expression of licentiousness, hedonism, materialism, and the like, is not at issue. The question is whether it necessarily has to be that. The question is whether it also could be an expression of complementarity, fecundity, and self-giving, if not in a strictly biological sense, still in a very real sense. If this is possible, then the question also arises as to what form the Church's pastoral ministry should take depending on the precise meaning that is given to sexual behavior. Should the ministry aim at avoiding or eliminating it? Should it attempt to direct it to religious and evangelical values. If the latter were chosen, then a different kind of pastoral ministry would be encouraged and a much different use of church resources would be involved than the ones proposed in the Vatican letter.

The Christian demand for self-denial

The document further urges the path of continence for homosexual people by treating more extensively the text of Paul that says those "who belong to Christ have crucified the flesh with its passions and its desires."[12] In this way, we are told, Christians have gained access to the fruits of the Spirit that in Pauline speech are opposites of the fruits of the flesh: Love, happiness, peace, patience, kindness, goodness, fidelity, meekness, and self-control. It is remarkable in this context that Paul does not mention a large number of children under this list of fruits of the Spirit. This seems to be a witty observation but it is in reality very essential because it provides another framework for the development of the concept of fertility in its Christian dimensions than the one given by the Vatican letter. A consequence is a different relationship between the order of creation and the imitation of Christ in his death on the cross and resurrection.

There is no doubt that in the context of the imitation of Christ, chastity has a general Christian meaning. Globally speaking, it is the virtue that makes us free for the gifts of the Spirit[13] while dealing with the body and human sexuality, liberating the person from the law[14] and elevating people out of the order of creation which is in labor until the revelation of the freedom of the children of God.[15] The virtue of chastity involves a perspective of salvation for all Christians—women or men, married or single, heterosexual or homosexual, lay person or ordained—in their dealings with their own sexuality.

Looking at it this way, Christians have not attained the fulfillment of the imitation of Christ if they only behave in a certain way. Nor have they when their behavior is considered to be morally correct. Theological or spiritual behavior must also be criticized as must every form of behavior because a fundamental dimension of human reality is left out of consideration if this is not included. This is the dimension of realizing values, and in this case it is a question of the values of salvation.

One cannot, from a kind of cathartic radicalism, turn this around so that behavior has no relevance at all. Behavior is a touchstone if we ask the question whether the professed values are indeed put into practice and the imitation is of such depth as to be a real unification with the living Christ. Only in the interaction of values and behavior does the process of imitation of Christ get its concrete outline and become incarnated, human reality.

And so we must also raise the question how the relationship between the moral and the theological-spiritual dimension should be conceived. If one accepts the view of the Vatican letter and considers homosexual behavior from a moral perspective as an "intrinsic moral evil,"[16] does one thereby deny any access to the fruits of the Spirit to those who behave in that manner? Furthermore, would this be so because they behave sexually?

The latter cannot be the conclusion. For it is true for heterosexual people that their sexual behavior as such is not a barrier to the fruits of the Spirit. Certain heterosexual excesses can be and even then only in varying degrees. The heart of the matter, then, must be that moral correctness (which implies sexual behavior for heterosexual people but only continence for homosexual people) is considered a necessary condition for sharing in the fruits of the Spirit.

It must be questioned whether such a strong emphasis on a work ethic for holiness and morality is supported by tradition. The concern of the teaching office for a certain moral order has a certain value and worth. But it is always relativized by the awareness of the particularity of the imitation of Christ. God's spirit blows freely and gives grace to whomever God wants. To reduce this realization to a harsh legitimation of the moral order which demands a necessary condition seems to be an attack on the genuine message of revelation. This would seem to be a social or even bourgeois curtailing of a perspective that darkens rather than enlightens the inscrutable mystery of God.

This also means that we have to be careful in urging the appeal to the "imitation" of Christ and its implied demand for self-denial for every Christian in moral matters. Every Christian is called to put off the old person so that the new one can grow into the full measure of the humanity of Christ.[17] This understanding cannot be used without further consideration either to legitimate definite moral insights in general or—certainly not in this case—to sweeten the bitter pill of enforced continence. It has to be made clear, first of all, why it is possible to develop a humanly dignified moral relationship (whether from the supposed unchangeable order of creation or not) involving the imitation of Christ and grace in heterosexual behavior, but not in homosexual behavior. It also has to be made clear whether the recommendations of continence really contribute to the renewal of the new person in an evangelical sense or only, as often seems, to an obsessive hardening of the old one?

The interfacing of different legal systems

The interest of the Catholic tradition in morality, which in itself is justified, turns out not only to generate tension with other dimensions of the same tradition but also to raise questions about the relationship of one particular moral system with others. These questions are defined where, through the democratic decision-making processes, those other systems have been embodied in certain opinions about the job of the state and its responsibility for the laws and for protecting its citizens from violence.

One can avoid the problem more or less by developing a variation on the doctrine of the two kingdoms. As a believer the Christian is subject to ecclesiastical laws; as a citizen of the state, to the laws of the state. Such a solution takes as its starting point the belief that the borders between both realms are clear. The principle of separation of church and state will, therefore, be strictly interpreted both in the public and private spheres.

Theoretically this would, perhaps, be possible. But in the actual situation there are many more borderline cases. It is clear, moreover, that the teaching office of the Church correctly is not ready in principle to have itself confined to strictly "churchy" issues. The message of Jesus Christ forces each Christian to testify to the world—whether this testimony is welcomed or not. This is also true even when the particular testimony involved goes against the goals and procedures of the civil or state authorities.[18]

Whoever accepts this principle, however, at the same time is confronted with the fact that those goals and procedures in a democratic constitutional state in which a large percentage of the population is Catholic also come to be accepted through the influence of those Catholics. Sometimes representatives of the teaching office seem to be more involved in a discussion with their own faithful than with governments when addressing political issues.

It is important to realize that not every religious approach, either in its moral importance or in the influence it exercises in civil society, has the same value. On the one hand are fundamental religious notions about absolute limits in shaping the common good, including respect for and protection of life, striving for human living conditions, and questions of peace and justice; on the other are ideas which have a different importance, ideas often discussed within the religious community itself, about personal morality and individual lifestyles.[19]

It must be said that the Vatican letter is not always as nuanced in this regard as required by the subtlety of the problems. It breaks the boundaries of in-house preaching in three points. In the first place, it suggests that the liberation movement of homosexual people outside the Church is characterized by a materialistic ideology.[20] In the second place, this statement has direct political relevance in number 10 which says that the legal protection given by civil authorities to homosexual persons (and which must be give in most democratic constitutional states) is an element of the process of social demoralization. Because of this protection it is understandable that violence against homosexual people in society increases.[21] Finally, the bishops are warned in number 14 against public (read: political) declarations which by their calculated ambiguity might obstruct the direct implementation of the Catholic view that is to be found in the Vatican letter on civil legislation.

The conclusion seems to be that the Church is playing, more implicitly than explicitly, a risky game. But it is this very implicitness that gets in the way. The letter isn't really clear whether there is a fundamental religious notion about an absolute limit in giving shape to the common good in the question of homosexuality which is comparable to the example of this given above. Are the rather more private notions about personal morality and individual lifestyles shared by large groups of people?

This lack of clarity about the relationship between public duty and private preference is worsened by reasoning from the "order of creation." As far as the political relevance of this model is concerned, neither the theoretical explanation of it nor the biblical sources used to describe it provide any points of departure for the general conclusions which are drawn. And surely not with the measure of certainty suggested in the above mentioned paragraphs of the letter.

The problem of historical and local limitedness

The document leaves no doubt about the fact that it views itself as an explanation of *the* Catholic teaching. It says that it represents *the* Catholic view that was always valid and always will be. It does refer to the problem of the historical origin of the teaching, but it limits itself to Scripture at that point. It resolves this problem by appealing to a harmony between the continuous condemnations of homosexuality in Scripture and the way this judgment was continued by the teaching office. It doesn't look for other possible traditions in Holy Scripture itself. Nor does it deal with the question whether there really is continuity in the several appropriate texts. It does not pose the question whether the problems dealt with in the Bible are the same ones as ours. The reason for a negative response to this last question is simply the fact that the biblical authors, whatever their opinion about homosexual behavior may have been, seem not to have had any insight into homosexual orientation.[22] There are no sources indicated for supporting the continuity of the official teaching other than the statements that are directly connected with the ones found in the letter itself. As for retracing the teaching backwards, there is only an encyclopedical continuity. This is said to be an expression of continuity in the teaching's content but no arguments are given showing this continuity.

Between the belief that God will keep the Church in the truth, including the functioning of the teaching office, and this very positivistic interpretation of the "continuity of truth" some questions arise. The model of an objective order of creation from which clear and unchanging laws for human life can be deduced does not answer these questions. This is especially so because the questions indicate how this approach is a dated one, although not necessarily wrong. Nevertheless, it is still a model that only with certain limitations expresses what is professed in the creed: "I believe in God, the Almighty, Creator of heaven and earth." That limitation, however, does not stand in the way of a very recognizable legitimating role for the model in ecclesiastical discipline. No definitive judgment about that model is given here, nor about the importance of ecclesiastical discipline. What it does indicate, however, is a limitation that in modern language refers to the question of historical consciousness.

This problem is not solved by indicating the alternatives that were developed in other times and places. The question is whether this model is allowed to claim here and now the deepest personal acceptance, that is, may it demand religious assent?

In this perspective the question about the plausibility structure of the model of the order of creation becomes pressing. In this context attention can be drawn to the fact that our culture has become more sensitive in respecting natural cohesion. But at the same time it experiences this demand for religious assent to the order-of-creation model to be in competition with the principle of human, free self-determination. The appeal to the timeless and suprahistorical character of a particular view does not evoke confidence as such, although one is not always capable of proving its datedness.

The datedness of the order-of-creation model has been proven convincingly by several theological studies. But again, with no more evidence than this, we cannot conclude that these insights are correct. We may prove, however, that the credibility of the attempt to legitimate the order-of creation insights is not enhanced by an appeal to their suprahistorical character for a contemporary religious self-understanding.

It may be clear that I am not happy with the Vatican letter on the pastoral care of homosexual persons. I judge the quality of the document to be poor. It is unacceptable that, at the level of one of the teaching office's most important structures, a problem that is so vital and concerns probably 5 to 10 percent of the human population, including the faithful, is treated so carelessly.

One can disregard this fact with the supposition that probably few people, let alone homosexual people, will take notice of the letter. But even if that were the case, the bishops would still have the responsibility to treat it seriously. And one thing will lead to another. Furthermore, I cannot see why homosexual people in general and religious ones in particular are not allowed to expect more from their Church than a condemnation of their orientation and untrustworthy demands about their behavior elaborated in an unsatisfactory manner.

This will probably not be a large problem for those religiously inclined homosexual people who have been able, in a harmonious process of self-acceptance, guided by an informed conscience, to develop an integrated way of life. We do have to be concerned a great deal, however, about those who under the pressure of conflicting expectations and longings, both within themselves and directed toward them, feel torn apart and lose a sense of their goals. That concern is even more urgent because it is well known how this experience of disintegration can harden itself into a lack of perspective and an attitude of bitterness. Thereby not only the quality of one's life but even that life itself are put in danger.

We can only have responsible pastoral care and serious directives for it insofar as that concern plays a role. That is hardly the case in the letter from the Congregation for the Doctrine of the Faith. It does not, therefore, offer a useful contribution to the religious task of facilitating the goal of the fully developed human person, that of praising God: *Laus Deo homo vivens.*

This quotation used here is deliberately ambiguous since *homo* in Latin means human being but also *homosexual* in Dutch. But this ambiguity is not meant to mislead the shepherds and the faithful. It is meant to make all of us aware of the experience of salvation in which we are all allowed to take part and which we make present for each other, precisely because we are called to be his Church.

Notes

1. See X. Thevenot, "Magistere et discernment moral," *Esprit*, 1985, pp. 231–44; E. Schillebeeckx, "Kerkelijk spreken over sexualiteit en huwelijk," in *Het Kerkelijk spreken over sexualiteit en huwelijk,* ed. T. Beemer et al. (Nijmegen/Baarn, 1983), pp. 220–24, especially: "Official teaching in the church is not the same as talking personally as a theologian; official teaching is essentially subject to a personal-ascetic reservedness" (p. 221).

2. See H. Faber, ed., *Handboek Pastoraat: Pastorale Perspektieven in een veranderende samenleving* (Deventer/Amersfoort, 1982), especially the introduction to part 4.

3. One does not have to adhere to the Freudian theory about the superego to be able to agree with this viewpoint. Buytendijk and Fortman, two Dutch authors, have occupied themselves with these problems in such a way that they have started a trend in pastoral theology and psychology.

4. The statement that the pope saw the document before it was published can

be taken as a suggestion that he was happy with it, but also as a sign that he doesn't want to treat the matter in an encyclical for the time being.

5. See no. 14 in the Vatican letter.

6. Catholic Council for Church and Society, *Homosexual People in Society* (published in Dutch; 's Hertogenbosch, 1979), p. 21.

7. No. 3 in the letter.

8. *De Volksktrant,* 31 January 1987.

9. See no. 7 in the letter.

10. See nos. 6 and 7 in the letter.

11. See no. 7 in the letter.

12. Gal. 5:22 and 24. In this context it is very remarkable that the confusing verse 23, "Against such things [the fruits of the Spirit] there is no law," is not quoted.

13. See also 1 Cor. 12:1–12; Eph. 5:3–20 (where the theological nucleus of the problem is to be discovered); and Col. 3:1–17.

14. Rom. 7:6 and parallels.

15. Rom. 8:21–22.

16. No. 3 in the letter.

17. *Gaudium et Spes,* no. 22, especially: "For, since Christ died for all, and since the ultimate vocation of [all human beings] is in fact one, and divine, we ought to believe that the Holy Spirit in a manner known only to God offers to every [one] the possibility of being associated with this paschal mystery."

18. *Gaudium et Spes,* nos. 83–90.

19. *Unitatis Redintegratio,* chap. 11, no. 11: "When comparing doctrines with one another, they should remember that in Catholic doctrine there exists a 'hierarchy' of truths, since they vary in their relation to the fundamental Christian faith." See also P. Franssen, "Geloof en zenden: Notitie over een veelgebruikte formule," *Tijdschrift voor Theologie* 9 (1969): 315–26.

20. See no. 8 in the letter.

21. See no. 10 in the letter.

22. Catholic Council for Church and Society, *Homosexual People in Society,* p. 15.

9

Morality and the Law: A Feminist Critique of the Vatican Letter

Mary C. Segers

The Vatican letter on the pastoral care of homosexual persons is the latest in a series of actions dating from 1984 which are of deep concern to American Catholics. These include: the Vatican 24 episode in which the Congregation for Religious threatened twenty-four nuns with expulsion from their communities because they signed a 1984 *New York Times* ad calling for open discussion of abortion policy; the censure of Catholic University theologian Father Charles Curran; the dehumanizing treatment of Archbishop Raymond Hunthausen, the Seattle ordinary who was stripped of jurisdiction over major matters in his archdiocese; and now the Vatican condemnation of homosexuality and of efforts to secure the rights of gay persons to human dignity and social justice. Together, these actions reflect a powerful impulse of the Roman bureaucracy to define orthodoxy. The letter on homosexuality should be understood as part of this series of events because its main intent seems to be to affirm loudly and clearly the traditional moral teaching of the hierarchical Church on the immorality of homosexual acts. It is but one more example of Rome's strenuous efforts to clarify church teaching to a faithful thought to be confused by the subtleties and complexities of post-Vatican II moral theology.

As a political scientist concerned with human rights, jurisprudence, and the law, I read the Vatican statement first with a view to public policy implications. I cannot be sanguine about these, for the Vatican letter takes a dim view of efforts to secure the civil rights of gay people by changing civil laws. The first part of this chapter questions this view. I argue that, in a pluralist society, the Church's position on civil law and the Church's moral teaching are separable and that, with respect to the rights of

81

homosexuals, the Church's jurisprudence need not and should not reflect its moral theology.

The second part of this chapter questions the Church's moral theology itself which declares the intrinsic immorality of homoerotic relations. Theological and ethical reflections upon the experience of same-sex love suggests that human sexuality encompasses a broad range of human experience manifested in a variety of personal relations of mutuality, intimacy, and respect. Here I have learned a great deal from the writings of Catholic lesbian feminists and I shall rely upon them to sketch in outline a critique of the Church's moral teaching on homosexuality. This chapter thus takes issue with statements of the Vatican letter concerning both the legality and the morality of same-sex relations.

* * *

To briefly summarize the letter's contents, the Church's teaching as stated in this document is that homosexual orientation and activity are not neutral, let alone good, but must be "seen as an objective disorder" and as leading to actions which are intrinsically evil. The Church's public policy position follows from this: that civil legislation should not be introduced "to protect behavior to which no one has any conceivable right" (no. 10). Claiming firm foundation in constant biblical testimony, the Vatican claims that the practice of homosexuality is morally unacceptable because it is self-indulgent (no. 7) and self-destructive (no. 12), it threatens to jeopardize the future and rights of the family (no. 9), and because it may seriously threaten the lives and well-being of a large number of people (no. 9). (Presumably, this is a not-so-subtle reference to the AIDS problem.) The Vatican statement deplores violence against homosexuals but then suggests that perhaps violence against gays should not surprise us since it is a backlash reaction to the successful enactment of gay rights legislation (no. 10). The document generally professes skepticism about using civil laws and statutes to protect the rights of homosexuals and recommends that, "in assessing proposed legislation, the bishops should keep as their uppermost concern the responsibility to defend and promote family life" (no. 17).

The Vatican letter is especially concerned with pastoral ministry and with implicit recognition by individual churches of organized groups, such as Dignity, which do not defend or promote traditional church teaching on homosexuality. Indeed, a recurring theme of the letter is a strong emphasis on defining Catholic orthodoxy and clearly articulating church teaching. The faithful must not be confused or misled by organizations which seem to undermine traditional teaching, which are ambiguous about it, or which neglect it entirely. Moreover, such groups should not be allowed to schedule religious services or use church buildings to carry them out (no. 17).

As a direct result of this last directive in the Vatican letter, Dignity masses have been ended in the dioceses of Brooklyn, Buffalo, Atlanta, New York, Pensacola, Florida, and Vancouver in British Columbia (Berger, 1987). In addition, bishops in New York, Chicago and Boston have consistently opposed gay rights legislation in their respective cities and states on grounds that the enactment of such statutes and ordinances constitutes moral approval of homosexual conduct.

* * *

The American Church's consistent pattern of opposition to gay rights legislation reflects, in my view, an interesting jurisprudential preoccupation with the function of law in civil society. Catholic thought emphasizes the pedagogical function of law—the role of law as teacher. This is a venerable tradition in legal philosophy, traceable to Socrates who referred to the laws of Athens as his "parents." On this view, law is an educational and socializing agent because the laws of society both reflect and reinforce a *consensus iuris*, a social agreement as to what is right and wrong. Those who hold this view of the law fear that, in the absence of a law prohibiting homosexuality, people will come to think that homosexual activity is morally acceptable. Similarly, any law which acknowledges and protects the rights of gay persons not to be discriminated against in employment and housing is said by Catholic bishops and some theologians to constitute approval of the practice of homosexuality.

Upon reflection, I see three obvious deficiencies to this way of conceiving the law. First, the Church's jurisprudence is inadequate here because it is based on the mistaken assumption that the legality of an action is conclusive of its morality. In a pluralistic society such as the United States, we reject any facile identification of legality and morality. We know that the fact that the law permits X does not necessarily mean that it is right to do X. This truism or common-sense notion applies, for example, to gambling, cigarette smoking, and the consumption of alcoholic beverages. Moreover, the Church itself quite properly insists upon a disjunction rather than a conjunction of positive law and moral norms in the matter of abortion; the fact that abortion is legal under the Supreme

Court's 1973 ruling in *Roe* v. *Wade* surely does not mean that abortion is now moral for American Catholics. If this is the case, then why should laws protecting the civil rights of gay persons be seen any differently—that is, why should such laws be construed as moral approval of homosexual conduct? The fact that behavior is legally permissible does not necessarily mean it is morally acceptable. A second, separate judgment must be made as to the morality of the conduct in question.

Second, it is illogical to assume that the legal protection of equal employment opportunity or equal credit opportunity or equal educational opportunity for gay persons automatically implies moral endorsement of the conduct of those protected. We make no such assumptions regarding the conduct of any other protected groups in American society—whether they are women, white men, racial groups, or ethnic minorities. Why then should we assume this with respect to gay persons? Gay rights advocates rightly insist that sexual morality per se cannot be the determinant of civil rights. Moreover, if the bishops want to make civil rights a function of correct sexual behavior, then logically they would have to insist upon the disenfranchisement of adulterous and promiscuous heterosexuals!

Third, I believe the Church's focus on the pedagogical function of law is wrong from the perspective of legal efficacy. That is, in the cases of both abortion policy and gay rights legislation, the bishops seem to care more about having laws on the books which censure actions regarded by the Church as immoral and less about whether such laws evoke compliance or are actually efficacious in preventing abortion and homosexuality. However, sound law making always looks to the consequences of legal prohibitions; it focuses on whether laws actually work and achieve their intended effects, not merely on whether they adequately register our moral convictions.

These reasons lead me to conclude that the American bishops' opposition to gay rights legislation is wrongheaded, shortsighted, and imprudent. It also seems to be not consonant with the spirit of the Gospels, since such episcopal opposition suggests that members of the American Catholic hierarchy care less about the dignity of individual gay and lesbian persons and more about communicating through law society's disapproval of homosexuality in the abstract. The recent Vatican letter reinforces the bishops' opposition to civil rights for gay persons. The American bishops would do well to look to their own earlier views. In 1976, for example, the bishops wrote: "Homosexuals, like everyone else, should not suffer from prejudice against basic human rights. They have a right to respect, friendship and justice" (National Conference of Catholic Bishops, 1976:34).

* * *

Thus far, I have assumed the validity of the Church's moral teaching on homosexuality and have asked only whether the Church should insist that public law reflect its moral theology. My answer is clear, I trust: with respect to the civil rights of gay persons, the Church need not and should not insist upon a strict conjunction of law and morals.

However, I now want to address directly the validity of the Church's view of homosexuality as expressed in the Vatican letter. I am prompted to do this by reading the thoughtful reflections and explorations of Catholic women, recently collected in two important anthologies: *A Faith of One's Own: Explorations by Catholic Lesbians* (Zanotti, 1986) and *Lesbian Nuns: Breaking Silence* (Curb and Manahan, 1985). This literature by women has helped me to think about same-sex love in ways not facilitated by the current media preoccupation with AIDS, "safe sex," and mostly male homosexuality. The Vatican letter succumbs to a similar tendency to focus on homosexuality as a male phenomenon and to ignore completely the experience of lesbian women. It is tempting to speculate why this is the case, but perhaps we can more plausibly attribute this to the familiar tendency of male writers to assume they are writing about human experience when they are really writing from the perspective and experience of men.

In relying upon the accounts of women presented in these two anthologies, I hope not only to compensate for the deficiencies of male-oriented accounts of homosexuality but also to apply a fundamental premise of modern theology and ecclesiology, namely, that theology today consists of communities of believers reflecting upon the implications of the faith based on Scripture, tradition, and their own experience. This method of doing theology is a post-Vatican II approach perfectly consonant with the notion of the Church as the People of God; it is assumed as well as illustrated in the newer approaches of liberation theology and feminist theology. As the institutional Church (the Vatican congregations and the American bishops, for example) turn their attention increasingly to topic areas such as the economy, reproductive technologies, marriage and the family, sexuality, and the status of women in society, they must rely increasingly upon the laity for guidance, for these are all areas in which the laity can speak directly from personal experience. An experiential approach to theological reflection is critical in areas pertaining to human sexuality. However, the Vatican letter gives no evidence whatsoever of consultation with the laity in this regard, and this deficiency seriously affects the credibility of the moral teaching stated in the document. I am not saying that the Vatican cannot rightly address a theology of sexuality, but that if it attempts to do so, it must listen to and incorporate the experience of lay and religious women and men in such matters.

In broad outline, the following themes emerge from a reading of the experiential accounts presented in *A Faith of One's Own* and *Lesbian Nuns;* these themes may be compared and contrasted with the statements of the Vatican letter on homosexuality. First, what emerges from these two anthologies is a very broad characterization of same-sex love as a strong affectionate relationship between persons which may or may not be sexual. For example, in *Lesbian Nuns,* Mary Mendola (1985), a former nun and now TV producer, writes:

> I prefer "homophile" to "homosexual" when speaking about love relationships in religious life that can and do go on for twenty or thirty years—but in no way include a sexual dimension. . . . What we are talking about here are homophile relationships within the context of a celibate commitment. . . . Our sexually-oriented society might learn a lot about loving from just such homophile relationships. . . . Maybe we get lost in our rigid definitions, forgetting that somewhere between celibacy and sexuality is a whole world of intimacy. [pp. 327–28]

Mendola is quick to note that, among laywomen and women religious, there are also love relationships which do include a sexual dimension. But physical sexuality seems not to be the essence of lesbianism, which has more to do with emotional intimacy, shared values and commitments, and shared moral aspirations. Another woman, speaking of her life as a religious in a community of sisters, writes:

> My friendships in the community are multileveled, diverse, and enduring. I love the women who have been with me and with each other through depressions, conflict with authority, firings, jail, prayer, celebrations, and growth in risk and seeking justice. . . . We want to express the great positive experience of being identified as Lesbians and as nuns. We are strong, caring, powerful women who live with—and love—other women. We share a common history and a constant search together. [Brady, 1985, 316–17]

What emerges from these accounts is a sense of the many diverse forms of human friendship and affection which bind people together in relationships and communities. This broad characterization of same-sex love accords with what we know from psychology about human sexuality. Many contemporary psychologists resist rigid categorizations of people according to sexual preference and instead stress sexuality as a continuum or spectrum of ways of relating. They deemphasize the physical dimension of sexuality and stress openness, vulnerability, intimacy, mutuality, and respect as primary in personal relationships. Many people develop same-sex friendships which display these qualities. Whether there is a sexual dimension to these relationships seems far less important than the existence of these other qualities.

Yet the Vatican letter seems to ignore or overlook completely these aspects of human relating and assumes instead a rigid, stereotypical categorization of people according to sexual expression. The Church cautions against a reductionist approach which describes everyone by reference to his or her sexual orientation (no. 16). Yet everything said in the document seems to contradict this. Use of the sexual faculty is said to be permissible only within marriage (no. 17), and it is said that homosexual activity cannot be held equivalent to the sexual expression of conjugal love (no. 9). It seems clear that the Church sees gay persons primarily in terms of the sexual dimension and only secondarily in terms of personal integrity and human dignity. This simplistic reduction of same-sex love to sexual expression fails to capture adequately the richness and depth of human relationships so apparent in these women's accounts. In my judgment, the Vatican letter betrays rigid, simplistic assumptions about human sexuality partly because it fails to take into account the experience of women such as these.

A second theme prominent in these accounts is the great emphasis these women place on personal growth and integrity. Their lives are characterized by a continuing search for alternative ways of relating to others, new forms of intimacy, alternatives to marriage and family traditionally conceived, new types of familial and communitarian arrangements. Their search is characterized by risk taking, willingness to grow and change, to explore self-identity and human relationships, to search for God in self and others. These women live on the boundaries of conventional society, on the growing edge of change and development. Because they do not conform to traditional conceptions of appropriate social roles for women (they are not conventional wives and mothers), their stories display a deeper, more vital awareness of the need to attend to personal integrity, caring, and growth.

Given these qualities, attitudes, and virtues, it is difficult to agree with the Vatican's characterization of these same-sex relationships as disordered, perverse, and somehow evil. What emerges from these women's accounts is not rationalization and justification of disordered, sinful inclinations and behavior but, rather, a creative rethinking of basic notions of spirituality and the Christian faith. The relationships these women describe appear to be virtuous rather than vicious and to be worthy, therefore, of the Church's blessing rather than its disapproval. In this regard, I find it interesting to compare the sentiments expressed in the Vatican letter with the statements of Episcopal Bishop John Shelby Spong of Newark, New Jersey. Bolstered by a diocesan report, Bishop Spong called on the Church to recognize and bless nonmarital relationships, including those between homosexuals. As he put it rather succinctly, "I find it difficult to believe that a church that blesses dogs in a Virginia fox hunt can't find a way to bless life-giving lasting relationships between human beings" (Goldman, 1987: B3).

A final theme prominent in these women's accounts is a deep concern for social justice. As theologian Mary Hunt (1986) states, "Loving well means doing justice" (p. 114). Hunt notes how the obligation to seek justice has taken center stage in twentieth-century Catholic thought and describes how many loving relationships have developed within the context of protest movements working for social justice. Two things are noteworthy here: first, that these Catholic lesbian feminists are actively seeking justice for the poor and oppressed instead of passively waiting for justice to be done to themselves and others; second, that their justice-seeking work is neither self-oriented nor self-sacrificial. In terms of integrity and self-respect, it is important to feminists not to selflessly repeat the sacrificial behavior traditionally expected of women through the centuries, but to work constructively for justice, not charity, for all including themselves. In this way, lesbian feminists as well as others can expect to benefit from the struggle against racism, sexism, poverty, homophobia, and heterosexism.

Needless to say, the social justice concerns evident in these women's accounts are precisely what is lacking in the Vatican letter, as I indicated earlier. These social activists are not deterred by some mythic possibility that gay rights legislation will undermine morality. On the contrary, they emphasize the moral intent of such legislation: to discourage, through threat of sanctions, hostile and discriminatory actions against gay persons. This is a matter of protecting the dignity and civil rights of homosexuals, not endorsing a particular lifestyle.

To summarize: The Vatican letter is not only inadequate from a jurisprudential perspective. It is deficient as moral theology because it assumes an excessively rigid, narrow, reductionist definition of sexuality; it holds to a negative conception of same-sex love as inevitably disordered and sinful; it does not attend satisfactorily to questions of social justice and civil rights for gay persons; and it seems to ignore and overlook women's experience. I believe Catholics can learn from lesbian feminists a more subtle, rich appreciation of same-sex love. The spirit and verve with which these women search for new forms of commitment and community can be especially instructive to those in static, conventional marriage and family relationships. And as for Vatican officialdom, I believe the hierarchical Church might learn from these women that, instead of issuing mean-spirited instructions to bishops which reinforce homophobia in the context of society's heightened fears about AIDS, the Church should be in the vanguard of the movement for social justice for all persons. Instead of pronouncing homosexuality to be evil, the Church might focus on healthy, committed same-sex relationships which provide the setting and conditions for moral and spiritual growth.

References

Berger, J. "Roman Catholic Mass for Homosexuals Is Banned." *New York Times,* 6 March 1987, B3.
Brady, E. "Lesbian Nun on the Boundary." In Curb and Manahan, eds.
Curb R., and N. Manahan, eds., *Lesbian Nuns: Breaking Silence.* Tallahassee: Naiad Press, 1985.
Goldman, A. "Newark Bishops Seeking to Bless Unwed Couples." *New York Times,* 30 January 1987, B3.
Hunt, M. "Loving Well Means Doing Justice." In B. Zanotti, ed.
Mendola, M. "Life-Long Lovers." In Curb and Manahan eds.
National Conference of Catholic Bishops, "To Live in Christ Jesus." In *Quest for Justice,* edited by J. Benestad and F. Butler. Washington, DC: United States Catholic Conference, 1981.
Zanotti, B., ed. *A Faith of One's Own: Explorations by Catholic Lesbians.* Trumansburg, NY: Crossing Press, 1986.

Part II
The Responses: Pastoral and Personal

10

Rome Speaks, the Church Responds

Jeannine Gramick

A steady stream of prominent newspaper headlines, editorials, commentaries, and Catholic voices criticizing the Vatican letter on the pastoral care of homosexual persons has appeared since its public release by the Congregation for the Doctrine of the Faith on 30 October 1986. In its 8 November 1986 editorial, the *Tablet*, a Catholic British journal, characterized the document as "violently hostile" to Catholic groups ministering to lesbian and gay people and noted that "not a word of appreciation is offered." In December 1986 the *Month*, a Jesuit British periodical, editorialized on the responsibility of church leaders "to develop a more truly authoritative theology and anthropology which can address . . . the reality of homosexuals in their living of Christian discipleship."

In the United States the critiques were no less stringent. New Ways Ministry publicly countered that "Catholic teaching flows from empirical data of the sciences and the experiences of people as well as from scripture and Church traditions. For the Vatican to ignore scientific research on human sexuality is to risk another Galileo affair where the Church's ignorance of scientific knowledge led to embarrassing condemnations which later had to be retracted." The National Coalition of American Nuns (NCAN) compared the treatment of lesbian and gay Catholics to the Vatican's disciplining of Charles Curran and Archbishop Raymond Hunthausen. NCAN noted that the Vatican was now "persecuting lesbian and gay Catholics . . . who seek the soothing ointment of reconciliation and healing from their church but who receive only burning salt on their wounds."

A theologian and psychologist team spoke of the deep wound of suspicions regarding sexuality being once again opened in the body of Christ and being aggravated by a document which has "injured an already

93

vulnerable part of the body Christian" (Whitehead and Whitehead, 1987, p. 126). Colman McCarthy, a leading Catholic syndicated columnist, articulated the feelings of a significant number of thinking Catholics when he wrote the week following the document's public appearance: "In a world all but paralyzed with wars, starvation, economic chaos, under-development and overpopulation, why is this global institution frittering away its moral force with homophobic rantings? What's the gain, short of supplying some minor satisfaction to those who crave authoritarianism? Where is the display of mercy and understanding of weakness that sym-bolizes the church on its best days?"

Only a minority of voices have attempted to justify and explicate the document's conclusions or to mollify its negative impact on the Catholic community. One apologist concluded, "On balance, despite its negative aspects, I think it amounts to a significant step—albeit a small, hesitant step—forward" (Williams, 1987, p. 259). One member of the U.S. episco-pal hierarchy drew the distinction between technical, precise language intended for the bishops and popular language of the general public. His further refinement between affirmations of a doctrinal nature and those which pertain to a social commentary was a subtle effort to admit serious deficiencies by acknowledging that the same measure of assent need not be accorded to different kinds of affirmation (Quinn, 1987).

Both before and after the public announcement of the CDF's letter, Fr. Robert Nugent and I traveled to more than fifty U.S. dioceses to conduct day-long educational seminars on lesbian and gay ministry. While open to people of any sexual orientation, the seminars drew mainly priests, reli-gious, parents, relatives, and friends of homosexual people, as well as lesbian and gay persons themselves. These workshops have enabled us to sense the prevailing moods and attitudes of grass-roots U.S. Catholics. What are some of the responses of various segments of the Church to the Vatican letter?

Response of Lesbian and Gay Catholics

On 1 November 1986 Dignity, the U.S. organization of approximately five thousand lesbian and gay Catholics, expressing shock and anger at the Vatican letter, issued the following statement:

> The document was promulgated with no prior consultation with lesbian and gay Catholics who have been able to reconcile our faith life with our sexuality; with no prior consultation with our parents who have received little or no help from the church to prepare them to

accept and love their lesbian and gay children; with no prior consultation with those priests, sisters, brothers, and lay persons who have ministered to and with us for almost 20 years.

How are we to interpret a document which demeans our very existence by calling us "disordered" and our loving sexual expressions "morally evil" but does not discuss providing pastoral care for thousands of our brothers who are dying of AIDS? How can the Vatican dare to call such a document pastoral? Where are the church's pro-life statements for lesbian women and gay men? Do we not rather need the "medicine of mercy rather than that of severity" as Pope John XXIII announced at the opening of Vatican II?

We are often criticized and challenged by other lesbian and gay persons who question how we can maintain allegiance to an authoritarian institution which has been one of the main sources of homosexual oppression throughout history. We have come to our church asking for the warm bread of nourishment and reconciliation but have received only the cold stones of condemnations and rejection.

We invite our official church leaders to enter into dialogue with us as Jesus engaged the Samaritan woman at the well. We thirst for the living water which Jesus promised us. So far the leaders of his church have shown us only an empty well.

In a letter to Cardinal Joseph Ratzinger, prefect of the Congregation for the Doctrine of the Faith, the Integrity/Dignity chapter of Madison, Wisconsin, stated well the frustration and pain of the lesbian and gay community: "We have been deprived of jobs and places to live, refused health care, abused in public, beaten in the streets, killed by drunks—and you want to deny us the protection of the law? The sins of society and the Church against gay people are far greater than any sin that can be committed by two people trying to express their love for one another."

Because of the Vatican letter, a number of U.S. bishops have expelled Dignity chapters from their churches. Some gay Catholics have reacted with determination and perseverance. In its letter to the Congregation, the Integrity/Dignity chapter of Madison said, "You can seek to keep us out of buildings, but we know that we are in and of the Church, and we cannot be driven from it. We will not cease ministering to one another in the spirit of compassion and understanding. We will continue to bear witness to one another and to the world that we are not 'objectively disordered' but are a part of God's good creation."

Two weeks after the release of the Vatican document, I received a long, moving letter from a dedicated lesbian teacher. It read in part:

I awoke to the newspaper headlines that the Pope was declaring war on the homosexuality issue again and that I was a moral evil. I was tempted to just give up again; it hurt so very much. About 1% of my life involves intimate relations with someone I love. The rest of the time I am a concerned and giving person in a human service occupation, trying to live a productive life. I cannot believe God would condemn me for something that is not of my own choosing.

I vowed at that moment not to let church leaders drive me away from Christ again. I love the church but detest its inflexibility and lack of humanism many times. I pray daily, will receive Communion and continue to grow closer to the Christ whom I know loves me very much. He has shown me this in too many ways to ignore.

Lesbian and gay Catholics, privately and publicly, have called the Vatican letter disgusting and vile. Many have left the Church because of it. One young gay seminarian formerly assumed that some deep truth could be garnered from "the cultural and religious accretions of Vatican documents on sexuality," but he now believes the writers to be so totally disconnected from human reality that such pronouncements themselves must be judged as objectively disordered.

It would be comforting to believe that the resolve to remain in the Catholic Church, despite the repeated pastoral insensitivity and rigid application of traditional viewpoints rather than compassion for the human condition, is a consistent response of lesbian and gay Catholics to the Vatican letter; yet I know otherwise. No one knows the heart, save God alone. Like different kinds of fabric sensitive at varying temperatures to the iron's heat, human psyches can tolerate different amounts of pain and rejection. Since the tolerance level for oppression endured by one person may be unbearable for another, no one can simply maintain that continual allegiance to a religious institution which treats one with minimal respect is conducive to everyone's spiritual health. One's own religious growth and nourishment may demand strategic separation from that institution.

Yet one hopes that lesbian and gay Catholics can bring themselves to forgive the pride, lack of compassion, and self-righteousness which are part of the scandals of the Roman Catholic Church. One also hopes they will realize that persons of faith seek others of similar beliefs with whom to minister, to worship, and to share community. Of sociological necessity, these faith communities require leadership and coordination; but when the systems and structures assume an importance greater than the very persons they were created to serve, the organization stands sorely in need of reformation. To a lesbian or gay Catholic feeling powerless to respond effectively to inadequate and alienating Vatican pronouncements, it is small consolation to state that such is the present period of church history.

Why Stay?

Since the Vatican letter, lesbian and gay Catholics are more seriously asking themselves, "Why remain in a Church whose highest authorities fail to defend and protect the civil rights of a persecuted minority and prefer to cast stones of fundamentalist bigotry instead of castigating the structured evils of violence and heterosexism which societies take for granted?" Why remain, indeed? Although separating oneself from a religious institution whose policies are set by such leaders makes eminent good sense, deep and personal religious convictions often outweigh logical reasoning. Pascal once said, "The heart has its reason of which reason knows nothing."

Lesbian and gay Catholics need to remind themselves, again and again especially in these times, that the pope and the bishops do not, of themselves, constitute the Church. While the episcopal magisterium possesses a definite and significant role in the faith life and ministry of the Church, all the people of God comprise the Church. We must allow no one to define us out of our faith communities. The Catholic Church belongs to committed lesbian and gay Catholics as much as to the episcopal hierarchy. Those who stand in dissent from traditional church teaching regarding homogenital behavior and from the new Vatican stance regarding homosexual orientation have the consolation that they are not opposing any essential elements of the Christian faith; Jesus spoke no words about homosexuality.

Why remain in a Church which officially teaches that the very core of one's sexual identity is flawed and disordered? In this same Church are some leaders who strongly disagree with the current direction of Vatican thought although most fear to voice this dissent publicly. In this same Church are ever increasing numbers of heterosexual Christians who question the truth or wisdom of Vatican pronouncements on many sexual issues, including homosexuality, because of the refusal of celibate policy makers to listen to the voices of the sexually experienced. In the United States these Catholics are manifesting their displeasure with Vatican sexual theology by decreasing financial contributions to the U.S. Church (Greeley, 1987). A number of Catholic social justice groups have issued "funny money" by which an individual contributes a "funny" dollar bill to the parish collection and gives legal tender instead to a Catholic organization working for the elimination of societal injustices based on gender or sexual orientation.

Why remain in a Church whose governing offices issue "pastoral" letters on homosexuality yet fail to mention the devastation and suffering of persons with AIDS except for an oblique reference of censure and blame? Yet to abandon this Church abdicates to these ecclesiastial authorities more power than they deserve. To claim one's Catholic heritage, culture, even birthright, and to allow no external force to snatch one's religious roots is to profess the persistent faith of the Canaanite woman whom Jesus praised (Mt. 15:21–28).

Why remain in a Church whose highest leaders ignore one's personal experience of sexuality because it contradicts long-established beliefs? This same Church was founded on Jesus, the Christ, who questioned, challenged, and disregarded some of the traditional teachings of his Jewish leaders. Their authority threatened by the truth within him, the religious leaders harassed Jesus, expelled him from the synagogue and ultimately secured his death by crucifixion. Through all this Jesus did not abandon his religious institution. "The disciple is not greater than the master. If they persecuted me, they will persecute you also" (Jn. 15:20).

Response of Heterosexual Catholics

The feelings of one woman religious attending an educational seminar on homosexuality immediately after the Vatican letter was made public typifies many reactions across the country. "Vicious, shameful, the last straw," she cried. Like the National Coalition of American Nuns, she viewed the letter as another Vatican attempt to stifle the U.S. Church.

Elinor Crocker, an officer of the National Federation of Parents and Friends of Gays who is a Roman Catholic mother of five children, represents the feelings of parents when she states, "I cannot comprehend the attack on my gay child's normal and loving life. Her relationship with her loved one is as strong, loving, and supportive as are the relationships of her heterosexual brothers and sisters. I cannot conceive of any reason for my church to sanction one child's life while denying that support to another. They are all children of God and I know God loves each of them equally. I do not believe that God intended any of us to live a lonely, unfulfilled life, nor do I believe that God expects anyone to live a lie, to pretend to be something they are not."

Saddened and dismayed by the Vatican letter, the great U.S. Catholic middle, not convinced by the mere repetition of sexual condemnations, is gradually moving to the left. Arthur Jones (1986) observed that "Catholic teaching has not yet proved its authority on or understanding of human sexuality. It is one thing for the institutional church to command. . . . , quite another to convince. . . . Try as the institutional church might, many Catholics are not in conscience convinced that current church teaching on human sexuality is dealing with the issues intelligently or compassionately" (p. 20).

In the last twenty-five years most U.S. Catholics have claimed their God-given freedom and have recognized the responsibility to search sincerely for truth and goodness. An episcopal pastoral letter on freedom and church teaching printed in the *West Texas Angelus* the day following the release of the Vatican letter assures us that "freedom and responsibility cannot be replaced by authority in the Christian life. Official teaching cannot replace the responsibility of Catholics to seek the truth in these teachings and to give their assent to that truth. And no one of us can simply sit back and wait for church authorities or theologians to figure things out or to make up our minds for us. This responsibility and freedom is nowhere more evident than in the areas where no final assurance can be given that God's own truth has been found" (Pfeifer, 1986: 2). In the area of sexual ethics, so diverse over time and culture, Catholics realize that there is no assurance that the final truth has been revealed. Since the Church's teachings on sexual ethics are not final, "both Church authorities and Catholics in general must be open to ongoing exploration and even revision when greater clarity emerges" (p. 2).

The movement by the great Catholic middle toward toleration and acceptance of homosexual issues was evident in a 1985 survey in which 51 percent of Catholics supported legalizing homosexual relations between consenting adults in private (Gallup and Castelli, 1987). Such a safeguard for private sexual behavior is the very protection to which, the Vatican claims, lesbian and gay persons have no right. Since legal and moral issues can and must be separated in nontheocratic societies, support for legalization of sexual acts between consenting adults in private does not imply moral approval of those acts. It is this separation of legality and morality which the Vatican has difficulty in comprehending. Yet in a 1987 *Los Angeles Times* poll, 34 percent of Catholics believed that homosexual behavior was not sinful (Chandler, 1987). Furthermore, a *National Catholic Reporter*/Gallup poll conducted during May 1987 found that only 34 percent of Catholics believed that the pope and other bishops should be the final authority concerning the morality of homosexual behavior; 58 percent believed that the pope, other bishops, and church teachings should be taken into account in arriving at a moral decision regarding homogenital behavior but that the final decision should be made by the individual (Fox, 1987).

These last statistics concerning the locus of moral authority and moral beliefs regarding homogenital behavior are of serious concern to Vatican officials who rightly detect in them, not civil policy issues, but a questioning and shift in Catholic attitudes. More than one-third of U.S. Catholics now dissent from the traditional moral teaching that all homosexual activity is intrinsically immoral; they believe that same-sex relationships can constitute an alternative and acceptable lifestyle. Since dissent is more widespread among younger Catholics where 39 percent under the age of forty disagree with the traditional teaching on homogenital behavior, it will likely increase in succeeding generations (Chandler, 1987). Moreover, the majority of U.S. Catholics, regardless of their private views on the morality of homogenital behavior, believe that the individual is the final moral arbiter and decision maker concerning personal homosexual acts.

The great Catholic middle believes that the individual should have a greater voice in moral decision making. Increasing numbers of Catholics are pointing out that the traditional teaching on homosexuality lacks credibility in part because it suffers from a sense of moral disproportion. Preoccupied, almost to the point of obsession, with genital activity, the Vatican teaching neglects to place sufficient emphasis, let alone mention, the body of episcopal teaching dealing with social justice, prejudice and violence against homosexual persons (Weakland, 1980; Roman Catholic Church of Baltimore, 1981; Washington State Catholic Conference, 1983; Quinn, 1984). Historically encrusted in a "pelvic theology" (Maguire, in press), the official teaching from Rome ignores the truly pastoral approach evident in many U.S. magisterial statements and pastoral plans for lesbian and gay ministry.

Many conversations further convince me that the great Catholic middle, however, does not consider homosexuality and heterosexuality of equal value. With a distinctly American sense of justice and fairness, the typical U.S. Catholic rankles at the suggestion of any double standards and thus believes that homosexual as well as heterosexual persons should be able to enjoy and sexually express a committed, faithful relationship. However, there is a suspicious reluctance to call homosexuality natural, to formally bless such unions by marriagelike ceremonies, or to consider homosexuality a part of God's divine plan for approximately 10 percent of humanity. My perception is that the great American middle, rightly or wrongly, believes the ideal meaning of human sexuality lies in the complementarity of the sexes. The moral acceptance of homosexual acts in loving, committed relationships by more than one-third of U.S. Catholics flows from a compassionate and compromising stance akin to the moderate theological school. They resonate with Curran's (1983: 165) analogy that homosexuality is to heterosexuality as being blind, deaf, or missing a limb is to a perfectly formed and functioning body.

Consultation

It seems that the Vatican failed to consult even episcopal documents on the subject. That such consultation of U.S. magisterial teaching on homosexuality was lacking is patently evident in the Vatican's condemnation of "civil legislation introduced to protect behavior" (no. 10) and its failure to mention the need for civil rights legislation to eliminate discrimination in employment, housing, and public accommodations.

Whether or not an individual's private sexual life conforms to official Catholic moral tenets, U.S. episcopal documents have been clear that "the State has no business demanding that gays and lesbians project publicly its [i.e., the Church's] given set of moral values. Hence, homosexuals who make public their lifestyle or who advocate homosexual orientation and acting out as completely moral should not be excluded from employment as long as their activity does not disrupt the public order. The State should protect them against discrimination occasioned by their lifestyle" (Washington State Catholic Conference, 1983: 53).

Unfairly characterizing lesbian and gay people as irresponsible or deceitful, the Vatican failed to take into account the faith experience of committed lesbian and gay Catholics. As the diocesan and regional hearings on women's issues illustrate, our U.S. bishops have learned that a document addressing the needs of a specific group of people cannot be credible without the consultation and input of the concerned group.

If lesbian and gay Catholics had been consulted, how would the document have been different? In 1984 the Catholic Pastoral Committee on Sexual Minorities (CPCSM) released the results of a survey of approximately two hundred lesbian and gay Catholics in the archdiocese of St. Paul-Minneapolis which asked lesbian and gay Catholics what they wanted from their Church. While these data are obviously not based on a random sample, I believe that they are fairly representative.

The primary need identified was a call to change the direction of sexual ethics from an act-centered to a person-centered theology. Since lifelong celibacy is not required of all heterosexuals as they can look forward to a life with a significant partner, it seemed unfair to the respondents to allow no faithful unions between persons of the same gender. If celibacy is treated as a special gift or charism for nuns, priests, and brothers who have extensive support systems to sustain them in their intimacy needs, why, they asked, is it legislated as a permanent precept for homosexual persons who lack similar supports? Since approximately 70 percent of all marriages between a heterosexual and a homosexual spouse end in divorce within the first three years, advocating such heterosexual marriages, they said, was an ineffective antidote to homosexuality and proved disastrous to the parties concerned, many of which included children. They asked their church leaders to bless their committed love relationships and to adopt a sexual ethics similar to the views of more progressive moral theologians (Maguire, 1983; McNeill, 1976). Even a move toward the opinions of more moderate moral theologians (Curran, 1983; Kosnik, 1977) would have been considered a step in a compassionate direction.

Since Vatican authorities seem unable or unwilling to nuance the official church teaching on homosexual activity, was the document on homosexuality the most benign pastoral letter that could have been expected? Of course not! The CPCSM study elucidated further needs which could realistically be met and should be wholeheartedly contained in any episcopal statement on homosexuality calling itself pastoral. The CPCSM respondents asked for education of the Catholic community on the subject of homosexuality, opportunities within the parish for healthy socializing experiences, a degree of visibility in the Catholic community, support systems for their families and friends, justice in employment, especially in church-related jobs.

These elements constitute a viable starting point for gospel-based pastoral ministry. Fortunately, the archdiocese of San Francisco has presented the Church with a model pastoral plan which, it is to be hoped, will be adopted in other dioceses (San Francisco Senate of Priests, 1983). Other U.S. dioceses have made commendable, if less comprehensive, efforts at implementing pastoral outreach to lesbian and gay Catholics (Roman Catholic Church of Baltimore, 1981; Dumaine, 1986). *An Introduction to the Pastoral Care of Homosexual People* from the bishops of England and Wales and the 1979 discussion document, *Homosexual People in Society,* from the Catholic Council on Church and Society of the Dutch bishops also show a compassionate attempt to understand the homosexual condition clearly lacking in the Vatican letter.

Vatican Strategy

If the Vatican's aim in this letter is to present a clear teaching on homosexuality and not simply to halt or reverse recent developments of that teaching that have occurred in the last ten years, it has certainly employed a poor strategy. Since 1975 the Vatican has simply reiterated its condemnation of homogenital acts in the belief that constant denunciations will confirm or compel assent in the hearts of dissenting Catholics.

Instead of claiming that "confusion" exists among Catholics on the teaching of homogenital activity, the Vatican should at least acknowledge that there is widespread dissent. If the language and tone of the official teaching belong to another historical age, does dissent not indicate that the Spirit is guiding the Church "to find new ways to communicate the truth of Christ" (Mugavero, 1976) to lesbian and gay people? The continuing search to discover how best to articulate truth in a specific time and culture requires the experience of the faithful and the results of the social sciences through dialogue with lesbian and gay Catholics and through consultations with respected scholars and scientists.

The problem of widespread nonacceptance will not be resolved by increasing authoritarianism. Church statements which ignore contemporary data and which demand acceptance on the basis of intrinsic authority weaken, rather than strengthen, genuine authority and contribute to the very lack of assent which they were intended to counter. Sincere questions as well as reasoned answers are valid components of orthodox teaching. Church authorities, as indeed all followers of Jesus, have not so much a mission to "defend Church doctrine" but to proclaim Jesus' message of forgiveness and salvation. To proclaim that message by means that are insensitive or disrespectful of persons produces a loss of credibility in those who proclaim the message and, at times, in the message itself.

Jesus' method was one of invitation, not coercion; one of "come and see," not compulsory compliance. If increasing numbers of Catholics do not accept the official church teaching that *all* homogenital acts are "intrinsically evil," it is doubtful that an unnuanced and simple repetition of the official position will effect any significant change in the growth of dissent on this question.

To follow in the footsteps of the humble Galilean requires a strategy based on a gentle persuasion of hearts. What has not been equally emphasized in the Church's teaching on homosexuality is the rampant sin of homophobia. By focusing almost exclusively on sexual behavior while lesbian and gay lives have been stunted or destroyed, the Vatican has failed strategically. Only by vigorously opposing all forms of violence which are detrimental to the welfare of lesbian and gay persons who are equal members of the body of Christ will the Vatican begin to regain its tattered credibility.

References

Chandler, R. "The Times Poll: Americans Like Pope but Challenge Doctrine." *Los Angeles Times*, 23 August 1987, p. 20.

104 · JEANNINE GRAMICK

Curran, C. "Moral Theology and Homosexuality." In J. Gramick, ed. *Homosexuality and the Catholic Church*. Mt. Rainier, MD: New Ways Ministry, 1983.
DuMaine, P. "Pastoral Guidelines for Ministry to Homosexuals in the Diocese of San Jose." *Valley Catholic*, March 1986, pp. 28–29.
Fox, T. "U.S. Laity Want Much Greater Say, Yet Remain Loyal, NCR Poll Finds." *National Catholic Reporter*, 11 September 1987, pp. 7–8.
Gallup, G., Jr. and J. Castelli. *The American People: Their Beliefs, Practices, and Values*. Garden City, NY: Doubleday, 1987.
Gallagher, J., ed. *Homosexuality and the Magisterium*. Mt. Rainier, MD: New Ways Ministry, 1985.
Greeley, A. *Catholic Contributions: Sociology and Policy*. Chicago: Thomas More Press, 1987.
Jones, A. "Natural Way Not Only Way in Family Planning." *National Catholic Reporter*, 19 December 1986, p. 20.
Kosnik, A., W. Carroll, A. Cunningham, R. Modras, and J. Schulte. *Human Sexuality: New Directions in American Catholic Thought*. New York: Paulist, 1977.
Maguire, D. "The Morality of Homosexual Marriage." In *A Challenge to Love: Gay and Lesbian Catholics in the Church*. Edited by R. Nugent. New York: Crossroad, 1983.
———. "The Shadow Side of the Homosexuality Debate." In *Homosexuality, the Priesthood, and the Religious Life*. Edited by J. Gramick. New York: Crossroad, forthcoming.
McNeill, J. *The Church and the Homosexual*. Kansas City, MO: Sheed, Andrews and McMeel, 1976.
Mugavero, F. "Sexuality—God's Gift." Diocese of Brooklyn. 11 February 1976.
Pfeifer, M. "The Freedom of Catholics and Official Church Teaching." *West Texas Angelus*, 31 October 1986, pp. 1–2.
Quinn, J. "Letter on Violence to Archdiocesan Deans," 1984. In J. Gallagher, ed.
———. "Toward an Understanding of the Letter 'On the Care of Homosexual Persons.'" *America* 156 (7 February 1987): 92–95, 160; reprinted in this volume.
Roman Catholic Church of Baltimore, "A Ministry to Lesbian and Gay Catholic Persons," 1981. In J. Gallagher, ed.
Senate of Priests, "Ministry and Homosexuality in the Archdiocese of San Francisco," 1983. In J. Gallagher, ed.
Washington State Catholic Conference, "The Prejudice against Homosexuals and the Ministry of the Church," 1983. In J. Gallagher, ed.
Weakland, R. "Who Is My Neighbor?" 1980. In J. Gallagher ed.
Whitehead, J., and E. Whitehead. "The Shape of Compassion: Reflections on Catholics and Homosexuality." *Spirituality Today* 39 (Summer 1987): 126–36.
Williams, B. "Homosexuality: The New Vatican Statement." *Theological Studies* 48 (1987): 259–77.

11

Compassion and Sexual Orientation

Benedict M. Ashley

Compassion means first to share the suffering of others without judging them (Mt. 7:1), to respect their human dignity, and to love them as if they were the Lord himself (Mt. 25:40). Second, it means to seek ways to minister to them so they may be healed if possible, and if not, then to transform their suffering into a blessing.

Compassion, however, does *not* mean helping victims deny their suffering or its real causes. Such evasions and illusions in the long run only make their suffering more destructive. It is a cruel kindness to encourage disabled or unfree people to deny their disabilities or compulsions. The truest compassion is *realism:* to face the fact of disabilities, to relieve the victims of false guilt, to assure them of God's mercy for real guilt, to reassure them of their human worth, to give them hope for a truly rich human life.

Homosexual orientation is a disability that prevents one not from loving sexually, but heterosexually, and therefore from the ability to make a permanent and procreative marriage commitment. That homosexuals may be in other respects quite normal physically and psychologically, professionally productive, and comfortable with their condition does not negate the fact that in regard to the very important ability to marry and have children they are disabled. It is a disability which has many degrees and variations. Some degree of homosexual attraction need not always prevent a successful marriage, but if exclusive, it makes marriage irresponsible and invalid.

Current propaganda and the mistaken compassion of certain psychiatrists and theologians have encouraged many homosexuals to deny their disability by arguing that homosexuality is just a legitimate variation of human sexuality, or even that it is the will of God. But sex was not created only for pleasure or to provide companionship. The Bible and Christian tradition have always taught that sex is for marriage only, and marriage is not only for the couple but for their children as well. Hence the Congregation for the Doctrine of the Faith calls homosexual acts "disordered," that is not ordered to marriage and children.[1]

God never wills anyone to suffer from the disability through impotence, sterility, or homosexuality of entering into marriage or of having children. He only permits such troubles, so that we will use our creativity to find their remedy or courageously bring spiritual good out of misfortune. Hence we must try to discover the causes of this condition. The still very inadequate research now available shows that the development of heterosexuality itself is very complex.[2] It involves both genetic and acquired dispositions, the latter rooted in early situations in the family and peer group. It is not strange that such a complex process in a considerable percentage of cases falls short of achieving the unambiguous heterosexuality maximally adaptive for the family and for society and human survival which depend on the family.

Can homosexuals achieve heterosexuality? Some therapists report a considerable percentage of patients who if treated early are able to do so, but present methods are not successful in the majority of cases.[3] Therefore most homosexuals, although their condition has different causes than chemical dependency, are in somewhat the same life situation, since their condition cannot be radically corrected, but must be lived with. Because it frustrates a profound need of human personality, it can be a very heavy cross. How is the homosexual to satisfy his or her normal needs for sexual satisfaction and intimate companionship? Not only are gays and lesbians sometimes deprived of their civil rights, but they find themselves socially restricted to friendships within the subculture of our cities. American society seems to regard permanent singleness or life with a same-sex companion as proof of active homosexuality.

What then are the options for persons who know they are homosexually oriented to a degree that would make marriage irresponsible? One is to satisfy sexual needs by casual relationships. Apart from the danger of AIDS (a tragic proof that promiscuity is biologically maladaptive[4]), such casual sex, whether heterosexual or homosexual, is unacceptable for Christians. Sex must be an expression of love and commitment, not an entertainment or an escape.[5]

The second option is a permanent relationship based on committed love. Many gays and lesbians hope for this with all their hearts; nothing is more natural and truly human than to want to give oneself in love and receive another's love in trust. Nor need we doubt many homosexual couples make such a commitment.

Yet two questions have to be asked. First, how realistic is it for a homosexual to expect to achieve partnership for life? Heterosexual marriages often fail even with the support of social approval, the male-female complementarity produced by evolutionary adaptation, and the mutual investment of children. What real chances then have most homosexual "closed couples" for permanence?

The best research available today seems to show that the great majority of such "closed couples" last but a few years and often are really "open" relationships.[6] Therefore no truly compassionate counselor can responsibly encourage a client to seek such a partnership, although the counselor may very well hesitate to break up an established couple, lest they return to promiscuity. In most cases the homosexual who seeks this solution is doomed to tragic heartbreak and disappointment, a life of seeking what he or she will never find, or be able to live up to.

More fundamental than this pragmatic reason, for a committed couple to use sexual acts which can never be in harmony with the purposes for which God made us sexual can never be an authentic expression of their love for each other, but only a substitute for what their deeper nature really requires. The homosexual orientation, like impotency, is a condition that makes true human sexual expression impossible. Persons sterile but not impotent, or those using the sterile period can, nevertheless, legitimately have intercourse since the act (unlike anal or oral acts or mutual masturbation) remains ordered by its very structure to transmit life even when, because of permanent or periodic sterility, this does not take place.

Of course to many today this reasoning seems far-fetched, but if they examine why it seems so, they will find that it is because they have come to think of sex simply as a one-to-one relationship only loosely related to the family. But biblical and Catholic teaching have always firmly held that God made sex for family life.[7]

The remaining option is celibacy. But is this a real option? Many do not believe anyone with normal libido can live without genital satisfaction, at least not without becoming neurotic, hostile, or emotionally withered. Or they believe successful celibacy requires a special "charism." It is probable that in a sinless world everyone would have married. But in our world of war, poverty, and social injustice where people bear the burdens of countless deprivations and defects, marriage is not the best choice for all. It is often preferable to choose not to marry so as to be freer to pursue a profession or ministry, or for the sake of religious contemplation and prayer. But celibacy is for everyone before marriage, and married couples may have to practice abstinence for health, birth regulation, or conditions of employment.

Thus homosexuals are not alone in being confronted with celibacy as the best or only moral possibility for their life.[8] Nor do they need a special charism to live as celibates. Although a special charism is required to accept the dedication required of priests and religious, for all Christians the graces of baptism and the other sacraments suffice to carry their cross whatever it may be. Jesus was compassion itself, and so he chose to be celibate to show that without any loss of human wholeness chastity is possible for every Christian.

Nevertheless, all of us, heterosexual and homosexual, to live chastely need the support of a community to minister God's grace to us. Ministry to homosexuals, as to other victims of disabilities, should have high priority in the Catholic Church. To be successful, however, it must be completely and unambiguously faithful to the Church's teaching on sexuality, and must avoid giving scandal to the heterosexual majority. Because heterosexuality is in part a learned process, and the spectrum of sexual orientation is wide, many heterosexuals are not secure in their orientation. They may feel homosexual attractions and at least unconsciously fear they may be homosexual and may project this fear as homophobia.

Such homophobic Catholics are scandalized at forms of ministry that seem to condone homosexuality. Compassion cuts both ways. We have to be compassionate to the struggling gay but also to the majority of people who fear that the Church is "getting soft" on homosexuality. The clergy are often accused of homophobia, perhaps because their dedicated celibacy leaves them uncertain of their own sexual orientation, or because they are in fact homosexually oriented and therefore chose the religious or priestly life to get support to remain celibate.

Most priests, however, have genuine compassion for homosexuals as for all they attempt to serve.[9] They want to encourage homosexuals who attempt to live the celibate life to continue to come to the sacraments for help. As for those who continue to live as active homosexuals because they sincerely believe that the Church is mistaken in its sexual teaching, priests can only respect their consciences and do what they can to keep them within the Church and in dialogue with those who accept this teaching. There is room in the Church for debate on difficult questions, but the bishops of the Church have the responsibility to witness to what they have received as the gospel in all its implications, without compromise or ambiguity.

Generally speaking, one's sexual orientation is a private matter. I believe the Church should support the civil rights of homosexuals and should preach that no one has any right to judge same-sex companions living privately. Such companionship without sex can be quite suitable for homosexuals and was common enough even in Victorian society without public suspicion. Nor should sexual orientation be a ground for discrimination in employment, provided that it not be made evident by public acts. But if publicized, then it is not discriminatory to exclude active homosexuals from positions which would seem to give approval to such behavior, especially to young people still struggling to achieve their own sexual identity.

The Church's ministry to homosexuals should include the following tasks. (1) We should be advocates for the protection of the civil rights of homosexuals. (2) We should preach on this subject to inform Christians of the problems of the homosexual and to create respect for their human dignity and compassion for their problems. We should also preach on the dignity of celibates, lay as well as priests and religious, and the freedom of all Christians to choose such a single life without stigma or suspicion. (3) We should provide counseling help both spiritual and psychological to assist those struggling with this problem, even when they are not yet ready to accept celibacy. (4) We should particularly reach out to help in the AIDS ministry. (5) We should foster support groups conducted in such a way as to protect the privacy of the members, to help them to find mutual support and friendship, but without ambiguity as to the teachings of the Church, and without any appearance of seeming to condone homosexual behavior.[10] (6) We should encourage research to find the causes and remedies of this disability. (7) We should give priority to the building of good family life, in which children will have the best possible opportunities to arrive at heterosexual maturity.

What I have written may outrage some who read it and seem to add to the already heavy burden of homosexuals who feel they have finally achieved self-respect and peace in living true to their own orientation whatever its nature or causes. I sincerely ask forgiveness of any of these if I have unintentionally offended them by language that may seem condemnatory, or lacking in sensitivity. My respect for them as persons has compelled me to write as objectively as possible and to share with them the truth as I see it.

I think the Vatican letter, with whose substance I entirely agree, has also tried to speak the healing truth. It can be criticized, just as what I have written can be, on details of expression or a lack of nuance inevitable in a document that had to be brief and directly to the point in order to clear up the ambiguities with which this complex question has been obscured.[11] The truth is not destructive but healing, if spoken and heard in mutual love. I extend that love to all those who suffer from this problem and I hope they may extend the same to me as one who seeks not to condemn but to minister.

BENEDICT M. ASHLEY

Notes

1. An editorial in *America,* 22 November 1986, pp. 313f., criticizes the Vatican letter: "Calling the orientation 'disordered' may be strictly consistent with the 1975 statement [*Declaration on Certain Questions Concerning Sexual Ethics*] that acts springing from such an orientation are disordered, but it goes further. It is bound to be questioned by those who will wonder what it means—morally—to speak of an orientation that is at one and the same time an 'innate instinct' (language of the earlier declaration) and 'an objective disorder' (language of the recent letter)." Was not the term "disorder" chosen precisely to indicate that the orientation is not "immoral" but only a difficulty for moral life? Would it be improper to call frigidity a disorder because it inhibits the duty of married love?

2. For the research referred to in this paper, see M. F. Schwartz (Masters and Johnson Institute), A. S. Moraczewski (Pope John Center), and J. A. Monteleone, M.D. (St. Louis University School of Medicine), eds., *Sex and Gender: A Theological and Scientific Inquiry;* (St. Louis, 1983); and also M. T. Saghir and E. Robins, *Male and Female Homosexuality: A Comprehensive Investigation* (Baltimore: Williams and Wilkins, 1973); A. P. Bell and M. S. Weinberg, *Homosexualities* (London: Mitchell Beasley, 1978); A. P. Bell, M. S. Weinberg, and S. K. Hammersmith, *Sexual Preference: Its Development in Men and Women* (Bloomington: Indiana University Press, 1981); J. Bancroft, *Human Sexuality and Its Problems* (Edinburgh: Churchill Livingstone, 1983); P. Blumstein and P. Schwartz, *American Couples* (New York: William Morrow, 1983).

3. See J. Bancroft, "Problematic Gender Identity and Sexual Orientation: A Psychiatrist's View," in *Sex and Gender,* p. 102–24.

4. How are we to minister to the AIDS victim who asks, "Is God punishing me?" A merely palliative answer will help little. We must help victims think the question through theologically. God who loves us no matter what we do punishes people only when they act against their own consciences, and then only to redeem them and warn others. When AIDS results from promiscuity, heterosexual or homosexual, engaged in by those who realize promiscuity is not worthy of human dignity, punishment may be deserved. The same is true if it results from chemical dependency willfully incurred with no effort to get treatment. If incurred by nonpromiscuous homosexual acts which persons engaged in against their own conscience, there is also guilt. In other cases there is no moral guilt on the part of the victim that God would punish. However, it is essential to remember that even when persons innocently do something *objectively* wrong God ordinarily permits them to suffer the consequences so they and others will learn from the mistake. "God always forgives, but nature never does." Since whatever is harmful to human beings is morally wrong, AIDS ought to make us ask ourselves honestly, "If promiscuity, heterosexual or homosexual, has such tragic consequences is it morally wrong?" and "If homosexual acts, even when nonpromiscuous, are especially open to transmitting such diseases, may they not also be morally wrong?" Yet the bottom line is that no matter into what mess we get ourselves God's mercy holds open the door of hope to all.

5. For the Catholic Church's teaching on the purpose of sexuality, I would recommend D. G. McCarthy and E. J. Bayer, eds. *Handbook on Critical Sexual Issues* (Garden City, NY: Doubleday Image Book, 1984) and R. Lawler, J. Boyle, Jr., and W. E. May, *Catholic Sexual Ethics* (Huntington, IN: OSV Press, 1985).

6. The research referred to in note 2 above shows that at present the data on the success of "closed couples" is still very inadequate. The most extensive is that of Bell and Weinberg and Hammersmith which seems to me to support my position: the average "closed" couple does not last very long or becomes "open" or simply ceases to be a sexual relation.

7. Both expositions in note 5 above contain a brief summary based on modern critical scholarship (minus the special pleadings of some theologians in the interests of a false compassion) for the Church's teaching.

8. C. Kiesling, O.P., *Celibacy, Prayer and Friendship* (New York: Alba House, 1978), is an excellent treatment.

9. I know of no objective research to support this statement, but I base it on many years of teaching candidates for priesthood and priests in practical ministry.

10. The *America* editorial complains that the official teaching on homosexuality "has been clarified sufficiently, and in the case of the latest Vatican document, more than sufficiently." But is the Congregation not forced to these repeated clarifications by the continued use of ambiguous formulations such as, "We believe that gays can express their sexuality in a manner that is consonant with Christ's teaching. We believe that all sexuality should be exercised in an ethically responsible and unselfish way" ("Dignity Statement of Position and Purpose," in J. Gramick, R. Nugent, and T. Oddo, *Homosexual Catholics: A Primer for Discussion* [Mt. Rainier, MD: New Ways Ministry, 1977])?

11. The *America* editorial also complains of the "pastoral deductions" from principles, which it would like to see replaced by "pastoral inductions" from actual cases. It especially objects (1) to the reference to AIDS and (2) to the statement that homosexuals should not be surprised at the violent public reaction to their work for civil rights. For the first reference, see note 4 above. The second reference is an attempt, perhaps not well expressed, to point out that it is a mistake to link civil rights to public approval of the "gay lifestyle," like the mistake of feminists who link civil rights to public approval of abortion. To demand civil rights is also to grant the civil rights of others to disapprove one's moral code and public behavior. The Congregation makes sufficiently clear, it seems to me, that such disapproval does not justify violence, any more than disapproval of abortion justifies bombing abortion clinics.

12

Speaking the Truth in Love

Peter E. B. Harris

During his address at the Quest 1986 Conference, a speaker commented that as homosexual Catholics involved in dialogue with the
rest of the Church, Quest's[1] members should be more concerned with
the "presumptions of the educated" than the "biases and prejudices of the
uneducated."[2] The letter from the Congregation for the Doctrine of the
Faith on the pastoral care of homosexual persons itself indicates that it is
written out of a deep concern to ensure that the pastoral care of homosexuals is not compromised by approaches and understandings which are at
variance with the Church's teaching. The principle is a sound one and we
must not forget that the Church does have a responsibility and a right
critically to engage the theories and ideologies of the time if it is to be
faithful to its own mission. But it would be unfortunate if this responsibility were seen solely to belong to only a certain section of the Church.
Every Christian must be called to this task by their baptism. We all need a
constant reminder of this if we are to avoid our role in the Church being
seen as simply a "them and us" situation.

Ultimately pastoral practice has to be based on and informed by good
theology which does justice to the gospel. Much has recently been said
about dissent in the Church and the case of Fr. Charles Curran has
provoked many to comment. The *Times* of London published an exchange between an English Roman Catholic theologian, Fr. Kevin Kelly,
and a Scottish Catholic bishop, Mario Conti, on this topic. The bishop
admitted that Father Kelly, while staying firm on official church teaching,
stood for something "person centred. . . , compassionate. . . , facing the
real situation in which many people find themselves today."[3] Francis
Thomas, in an official intervention to that correspondence, allowed, "there
is room for serious probing and questioning, but not for the kind of open
dissent that leads nobody forward."[4] Father Kelly went on to say that
"facing issues honestly . . . is entirely desirable . . . [and] underlying
issues of methodology and responsibility must be central to the dialogue."[5]
Indeed they must.

Bearing this in mind we can recognise that the last twenty years have seen a great deal of discussion about both the nature of homosexuality and the political and social rights of homosexual persons to choose lifestyles without the fear of discrimination. A positive gay identity has emerged and gay liberation movements have been vital not only for carrying on the political and social debates but also for changing gay consciousness as no longer something to be disguised or ashamed of, but something which is essentially as unremarkable as being heterosexual. The Church, as well as society, owes a profound debt to any group or movement which identifies injustice or discrimination and works for the safeguarding of their own rights.

The Church no longer controls society's agenda of issues and is frequently found rather desperately trying to formulate principles with a theological and moral vocabulary which no longer has common currency. Nevertheless, in the 1975 "Declaration on Certain Questions Concerning Sexual Ethics" the Church reflected meaningfully on its responsibilities: "The traditional doctrine [of sexual morality] must be studied more deeply. It must be handed on in a way capable of properly enlightening the consciences of those confronted with new situations and enriched with a discernment of all the elements that can usefully and truthfully be brought forward about the meaning and value of human sexuality."[6]

The current debate about homosexuality reflects these problems in a particularly intense way for whilst homosexual Catholics have been liberated and have found their voice within the Church, the expression of lifestyles realising this new-found confidence and freedom places them in conflict with the Church's traditional understanding of homosexuality and its genital expression. Not only do homosexual Catholics have to cope with finding authentic lifestyles in society at large but also have to live out their faith within the community of the Church, a Church whose language of understanding is, in this case, alienating. Many homosexual Catholics cannot find in that understanding their own experience of God's presence and love. For all its talk of what Christian liberation means, the CDF letter seems unwilling to let the Church itself address the question as to what sort of behavior most expresses the Christian life and calling. Such analysis as the CDF letter does give does not do justice to the reality of human sexuality. The language is such that it remains foreign to the People of God and no longer corresponds to the way they think of themselves or experience human relationships. There is much rethinking to be done and only when it has taken place will the Church be able to offer once more the fullness and richness of its teaching, addressing the modern world with credibility. However, let us not forget that in this context homosexuality is only one part of a wider problem.

But what of the lived experience of gay Catholics themselves? I am only qualified to speak of our experiences here in Britain, but it is my conviction that what we, as gay Catholics, have to offer the Church has come from our distillation of our concept of Church itself. For so long gay Catholics have seen themselves as a marginalized group. Indeed, the 1986 National Conference of Priests of England and Wales in choosing for its theme "Marginalized People" called attention to the plight of homosexuals in the Church and the Church's need to end such discrimination. As a sign of this, Quest was asked to send an official observer to the conference and in its submissions the conference requested the bishops to reissue their 1979 "Introduction to the Pastoral Care of Homosexual People." But as long as people are prepared to continue to see themselves as a marginalized group, waiting for the Church to minister to them, they will remain a marginalized group. Once we see the relevance of ministry in our own lives, then true participation in Church begins and we become, truly, one of the People of God. It is a matter of taking the initiative and dealing with the problems and questions that face us, ourselves, and not waiting for someone else to deal with them for us. As Paolo Freire would have us realize, "conscientization" is the beginning of our redemption.

Quest has never seen itself as a pressure group. It is a forum, encouraging dialogue among its members and offering their experience to the rest of the Church so that the Church can continue to grow and discern its message for all humankind. There is no doubt that Quest's attitude is rooted in a recognition of the Church's teaching role, but it may be that there are occasions when the Church that teaches has to start to learn again. God in the world has to be looked for in history and experience and we, the people, are the Church. In his commentary on the documents of Vatican II, Vorgrimler speaks to this theme:

> [Vatican II] has indeed touched upon a matter of the utmost importance for the Church of tomorrow. Drawing on his lay knowledge of the world and the milieu, the secular layman is to build the Church of tomorrow along with his pastors. He is to reveal his world to them, a world ever more closely knit, ever changing and evolving, its preoccupations and distress, its feelings, its sense of what life is about . . . [he is] to present theologians with new problems day in day out and efficaciously help in finding their solution . . . in all the subtle complexities which the cure of souls involves nowadays, so that those who hold priestly office may speak with more assurance and more to the point . . . and the Church itself be better adapted to the situation in the world.[7]

These words well express the spirit of Quest. It should be kept in mind that Quest's constitutional purpose is "to preach the Gospel of Our Lord Jesus Christ so as to sustain and increase Christian belief among homosexual men and women." As part of this work Quest welcomes all opportunities for dialogue within the Church in the "spirit of truth and love" (Eph. 4:15) of which the CDF letter speaks.

In approaching dialogue Quest has always borne in mind the words of Pope Paul VI:

> A characteristic of the dialogue is meekness. . . . The dialogue is not proud; it is not bitter; it is not offensive. . . . It is peaceful; it avoids violent methods; it is patient; it is generous. . . . In the dialogue one discovers how different are the ways which lead to the light of faith, and how it is possible to make them converge on the same goal. . . . The dialogue will make us wise.[8]

The CDF letter rightly claims that Scripture "bids us speak the truth in love," and the Catholic Church makes demands in truth and out of love, for the Church is concerned with our destiny. But there are different forms of truth, and truth itself is found in different ways. Truth changes and deepens in time. Truth can be found through speculation, insight, reflection, and a sense of growing, but we all need to ask ourselves how we arrive at truth and love. We also need to ask what sort of truth we are looking for and what sort of love we are seeking. And if we ask those questions honestly we must be prepared to hear the truth and accept the love. We have to ask ourselves if we are ready to hear the truth from anywhere and whether we are ready to accept love in the way that it is offered rather than the way we would like to receive it. At the same time, we must be ready to help others speak *their* truth and *their* love.

Along with this we have the need to be united and to try to bring together the areas of our lives which are marked by division. In this context we must consider the division of being gay and Catholic. How do we find ourselves in a Church that tells us what we are, in a Church which makes demands in truth and out of love? Must being gay also mean division and pain? We have the task of trying to put together the two things: being gay and being Catholic; it's a lifetime's work that we are being called upon to do, and primarily we must live a life worthy of the gospel. We are all in the process of coming out to God and to one another, and we must be prepared to walk with one another and be patient with one another. Theology does not necessarily provide all the answers; indeed, there may not be answers, only a new shaping of thoughts. "Let us speak the truth in love" is, after all, an invitation as well as a command.

Love and truth are common words and we often talk of the truth as setting us free. But does it? Truth and love can be threatening and are also a risk, and we have to ask ourselves whether we are willing to take the responsibility of speaking the truth in love. If we are, then we must speak them responsibly and with depth, according to the grace given by God. To speak the truth is to decide to step out and to commit oneself in love.

Both the CDF letter and the AIDS crisis present a new situation. They are a challenge and they raise serious questions. Of recent months many have asked, "What exactly *is* the CDF letter trying to say to us?" There are some positive points. There is a debate which challenges the contemporary world. The Church asks: "What does it mean to be free?" Is the gay lifestyle a liberation or an illusion? Our liberation is to hear the gospel and live it. This is a working out of our salvation and much has happened that has forced gay liberationists to rethink their liberty.

The Church has also said that we must deal with the whole person, which is the basis for pastoral care. Pastoral care which falls short of this is not according to the teaching of the Church. Also such pastoral care is the responsibility of the whole Church. All are to see themselves as called to care for the homosexual in the Church today.

But we are left with many negatives too. Has the whole truth been spoken, or is it only one version of the truth? Has it been spoken in love? Gayness is not a matter of choice. Neither is the only expression of homosexuality a genital one. Homosexual "activity" is a much wider concept than mere genitality. Both the CDF letter at one end and the gay liberationists at the other seem obsessed with choice and genitality; both parties do a disservice to the gay Catholic, who is, above all, a person who has a right to consideration for what he or she is rather than what they might do. As with heterosexuals, gay persons who enter into relationships are called upon to seek to "sustain each other, heal each other and help each other to grow. Insofar as they do this they make real for each other the work of the sustaining Father, of the redeeming and healing Son, of the transforming Spirit. A truly Christian vision [of this] can be found in the person of Christ; accepting, caring, reconciling, healing; calling and challenging, suffering and enduring, trusting and persevering—and all for love."[9]

And this is the very witness being given by so many gay Catholics in their everyday lives. Gay Catholics who have come to recognize the special gifts of God in their lives and who have set one foot in front of the other to travel on that journey that begins with the first attempt to speak the truth in love. Neither the Church, as represented by the Congregation for the Doctrine of the Faith, nor the gay liberationists have really seemed to be seeking to help the homosexual person find fulfillment; that fulfillment—spiritual or temporal—which is something unique to each individual and which brings to fruition in them what they really are, not what they seem to be.

The qualities which mark Christian life and thought are faith, hope, and love. Whatever the outcome of the present dialogue we should not compromise on any of these but rather take the opportunity which the CDF letter provides for deepening our faith, working in hope, and living in love with the Church. More than most we know that we belong to a Church which does make mistakes and is a community of sinners but it is to this very Church that God has called us and given us a mission—not for ourselves alone but for all those who will come after.

The fathers of the Second Vatican Council said, "The Church seeks but one solitary goal: to carry forward the work of Christ himself under the leading of the befriending Spirit. And Christ entered this world to give witness to the truth, to rescue and not to sit in judgment, to serve and not to be served."[10] As gay Catholics we must constantly recognize our own worth and the value of the contribution we make to the Church. We must recognize that we are present in the Church because we have answered a call. The Incarnation is as active in our lives and our ministries as in any other part of Christ's body. The Church needs to be asked to help us to make ourselves, and the experience of being gay, into a grace. That is liberation and a witness to God. God chooses us to speak truly and in love for him. We must love the church and teach it to love us. It must not be allowed to become an institution which dictates where and how God acts. On the contrary, the Church challenges us to move from where we are now into the transcendent, for the Spirit moves in us and in the Church.

Quest stands for holding things together and letting people find their truth in love. Each of us is the Church for which we take the corporate responsibility. In order to find our truth we must respect the truth of the whole Church. "The joys and hopes, the griefs and anxieties of the men of this age, especially those who are poor or who are in any way afflicted, these too are the joys and hopes, the griefs and anxieties of the followers of Christ. . . . That is why this community realises that it is truly and intimately linked with mankind and its history."[11]

In these profound opening words of the Pastoral Constitution on the Church in the Modern World the fathers of the Council committed the local as well as the universal Church to human history, the histories of individuals and groups as well as the histories of nations. It is this solidarity which is both the beginning and the goal of the Church's ministry. Any ministry which is to be effective must not only enter into the dialogue of salvation with the movements and philosophies which form the mind of the times but must be preceded by a deep and accurate listening, that it may identify and discern the various spirits which are at work. Pope John Paul II said that "to look into the eyes of another person and to see the hopes of a brother or sister is to discover the meaning of solidarity."[12]

Both "An Introduction to the Pastoral Care of Homosexual People" and the CDF letter begin to set out the direction of a caring ministry to homosexual persons within the Church. They indicate how necessary such a ministry has become at the present time; they offer us all a time for healing. The Church already has at its service a wide range of expertise and experience in its pastors and people. It is vital that in its development of pastoral care (CDF letter, no. 15) the Church enlist the advice of those groups who have experience of this ministry, especially the experience of homosexual persons themselves.

The time has come for the Church to address itself to the problems of people who are homosexual rather than those who are seen to indulge in homosexual acts. It is the former who are trying to struggle into the heart of the Church, but it is apparently only to the latter that the hierarchy of the Church has so far seemed willing to address itself.

Notes

1. Quest is a British organization under lay leadership for gay Catholics.
2. Robert Nugent, SDS, "Struggling into the Heart of the Church," Quest 1986 Conference address, University of Leeds, 19 July 1986.
3. Mario Conti, "A Flawed Sexual Ethic," The Tablet, 6 September 1986.
4. Francis Thomas, Letter to the Editor, the London Times, 3 September 1986.
5. Kevin Kelly, "Sexual Ethics and the Vatican," the London Times, 30 August 1986.
6. Sacred Congregation for the Doctrine of the Faith, "Declaration on Certain Questions Concerning Sexual Ethics" (Washington, DC: United States Catholic Conference, 1975), p. 15.
7. H. Vorgrimler, ed., Commentary on the Documents of Vatican II, vol. 1 (New York: Herder and Herder, 1968), p. 29.
8. As quoted by Bishop Walter Sullivan in his introduction to A Challenge to Love: Gay and Lesbian Catholics in the Church, edited by Robert Nugent (New York: Crossroad, 1983), p. xiii.
9. Bishops of England and Wales Secretariat, "Pastoral Care of Marriage and Family Life," 1986.
10. Gaudium et Spes, no. 3.
11. Ibid., no. 1
12. Pope John Paul II, "Message for the Twentieth World Day of Peace," December 1986.

13

Pope John Paul II's
Theology of the Body

Ronald Modras

The Vatican letter on the pastoral care of homosexual persons may have been signed by Joseph Ratzinger, cardinal prefect of the Congregation for the Doctrine of the Faith, but its contents and terminology bear the marks of Pope John Paul II. Not only approved but obviously also authorized by the pontiff, the letter is infused with his thinking and constitutes but one more item on the already considerable list of pronouncements that have emanated from this pontificate relating to sexuality. It contributes but one more reason for puzzlement as to the cause for what appears at first glance as almost an obsession with the subject.

Not only the existence of the letter but its language and ideas can be clarified when perceived within the framework and from the background of Pope John Paul II's theology of the body and human sexuality. Time and again the letter speaks of "the truth" about the human person, a phrase that has become a hallmark of his discourse. The letter maintains that homosexuality is to be properly understood from the standpoint of the first chapters of the biblical book of Genesis, the subject of a lengthy series of papal addresses. Both in those addresses and the Ratzinger letter, reference is made to the "spousal significance" of the body, now "obscured by original sin." The letter, like the pope, identifies love as self-giving born of self-denial. Most telling of all, however, nowhere does the letter speak of homosexuality in terms of nature nor are homosexual acts described as being contrary to natural law or as sins against nature. Instead, the letter makes the highly controversial and problematic claim that the homosexual condition itself, although not a sin, is an "objective disorder."

Space does not allow a lengthy let alone exhaustive elaboration of the pope's anthropology as it impinges on sexual morality. Only the more

119

salient features can be outlined as they relate to the Vatican letter. Even so modest an essay, however, may serve to clarify the foundations and fuller implications of the often obscure, sometimes ambiguous references in the pope's theology of the body and human sexuality.

Thomistic Personalism

If the pope's theology of the body is sometimes ambiguous, it is because it can appear so revolutionary and original at first. He uses the language of personalism and the phenomenological method of description in his analyses of sexuality. He speaks rarely about nature and often about persons, personal dignity and responsibility, and so appears to have broken with his neo-Thomistic training with its insistence upon immutable natural laws. Upon closer examination, however, the pope is a skillful and energetic exponent of the neo-Thomistic natural law ethic, as he translates it into personalist categories and calls it "Thomistic personalism."

Karol Wojtyla wrote an article under that title in 1961.[1] In it he described personhood as the "highest perfection" in the created order, but time and again spoke of human emotions and feelings as something to be dominated and subordinated by the rational will. So too in his book, *The Acting Person*,[2] Wojtyla describes human transcendence and spirituality in terms of self-domination. Although he constantly refers to personhood with its connotations of unity and integration, Wojtyla still maintains the old Platonic dualism with its suspicion of the body and its passions. The soul, for him, is the principle which allows us to possess and govern our bodies like a "compliant tool."

Wojtyla espouses a stratified concept of the human person. Like the pagan Stoics and medieval schoolmen, he views the emotions as dangerous if not evil. They are part of our "lower" sphere, requiring control by the "higher" sphere, the intellect and will, in an "absolute manner" if need be (p. 315, n.72). Such self-control constitutes, for Wojtyla, authentic spiritual power and is, he writes, "probably the most fundamental manifestation of the *worth* of the person" (p. 264). It is difficult to conceive of a higher valuation of the category of control.

His stratified, dualistic body-soul anthropology lies at the basis of Wojtyla's *Love and Responsibility*,[3] the fullest exposition of his thinking on sexual ethics before he became pope. Here too, although he uses words like "person" and "love" liberally, his understanding of those terms is hardly that of his readers. Like his arguments, his definitions refer constantly to nature. Like his neo-Thomistic teachers, he describes the sexual urge as a specific force of nature whose natural end is procreation. True love, he argues, is not an emotion. It is the virtue or habit of goodwill *(benevolentia)*, whereby the rational will affirms the value of a person. Such affirmation requires "subordination" to the laws of nature. "In the order of love a man can remain true to the person only in so far as he is true to nature. If he does violence to 'nature,' he also 'violates' the person by making it an object of enjoyment rather than an object of love" (p. 229). With love so linked to nature, one can see why Wojtyla attacks artificial birth control so aggressively. Procreation is not distinct from love, nor love from procreation. Contraception has "a damaging effect on love" (p. 53), and "the correct attitude toward procreation is a condition for the realization of love" (p. 226).

Karol Wojtyla has never been one for offering empirical evidence for such claims. Instead, his argument is philosophical, an appeal to the moral imperative first formulated by Immanuel Kant: a person must not be *merely* the means to an end for another person. Artificial contraception, he contends (and a fortiori homosexual activity), is a mattter of two people using one another for "mutual, or rather, bilateral 'enjoyment.' " This is not love, he concludes, but utilitarianism. If there is a weakness in Wojtyla's argument, it hinges upon the word *merely*. Although he states the Kantian imperative correctly the first time he quotes it, he thereafter regularly omits the crucial word *merely*. We cannot help but make use of other persons as means, as we deal with each other. The pope uses cardinals the way the rest of us use mechanics and grocery clerks. Kant's principle forbids using persons "merely" as means without recognizing their value "at the same time as an end." Wojtyla simply asserts without further argumentation or qualification that "anyone who treats a person as the means to an end does violence to the very essence of the other" (p. 27).

In treating of the erotic and emotional aspects of sexuality, Wojtyla says at first that the benevolence or goodwill that is genuine love can "keep company" with the love that is desire, so long as desire "does not over-whelm all else" (p. 84). Further into his exposition, however, the language becomes more negative: the will "combats" the sexual urge and "atones" for the desire to have the other person. Genuine love is the antithesis of emotional desire, and a couple "must free themselves from those erotic sensations which have no legitimation in true love." Wojtyla describes love as a "duty" whereas sexual desire or concupiscence "means a constant tendency merely to 'enjoy' " (p. 160).

Assisting us in performing our duty is the virtue of chastity, which "implies liberation from everything that 'makes dirty.' Love must be so to speak pellucid." Wojtyla does not explicitly describe sexual feelings as dirty, but he does imply it when he writes that "sensations and actions springing from sexual reactions and the emotions connected with them tend to deprive love of its crystal clarity" (p. 146). Sexual emotions or enjoyment are not evil in themselves, but only if dissociated from procreation. God's attitude toward contraception is comparable to that of a father when his child, to whom he gave bread and jam, throws away the bread and eats only the jam (p. 309, n.66).

Long before becoming pope, Karol Wojtyla evinced an unremitting interest in sexuality. In 1971 he wrote about concupiscence, which we may here define as spontaneous sexual desire, as destroying human dignity and impoverishing the world. Even concepts like salvation are more fully intelligible in the context of "overcoming concupiscence."[4] Clearly, birth control and homosexual acts are not peripheral matters of secondary importance to him. Sexual ethics, he wrote in 1978, possess "such powerful anthropological implications" that it has become the battlefield for a "struggle concerning the dignity and meaning of humanity itself."[5]

Sexual Desire and Disorder

Less than a year after becoming pope, Karol Wojtyla began a remarkable series of addresses on the first chapters of Genesis.[6] Pilgrims and tourists who had come to a general audience to catch a glimpse of the pope were accorded an erudite theological exposition on marriage, sexuality, and original sin. The addresses, accompanied by elaborate footnotes, bear all the features of a book the pope had been writing prior to his election. The work is not one of biblical scholarship; the pope does not pretend to be a biblical scholar and only infrequently relies upon modern biblical exegesis. The talks comprise a "catechesis," as they are subtitled, on the Book of Genesis, or rather on a particular school of interpreting Genesis, namely, that of Saint Augustine. (Jewish, Eastern Orthodox, and contemporary historical-critical interpretations are quite different.)

Although he acknowledges that the first chapters of Genesis have a "mythical character" (p. 28), the pope treats the creation stories as if they were history, or, as he calls them, "revealed theological pre-history" (p. 37). The reader may be confused at first, since one is not altogether sure whether Adam ("humankind") is regarded as a historical individual engaged in historical events or a symbolic representation of ourselves in our present human condition. In either case, the pope uses the creation stories not so much for substantiation as for inspiration or a jumping-off point for his own personal reflections. Those reflections in no way contradict his earlier ideas but rather restate them. Once again he affirms the importance of self-control but now in terms of the ability of a person's self-gift to another, described by the pope as the "nuptial" or "spousal" meaning of the body.

The pope can be profound as he expounds upon our call to a "community of persons" achieved by self-giving. More problematic, however, is his discussion of the spontaneous sexual desire that Catholic theological tradition has come to call concupiscence.[7] Together with the Genesis story of Adam and Eve, the pope conjoins the words of Matthew 5:28 ("Everyone who looks at a woman lustfully has already committed adultery with her in his heart") and of 1 John 2:16 ("For all that is in the world, the lust of the flesh, and the lust of the eyes, and the pride of life, is not of the Father but is of the world"). The pope interprets these texts not within their own distinct historical contexts but in the light of one another, assuming that they share a common theological vision and attitude toward the body and its sexuality. The attitude is very much that of Augustine as the Pope describes the sin of Adam and its sexual consequences in terms of "cosmic shame" (p. 48).

Absent are any references to "mythical character" as the pope draws an historical "state of original innocence" from the first chapters of Genesis (p. 71). Adam is obviously not a symbol but a historical individual and his sin an event whose "cosmic shame" is indicated by our sexual shame. The pope not only interprets the Genesis story historically but assumes that the nakedness of Adam and Eve implies their original "self-mastery" and "self-control" over their sexual organs (p. 51). They were created "above the world of living beings or 'animalia' " (p. 52), capable of "disinterested" self-giving without any taint of the selfish "enjoyment" that is the negation of the "nuptial meaning" of the body (p. 83). The loss of original innocence resulted in a "constitutive break within the human person, almost a rupture of man's original spiritual and somatic unity" (p. 50). As a consequence of that first sin, our bodies are marked by the "humiliation" that is spontaneous sexual desire or concupiscence (p. 50).

The pope uses words like "imbalance" and "distortion" (p. 72) to describe the concupiscence or "lust of the flesh" that is now a permanent element or "disposition derived from man's sinfulness" (p. 145). The human heart has become a "battlefield" between the "sincere giving" that is love and the lust that seeks to "appropriate" another as an object of enjoyment (pp. 75–77). Because of that first sin, " 'the desire of the body' is more powerful than 'the desire of the mind' " (p. 84). We can become gifts to and for one another (the "nuptial meaning" of the body) only if we have self-control. Concupiscence "limits" and "reduces" self-control (p. 77) and makes us "ashamed" of our bodies (p. 53).

Here, within the context of concupiscence as the pope understands it, we can properly understand the controversial reference in the Vatican letter to homosexuality as a "disorder." The word should not be taken to mean a psychological or even a moral disorder, since the letter makes clear that the homosexual condition is not a sin. Within the framework of the pope's theology, however, homosexuality is the result of sin. God simply could not, would not, and did not create homosexuals as such. The homosexual condition is a result of the first sin, an aspect or form of the concupiscence that is the condition of us all. Unwilled, spontaneous sexual attraction or desire for someone of the same sex is a "disorder" in the same way that unwilled, spontaneous sexual attraction or desire for anyone is an "imbalance" and "distortion."

According to the pope's theology of the body, it is a disposition "derived from man's sinfulness" that we do not have our sexual inclinations and desires completely under our rational control. It is a "disorder" and "distortion" since, for the pope as for Augustine, sexuality was created for procreation, not enjoyment. Homosexual persons are bound to combat and control their erotic impulses the same way that heterosexual and even married persons are. Disinterested self-giving is the only love that is genuine, and homosexual acts, like birth control, are the antithesis of such love.

Pope John Paul II's language is abstract, at times turgid, and often ambiguous. He created an outcry when he stated that it was possible for a husband and wife to commit adultery with one another "in the heart" (8 October 1980). Apologists hurried to point out that such adultery "in the heart" results from spouses using one another for "mere satisfaction" of their sexual needs. To quote the pope completely: "Man can commit this adultery 'in the heart' also with regard to his own wife, if he treats her only as an object to satisfy instinct" (p. 145). What the apologists usually fail to point out is that, for Pope John Paul II, birth control is precisely an example of spouses using one another for "mere satisfaction" and therefore is a matter of adultery "in the heart."

Pope John Paul II is an attractive and charismatic evangelist of Thomistic personalism and the theology of the body and sexuality he derives from it. The idea, however, of a historical Adam in complete control of his sexual organs cannot help but pose some difficulties for contemporary biblical scholars. Psychologists will question whether a completely self-giving love is possible, and if complete rational self-control to the detriment of spontaneity is altogether desirable. Karl Rahner, the foremost Catholic theologian of our century, has pointed out that concupiscence is natural, since, according to Catholic tradition, freedom from it is preternatural and so not required by human nature. If Adam in the Genesis story was free from concupiscence, it did not stop him from sinning. It follows, moreover, that if concupiscence limits our self-control and thereby our totally free self-giving to virtue, it also limits our totally free self-giving to vice. If it keeps us from being angels, it keeps us from being demonic as well.[8]

But it is not biblical scholars, theologians, or psychologists who pose the greatest resistance to the pope's theology of the body. The pope speaks to the masses of Catholic faithful, and it is the masses of the faithful he will have to convince. His persuasive powers are considerable, but he will have to confront more thoroughly something to which homosexual persons and married couples practicing birth control both appeal. The pope is intelligent and articulate, but he has to contend with something more formidable than ideas. Whether it is a matter of describing birth control as adultery "in the heart" or the homosexual condition as a "disorder," the greatest challenge to the pope's theology of the body and its sexuality is people's experience. What the pope approaches from the outside and calls lust, they live on the inside and call love. More than anything else, it is the experience of their lives, reflected on in faith and sustained by the sacraments, which lead them respectfully to disagree.

Notes

1. "Personalizm Tomistyczny," *Znak* 13 (1961): 664–76.
2. *The Acting Person* (Dordrecht, Holland/Boston: D. Reidel, 1979).
3. *Love and Responsibility* (New York: Farrar, Straus & Giroux, 1981).
4. "Notatki na Marginesie Konstytucji 'Gaudium et Spes,'" *Atheneum Kaplanskie* 74 (1970): 3–6.
5. "Antropologia Encykliki 'Humanae Vitae,'" *Analecta Cracoviensia* 10 (1978): 13.
6. The addresses first appeared in English translation in *L'Osservatore Romano*, English Edition. They have been subsequently compiled and reprinted as a series in book form by the Daughters of St. Paul: *Original Unity of Man and Woman, Catechesis on the Book of Genesis*, with a preface by Donald W. Wuerl (Boston: St. Paul Editions, 1981).
7. *Blessed Are the Pure of Heart, Catechesis on the Sermon on the Mount and Writings of St. Paul*, with a preface by Donald W. Wuerl (Boston: St. Paul Editions, 1983).
8. K. Rahner, "The Theological Concept of Concupiscentia," *Theological Investigations*, vol. 1 (Baltimore: Helicon, 1961).

14

Rights, Responsibilities, and Homosexuality

Carolyn Osiek

At least since the beginnings of the Church's social teaching for the modern world at the end of the nineteenth century, the institutional teaching Church has seen itself as defending rather than attacking human dignity and human rights. This self-perception is reflected in the Vatican letter (nos. 11 and especially 16). Indeed, its nineteenth-century history of championing human rights, as interpreted by the Church itself, against what were considered the excesses of liberalism, rationalism, secular humanism, socialism, and totalitarianism, is impressive. In fact, at certain times and in certain places the Church has been, and still is, the only power strong enough to defend human rights against institutions that threaten to destroy them. Thus it is quite ironic that some persons find their human dignity and rights under attack by that same Church.

In the twentieth century the same kind of approach has been tried with regard to issues such as feminism and birth control. The argument has proceeded thus: the Church speaks out for the fundamental dignity and rights of the human person against a godless society that will, in the name of a false freedom, really bring enslavement to selfishness and sin. Here the Church sees itself as champion of the true person, of the deepest qualities of human community, and of God's intentions for humankind.

The same presuppositions are evident in the present Vatican letter on homosexuality. It is as if the Church feels the responsibility to save homosexual persons from themselves and from a pernicious libertine society that will undermine and ultimately destroy their true dignity and rights.

If this approach no longer works in the late twentieth-century Western world, it is because too much has changed. An erosion of the credibility of authority has made it difficult to trust that any institution has the welfare of its members as first priority. Paternalism, in other times and places a welcome alternative to totalitarianism, is not appreciated in a society of persons for whom autonomy is a very high value and democracy is taken for granted. The traditional theory of natural law as expression of God's design does not hold up well under the pressure of the scientific and technological revolutions in which the potential for human interference in the harmony of the universe seems limitless. In short, in a society like ours, the Church with its present policies is no longer seen as defender of rights, but as restrictor of those rights; no longer as alternative to oppression, but as oppressor.

Thus a document like the Vatican letter seems strangely archaic and oppressive to those who would find helpful something more in keeping with, for example, the contemporary social sciences. Rather than advance in that direction over previous church pronouncements on homosexuality, this one seems actually to take a step toward more extreme polarization by declaring not only that homosexual activity but even homosexual "inclination," though "not a sin," is a "tendency ordered toward an intrinsic moral evil" and "thus the inclination itself must be seen as an objective disorder" (no. 3), and as "essentially self-indulgent" (no. 7). The letter does not clarify how a tendency that is an objective disorder can be ordered to moral evil without itself being sinful. What would be missing, according to traditional moral theology, is full knowledge and consent of will, but these criteria are usually applied to specific acts, not to an inclination or tendency. Nor does the letter elaborate on how an inclination can be essentially self-indulgent, yet not a sin. Here it would seem that a theology of objective sin and a theology of grace are being held uneasily side by side. The letter stops just short of saying that homosexual orientation is sinful but comes closer to making that connection than any recent Church pronouncement on the subject.

There can be no doubt that the whole letter has caused profound dismay among many American Catholics, and not only among those in the homosexual community. But should it have come as a surprise? It does so, I think, to the extent that we lose sight of the fact that Catholic church law and teaching start from a very different set of assumptions than do American law and social theory. Put in the context of Roman philosophy of the person in society, the Vatican letter, though just as dismaying, is perhaps less surprising.

The social philosophy behind the American democratic experience and behind traditional church social teaching have the same starting point: humanity is creature of God, and that is the basis for human dignity. From that fundamental conviction, the two diverge into different paths. In the American experience, based on common law, that God-given dignity is the basis for individual human rights. All created equal, "they are endowed by their Creator with certain inalienable rights. . . ." Sexuality is a function of the exercise of these rights: the right to communicate and express oneself in love. From these rights flow the responsibilities necessary to safeguard them for each person. The good of all individual persons together constitutes the common good. Thus human dignity means rights, for which exist responsibilities, and the sum of the good of each individual makes up the common good.

For the Roman law tradition, God's gift of creation of the human person necessitates first of all the response of the creature, that is, the responsibility to live according to the will of the creator. Primary among these responsibilities is that of safeguarding the common good for the sake of the individuals which constitute it. Persons then have those rights which will enable them to fulfill these responsibilities. Sexuality is a function not of right but of responsibility; in this case, the responsibility to contribute to the common good by providing offspring. The traditional church teaching that the primary purpose of marriage is the procreation of children, and that sexual activity is legitimate only there, is to be understood in this context. From the perspective of the modern world, this seems like a strangely mechanistic approach to sexuality, indeed quite cold and impersonal, and far from any notion of human dignity.

Vatican II's Pastoral Constitution on the Church in the Modern World seemed to hint at some departure from this unilateral view of marriage and sexuality (*Gaudium et Spes,* especially no. 50) by suggesting that the mutual relationship of spouses is just as important an end. Canon 1055.1 of the new *Code of Canon Law* confirms this by stating that marriage is ordered toward a double end: the conjugal good of the spouses, and the procreation and upbringing of children—both equally important. However, both during the Council and ever since, there has been strong resistance to this departure from previous teaching, resistance logically based on the fear that affirmation of sexuality as relationship opens the way to a reexamination of the entire philosophy of human nature and all the positions built on it.

Church custom has long implicitly admitted that marriage and sexuality have another purpose than reproduction by permitting the marriage of infertile persons (reconfirmed in canon 1084.3). In spite of this, the Vatican letter classifies homosexual activity as "not a complementary union, able to transmit life; and so it thwarts the call to a life of that form of self-giving which the Gospel says is the essence of Christian living" (no. 7). This is in effect a return to the traditional position about sexuality: if it lacks the potential for procreation, it has no good purpose.

These discrepancies notwithstanding, something like the present letter must be seen within the broader context sketched above. The heart of the argument has to do not with Scripture or natural law, but with the relationship of sexuality to individual rights and responsibilities and of these to the common good. The real fear is voiced at the end of number 9: "the view that homosexual activity is equivalent to, or as acceptable as, the sexual expression of conjugal love has a direct impact on society's understanding of the nature and rights of the family and puts them in jeopardy." The threat is not to individuals but to the family, and thus to the common good. It is clear that by homosexuality, irresponsible promiscuity is assumed: it "may seriously threaten the lives and well-being of a large number of people" (no. 9); self-denial in conformity with the Lord "will save them from a way of life which constantly threatens to destroy them" (no. 12).

If the family is threatened, the argument goes, the common good is at stake, individual responsibility for the common good is being neglected, and therefore the rights of those who neglect it have only relative value. The political theory which emerged out of medieval Christendom was able to affirm, within a closed system of authority and truth, that "error has no rights." At Vatican II and in the theological developments just prior to the Council, that maxim was repudiated in favor of the hard-won, and in some corners grudgingly accepted, Declaration on Religious Freedom. Here, really for the first time the Church officially accepted the idea of the separation of church and state, in which the state lacks competence to enforce conformity of belief and the church to enforce one form of government over another. The area of public morality falls uneasily between the two as we have seen so clearly in issue after issue in recent years.

Within the social theory described above, the question of the rights of those who are considered to be in error, much less of those possessing an inclination "ordered toward an intrinsic moral evil," are very unclear. Public harassment of homosexual persons is deplored and condemned "because it endangers the most fundamental principles of a healthy society" (i.e., the common good). Yet theirs is "behavior to which no one has any conceivable right" (no. 10). Thus it would seem that a right to physical and moral security is upheld, but not a right to privacy. Rights to housing and employment go unmentioned in the letter, but the opposition of local bishops in several recent attempts to enact city legislation in that regard yields a negative answer. In matters of morality, it would seem that error has limited rights, only those negative rights which would defend such persons from direct harm. To allow such persons extended positive rights would be to place the common good in danger.

Despite a few flaws in the logic, there is a unified line of argument here. It is based on the assumption that the common good must be defended by all means and cannot be sacrificed for the good of individuals who act contrary to it. In this case, the common good is the flourishing of family life. Sexuality exists for the sole purpose of contributing to that common good, thus for reproduction within marriage. On the success of this purpose, the survival and prosperity of society (and so also of the Church) depend. Moreover, there is a further assumption that even the ultimate good of individuals who claim a different kind of right (i.e., homosexuals) lies in conformity to what is posited as the way to upholding the common good. At the deepest level, they do not know what is best for them.

Let us for a moment examine more closely these assumptions. First, is the common good the goal of all effort, that which is to be preserved above all? Both systems, Roman and common law, would say yes. The point of difference lies in the means for achieving that goal. Common law will be more sensitive to the violations of individual rights in the process since in its system the common good is the sum total of the good of each citizen. Roman law will be more sensitive to the effect of the action of individuals on the whole of society.

Second, is the common good to be equated with family life? This is too facile an assumption anywhere in the modern world today. The classical image of the nuclear family represents only a small portion of the population in a place like the United States. Single-parent families, remarried heterosexual persons with complicated relationships to children and former spouses, childless couples (whether heterosexual or homosexual), homosexual couples with children, singles of both sexes living alone, and persons of both sexes and orientations living in voluntary community situations make up today's complex society. It is no longer adequate to simply say that "the family" is the basis of society without making a number of qualifications. So the common good has to be understood much more broadly as the happiness and prosperity of all persons, in whatever kinds of relationships they choose to live, exercising their personal rights with due respect for the rights of others.

Third, is homosexuality a threat to the family? There are ugly stereotypes conjured up by such a statement: of pedophiles and kidnapping, of ugly and painful deeds perpetrated far more frequently by heterosexuals than by homosexuals. But with stereotypes, facts are of no importance. There is the fear of adolescent promiscuity, again far more pervasive in the predominant heterosexual population, a terrible and growing social problem. The idea that homosexuality is a threat to the family seems to be based on a number of false assumptions. It is to suggest that persons are free to choose their sexual orientation and are more likely to choose a homosexual lifestyle out of "lust" or "selfishness." It suggests that a homosexual lifestyle is somehow more appealing and will run competition with marriage as choice of a state in life; that homosexuality is connected with "vice" in a more general sense, as opposed to the "virtue" of heterosexual lifestyle. In summary, it seems to attribute to the power of homosexual example the ability to exert far more influence on children than it in fact can. We are dealing here at the level of irrational fears and collective homophobia under the guise of philosophical assertions.

Fourth, is homosexuality then in any way a threat to the common good? It would have to be demonstrated that homosexuals in some way violate the pursuit of happiness and prosperity and the exercise of personal rights on the part of someone else. Certainly the bizarre public behavior of some in the gay community is offensive, but no more so than that of heterosexuals whose behavior is just as bizarre. The issue there is not homosexuality but disturbing the peace. If the common good is understood as the happiness and prosperity of all citizens, then the right to live in the kind of relationship to which one feels called, provided it does not do violence to the personally chosen relationships of others nor to their civil rights, would seem to be not a threat but in fact a contribution to social stability and thus to the common good.

Fifth, it can be affirmed that sexuality exists for the common good, that is, for the happiness and prosperity of persons in society. The Church is just beginning in this century, under the influence of the social sciences, to affirm the personal dimension of sexuality beyond its societal function. Sexuality is not to be treated cheaply or taken for granted. To assert that its sole purpose is procreation is perhaps, from a modern perspective, to do just that. To say that it is part of the mysterious ability of human persons to give themselves to each other in mutual love opens up new horizons for understanding its role in the mystery of human relationship to other persons and to God.

Sixth, it is certainly true that the survival of society and of the Church within it depends on the function of sexuality. In any culture that has so far appeared, the majority of the population contribute to that function by entering into heterosexual marriage and producing children. There is no indication, with the present sense of crisis about world overpopulation, that this trend is slowing down. The problem lies in the assertion that the more common way is the only right way or the only way intended by God. This argument is most strongly based on the theory of natural law which has been badly eroded by modern discoveries of the vagaries of natural forces and patterns.

Finally, can we in the twentieth century be comfortable with the idea that some mentally competent adults are incapable of knowing and choosing what is best for them, so that they need a benevolent institutional authority to guide them and save them from the ruin to which, from its point of view, they may be hastening? While it is certainly true that some people in our society unconsciously choose the very things which are not for their good, the facts make it impossible to responsibly suggest that such a tendency is inherent in any one group of persons on the basis of a common orientation. To make such an assertion is to fall back into a patronizing paternalism which will undermine the very dignity of human nature which so needs to be emphasized. Again, we are dealing here with irrational stereotyping and homophobia.

If these suppositions are critically examined, one need not be surprised by the official Church's teaching on homosexuality or by its reaffirmation in the present Vatican letter. The letter's intention is not to attack homosexual persons but to minister to them, though they will hardly feel understood or welcomed by it. They are unfortunately caught, as are American Catholics on a variety of contemporary issues, between two worlds of social theory and experience that have yet to fully meet one another in a good number of other domains as well. What is more serious, though, is the appeal to some unexamined presuppositions which no longer (if they ever did) hold up under careful scrutiny. Such discrepancies indicate that the whole theory of common good and the role of individual rights within it need to be reworked under the pressure of a rapidly evolving new world culture. Until this is done, such impasses about religious and moral questions will continue to occur.

15

Please Don't Shoot
the Bearer of Bad Tidings:
An Open Letter on
Cardinal Ratzinger's Document

Peter Hebblethwaite

Dear Reader,

Forgive me if I put what I have to say in the form of a letter. It is designed to make it a more personal statement. A formal essay might suggest an omniscience that those in my trade (Vaticanologist) like to assume but do not actually possess. A letter may come closer to the truths that lie well this side of omniscience. And what I have to say really is very tentative, even if trenchant in its expression.

I ask myself, first of all, why I have never written on homosexuality before. The answer is quite simply that I didn't know what I thought about it. I was confused. So I preferred to dodge the question. In the long period of Jesuit training (1948–65) I had the usual intense friendships common enough when males are isolated for long periods from desirable women. Being in the Jesuits was rather like being in the navy or in prison. But I never thought of myself as anything other than heterosexual. Perhaps that illustrates the dominant power of the culture.

George Tyrrell, about whom so much has been written recently, reported that when he was locked away at St. Beuno's "on a pastoral forehead in Wales" (where Gerard Manley Hopkins wrote *The Wreck of the Deutschland*), he imaginied he was a homosexual; but on arriving at Farm Street in London's Mayfair, he soon discovered his mistake. I understood that experience.

Tyrrell, by the way, wrote a privately published paper for the guidance of Farm Street confessors on the treatment of homosexual people, or as they

133

were infelicitously called in the jargon of the times, "Uranists" (presumably after the Greek God, Uranus). This was in the Oscar Wilde period when incense and vestments and conversion were all the rage, and evidently enough homosexual people passed through the Farm Street church confessionals to make such a handbook necessary. It was published by the long defunct Manresa Press, Roehampton, by Brother Griffin around 1905. I regret to say that I have lost my own personal copy. Some scholar ought to ferret it out, but I fear it won't bring anyone much comfort.

Indeed, scanning the horizon from my place at Oxford, I don't see much consolation anywhere for the gay community. The expression "gay community" is itself under attack. John McNeill concedes that though the term "community" suggests a warm and welcoming group, "the reality of the gay life-style . . . is often an impersonal unloving fantasy sex."[1] In any case, "gay community" seems to point toward a separated world radically cut off from more basic human communities. We do not want to end up with a gay-Church and a youth-Church and Rosemary Radford Ruether's woman-Church that would be incapable of reestablishing links with what Avery Dulles calls "the community of discipleship."[2]

Now to the "Letter to the Bishops of the Catholic Church on the Pastoral Care of Homosexual Persons" from the Congregation for the Doctrine of the Faith. That title itself is a bit of a mouthful. But I want to note three features about the title: (1) it is addressed to bishops who presumably know how to read such documents. It is not addressed directly to gay people who are unfamiliar with this style. That's only a little squeak of consolation, I admit, but it's better than nothing; (2) it is concerned with the "pastoral care" of such people; it is not, therefore, despite appearances, a theological or metaphysical pronouncement, valid for all ages and climes on the homosexual condition; (3) it does not distinguish between men and women and by speaking of "homosexual persons" concedes that they actually do exist as a possible variant of the human condition. Big deal I hear you cry. For there can be no doubt that the document displays an overall *hostility* to homosexual acts, or better, homogenital acts, whether embarked upon by women or by men. Why? Such acts, says the letter, are "deprived of their essential and indispensable finality, as being 'intrinsically disordered,' and able in no case to be approved of" (no. 3).

This involves a certain view of the natural law. Shakespeare has many passages, notably in his tragedies, where nature is topsy-turvy. But we can all write essays on the 120 senses of "nature" and their deep ambiguities. What is not ambiguous, I believe, is the Thomistic treatment accepted by the Church. Human acts, in order to be properly and fully human, have to correspond to their specific purposes. They are *ordered* to certain ends. We cannot abandon or reinvent such ends. This is the grounds for the severest statement in the letter: "Although the particular inclination of the homosexual person is not a sin, it is a more or less strong tendency ordered toward an intrinsic moral evil; and thus the inclination itself must be seen as an objective disorder" (no. 3).

In the natural law terminology used here, to speak of an "objective disorder" is to speak of something not intended by God for creatures, something not part of the divine plan for fully human persons. It is a falling short, a missing of the mark, an aberration; in short, a sin. It is fair to add, however, that number 15 which speaks explicitly of sin, does not exploit the distinction between mortal and venial sin. It would be rash to conclude that "mortal sin" has finished its honorable career and is now in the lumber room of discarded notions. But in practice "grave sin" seems to have replaced it.

Natural law arguments appear most strongly in what I take to be the central contention of the letter: "The Church, obedient to the Lord who founded her, and gave to her the sacramental life, celebrates the divine plan of the loving and life-giving union of men and women in the sacrament of marriage" (no. 7). It is difficult for a Catholic Christian not to recognize that as mainstream church teaching. But once you have accepted that, then the letter's conclusion seems inescapable: "It is only in the marital relationship that the use of the sexual faculty can be morally good. A person engaging in homosexual behavior therefore acts immorally" (no. 7). That is what "intrinsically disordered" means.

Now the only way to challenge or invalidate the judgment is to deny the principle on which it is based, to deny, that is, the necessary nexus between sexuality and procreation. The *Quest Journal,* published in Britain, has a commentary on the Vatican letter which has the merit of taking it seriously. Yet when it reaches this crucial question of the finality of sexual acts, it falters and stammers. "No one maintains that homosexual intercourse is procreatively ordered in the biological sense that the partners can conceive a child. What is absent from homosexual acts is not *their own finality* but *another* finality, viz., that which is proper to heterosexual acts."[3] In so far as I understand it, this statement seems to mean that it is futile to ask of homosexual acts that which in the nature of things they cannot deliver and note that "nature" here makes a respectable comeback. Now that seems to me to be tautological and, therefore, like all tautologies, true.

But it does nothing to remove—and much to intensify—the contention of the Congregation for the Doctrine of the Faith. Deprived of procreation, the *sole finality* of homogenital activity is as body language of love, at its best. That is not to disparage it so much as to define it. The same may be said of many individual acts of heterosexual lovemaking; they will not always result in conception and, indeed, if you get your thermometer and calendar working together efficiently, cannot result in conception. But Catholic theology has never taught the evident absurdity that every sexual act should result in procreation, rather that every sexual act should be at least open to that possibility as *Humanae Vitae* says. Thus the occasionally nonprocreative acts of heterosexuals cannot be reduced to or made the norm for the necessarily nonprocreative acts of homosexual persons.

My wife Margaret read what I have so far written and charged me with "hypocrisy" and fraudulence. She claims this because I have based my argument on *Humanae Vitae,* an encyclical in which I do not believe. What I *think* about *Humanae Vitae* is rather complicated and not strictly relevant here. But I reject her accusations for the following reason. Suppose a heterosexual couple marry and announce that they are never ever under any circumstances going to have children, even though they are potent and fertile. That would be an *invalid* marriage. The same principle, it seems to me—that the deliberate option for sterility makes a marriage invalid—is the reason why homosexual marriage is excluded by the Church and why homogenital acts are frowned upon.

This is where the crunch comes. Unless the Congregation can be persuaded to budge on the sexuality-procreation (as possibility) connection, there will be no place for active homosexual people in the Church. And the Congregation, mark my words, will not budge on this one. Of course, there is homosexuality in the Roman Curia, even if not all Roger Peyrefitte's tales are to be believed. But it is always perceived as a threat, a menace, a great surging wave or disorder coming from below (or from Naples). One of the mistakes some gay movements make is to encourage the belief that the present position of the Vatican comes about only because we have a tough-minded macho pope or a Bavarian inquisitor as prefect of the Congregation. Please, do not count on such personal factors. Yet people go on trusting in such mirages. For example, *Quest* has stated publicly that the views of one Pope will rarely embrace the whole Catholic moral tradition; the emphasis will vary from one pontificate to another. True enough. But what are the parameters of emphasis? With great respect, I find *Quest* here very naive. Its editors fall into a trap that I have fallen into occasionally. Every time I have got the Vatican wrong (and it has happened), it was because I allowed my heart to rule my head. I imagined that what I *wanted to happen* was actually *going to happen.* There is no surer path to self-deception. In 1976 I never really thought that

Cardinal Basil Hume of Westminster was a serious contender for the throne of Peter, but I liked the idea and so allowed for its possibility. I am now sadder and wiser. It seems that Cardinal Joseph Ratzinger had such extravagant expectations in mind when, after putting the boot in vigorously, he summons the entire Catholic community to rally round and help its homosexual brothers and sisters, but "without deluding them or isolating them" (no. 15). I suppose Fr. Thomas Herron, of Philadelphia, the leading American on the Congregation's staff, translated that. He has a redundant "them" (the first one).

What are we going to do with this document? One approach is to treat it as absurd and ridicule it. This is nearly always possible. One of the basic rules of controversy is to select the weakest points in an opponent's position, concentrate on demolishing *that,* thereby giving the fallacious impression that the whole case has been obliterated. I know this because I confess to having used this controversial technique in tight dialectical corners.

For example, Dan Grippo enjoyed himself hugely and entertained us by proving that Cardinal Ratzinger did not understand the Old or the New Testament, still less the meaning of *malakoi* and *arsenokoitai* in 1 Corinthians 6:9.[4] This led Fr. Roland Calvert to write that "there was more substance in one paragraph of Grippo's article that in Ratzinger's entire statement."[5] This is no doubt true. But it does not make a scrap of difference. For the CDF letter does not depend on the interpretation of *malakoi* or *arsenokoitai.* It does not stand or fall upon the woefully inadequate scriptural exegesis found in number 6. All such attacks leave the main target undisturbed. For this document is based, to repeat, on the sexuality-for-procreation approach.

And the document still stands erect though tattered when you have proved that it is uncompassionate, unevangelical, unjust, fraudulent, biased, and discriminatory. One passage is definitely sinister: "When civil legislation is introduced to protect behavior to which no one has any right, neither the Church nor society should be surprised when other distorted notions and practices gain ground, and irrational and violent reactions increase" (no. 10). In other words, you've got what you deserved.

But this is extraordinary language in a Christian document. It appears to rationalize, if not condone, the ousting of gay teachers or the beating up of gay people or (dare I say it?) the wearing of pink triangles as insisted on by the Nazis in Hitler's Germany (something with which Cardinal Ratzinger, born in 1927, would have been familiar). When in December 1986 and January 1987 three dioceses in the United States expelled chapters of Dignity, a Catholic organization for homosexual people and friends, the national president, James Bussen, "angrily asked if those dioceses also support the document's implicit sanction of violence against gay people."[6] Such reactions are natural (there's another meaning of the term). The Roman Curia, we instinctively feel, ought to write letters that are models of pastoral compassion and evangelical understanding. How else can Rome claim to be *Mater et Magistra* (Mother and Teacher)? Here it is behaving more like an irate father and judge. This letter is appalling in tone. Yet complaining about its aggressiveness could be a distraction from, or an alibi for, ignoring its central point.

That would not be much consolation for Gabriel Moran who dubs the letter "one of the most duplicitous documents in the modern era of the Catholic Church."[7] He seeks to show that it is incoherent in its use of "orientation," which is slipped in alongside "inclination" and "condition" in number 3, while being bizarrely equated with acting out compulsively in number 11.

This provides me with an opening here for a discussion of what some might consider the node of this debate: What is meant by "sexual orientation"? It was regarded as a great triumph to have got Pope John Paul II to say to the bishops of the United States assembled in Chicago in October 1979 that they had rightly stated that homosexual activity, as distinct from homosexual orientation, is morally wrong. That was considered "progress" at the time. But progress is always relative to what went before and will come after. The ground that appeared to have been gained in 1979 was lost by the 1986 CDF letter.

What is the explanation for this setback? To answer this question, we need a little bit of history. The first statement of the Congregation on homosexuality came in *Persona Humana,* or "Declaration on Certain Questions Concerning Sexual Ethics," dated 29 December 1975. This document has generally been considered better than the recent CDF letter. Yet if it admits to the reality of a "homosexual orientation," it does so in grudging terms and different language. *Persona Humana* first mentions "temporary homosexuals who can expect to be cured."[8] Then a second type "consists of homosexuals whose condition is permanent and who are such because of a constitutional defect presumed to be incurable."[9] It is clearly a lamentable misfortune to be so afflicted. And if you try to argue that "the condition of the second type of homosexual is so natural that it justifies homosexual relations for them,"[10] then *Persona Humana* warns that you are gravely mistaken. Hence its conclusion: "Sexual relations between persons of the same sex are necessarily and essentially disordered according to the objective moral order."[11]

But if that is the case, and it is, why did people get the *impression* that this 1975 document represented progress? Part of the answer is because gay groups wanted some good news from Rome and thought they could find it in this document. With a dash of imagination, one could turn the unfortunate "permanent condition" into the scientifically founded "sexual orientation." The next step was to expand on *Persona Humana*'s observation that "sexuality pervades the whole of life"[12] and draw the obvious conclusion that this must be as true of homosexuals as heterosexuals. Then the declaration's appeal to "psychology" and the sciences generally and the invitation that people should "apply their intelligence to the discovery and constant development of the values inherent in human nature"[13] seemed to hint that some sort of change was contemplated. I am not attributing bad faith to anyone. If I had wished to commend the homosexual case, I would have treated the text in the same way, easing it gently in my direction.

In any case, from a *pastoral* point of view, there were some loopholes through which an experienced casuist could help one leap. If homogenital relations were "essentially disordered in the objective moral order," did that not leave some leeway for those still splashing about in the *subjective* moral order? And the "lesser of two evils" maxim could be invoked. For example, it would make little moral sense to break up a stable homosexual relationship if the alternative were promiscuity and one-night stands. The rest of that story you know.

One other development was the espousal by the U.S. bishops of the "orientation is OK; acts are not OK" for which Pope John Paul II praised them. I would suggest that the reason it has been abandoned is because it was unworkable. For it put into the hands of gay persons an extremely powerful and indeed, on one level, irrefutable argument. All *theologos* is ultimately talk about God. But what "orientation is OK; acts are not OK" said was that God created human beings who were doomed to frustration in the whole of their lives since, as *Persona Humana* asserts, sexuality "is the source of the biological, psychological and spiritual characteristics that make a person male or female."[14] A God who can create such frustrated creatures has to be a sadistic monster.

This was all the more powerful an argument for the survivors of Thomism. For the whole structure of Aquinas's ethics reposes on the relationship between function and God-intended purpose, and pleasure or delectation are the sign that we are in the presence of a well-ordered appetite. This is still the basis for the procreation-sexuality link which I consider so important. But if God has created people who are so blighted that pleasure and delectation come only in some nonprocreative way in which they are not allowed to be engaged, then God is a very cruel God indeed. God has made a botch of creation.

There are only two ways out of this dilemma. Either you say that those of a homosexual orientation have a perfect right to loving sexual fulfillment just as much as anyone else—and that lets God off the hook—or you elude the distressing conclusion that God is a tyrant and a bungler by abandoning the "orientation is OK; acts are not OK" argument altogether. This is precisely what we see happening in the CDF letter.

Of course, to make the "homosexual orientation" disappear in a puff of smoke, the magician Ratzinger has first to get rid of whatever scientific evidence would go counter to what he wishes to do. So the letter appeals to "the more secure findings of the natural sciences" (no. 2), by which it means those that go his way. There are bound to be some that do, since the study of human sexuality is not an exact science like physics. But in any case Cardinal Ratzinger is not concerned about scientific detail or arguments because he offers none. Nor does he really need to since he believes that "the Church is in a position to learn from scientific discovery, but also to transcend the horizons of science" (no. 2). Oh, dear! We know what *transcend* means: he is going to soar above contrary evidence and ignore it completely. The Baron Friedrich von Hügel used to way that Roman documents never conveyed information; such was not their purpose. They communicated instead a powerful atmosphere. This one certainly does that. Great waves of moral disapproval swirl over the reader and crash upon the shore of our fragile hopes.

Yet is the document's position completely crazy? Moral norms may be shaped without being determined by science. Some rather odd doctrines have been propounded in the name of science. For example: Francis Galton invented "eugenics" with the idea of improving the human stock by encouraging child-bearing among the more intelligent who were fair-haired and blue-eyed. It gave the superior people the right to exploit and oppress "lesser breeds without the law." We all condemn today such doctrines as perverse. But they were once the latest scientific fashions.

It is time to conclude. I warned you that I would not bring much consolation. You may remember the passage of the Victorian poet, Arthur H. Clough, that Winston Churchill quoted at the worst moment of the Second World War: "I tell you naught for your comfort, naught for your desire, save that the skies grow darker yet, and the seas grow higher." What, then, is to be done? You didn't ask for my advice, and I have no business preempting what your own answer might be. But I feel a responsibility to offer some unsolicited advice and here it is.

Don't leave the Church even though you may feel that in practice it is excommunicating active gay people. Why not? Because you, too, are Church, and are validly baptized and confirmed, part of the gathering from East and West, North and South, summoned by the proclamation of the gospel. I am echoing here Karl Barth. We sometimes imagine that we come together to read the gospel. Wrong. It is the Gospel that brings us together. It produces a people, the new pilgrim people of God. You can't drop out of a people. Period.

You might have read the articles in the *New York Times* just before Christmas, 1987, where the writer, E. J. Dionne, quotes James P. McFadden, president of a conservative Catholic group based in New York. McFadden holds that "one of the Church's greatest problems is that the dissidents don't leave." McFadden, ignoring history, praises Martin Luther "because he knew when it was time to go." So rule one is: do not give McFadden and his ilk the satisfaction they seek.

Rule two is: be holier than Cardinal Ratzinger. True, his insulting tone and manipulation of evidence would try the patience of a saint. But don't descend to that level. Don't reply in kind. I have just been sent an account of a meeting of Italian gays called David and Jonathan who met in Treviso. They have charged Cardinal Ratzinger with "vanity, arrogance and blindness." There is a problem here. Pope John Paul II has made it perfectly clear that he stands four-square behind Cardinal Ratzinger. The cardinal is not uttering his personal opinion in this matter. I think I would have some difficulty with paper primacy if I found that the pope was "vain, arrogant and blind." That's maybe my problem, not yours. But trading insults with the Congregation will confirm Cardinal Ratzinger in his worst fears. The angrier you are, the more he will feel vindicated. Adopt the tactics recommended by Jon Sobrino in defence of liberation theologians: beat the Congregation by superior holiness.

What does this mean in practice? In pastoral practice, for example? I don't honestly know. But I do think we can all ponder Cardinal Ratzinger's hard saying: "The cross, for the believer, is a fruitful sacrifice since from that death comes life and redemption. While any call to carry the cross or to understand Christ's suffering in this way will predictably be met with bitter ridicule by some, it should be remembered that this is the way to eternal life for all who follow Christ" (no. 12). For *all*. We all carry differently shaped and differently sized crosses, but carry them we must. The peculiar configuration of the gay cross is that it involves suffering at the hands of the Church. Then I recall what an old French Dominican, Hugo Clerissac, said at the height (or depth) of the modernist crisis: "It is easier to suffer *for* the Church. The difficult thing is to suffer *at the hands* of the Church."

Rule three is this: while being as holy as you can and carrying your cross sturdily, continue to argue for change, and *admit* that that is what you are doing. When Cardinal Ratzinger advised bishops to be "especially cautious of any programs which may seek to pressure the Church to change her teaching, even while claiming not to do so" (no. 14), I do not think he was drawing a caricature. I have always admired the Jesuit priest John McNeill because he did not disguise the fact that while the tradition was against him, he tried to show it was based on cultural judgments that are not part of revelation. McNeill's obedience, when he was silenced, was also edifying. I watched this from the Roman end, and can assure you that it took enormous courage on the part of Pedro Arrupe, then general of the Jesuits, to go on defending his man to the end. Arrupe's principle was always: "I will defend you as best I can, but please make it easier for me to defend you."

Rule four: be guarded in making claims. Sometimes the claims are statistical as when *Quest* estimates that there are two-hundred-million homosexual persons in the world.[15] No doubt such a "guesstimate" is routine in gay circles. I don't know how "scientific" it is. It seems to suggest that two hundred million people can't be wrong, a proposition for which I see no evidence at all. The Kinsey Report revealed that a high proportion of the population got up to all manner of sexual activities, but no one ever thought of it as a moral handbook. Questions of morality are not answered by a Gallup poll.

Sometimes the claim is made that wonderful people we all know about, including candidates for beatification, were "really gay." This has been said of both John Henry Newman and Giovanni Battista Montini, who became Pope Paul VI. As someone engaged on a major biography of Montini, I see the point of wishing to annex him. But at the same time I have great difficulty in knowing what it means to say of him or anybody that he or she was "really gay." A gay member of a religious order in Rome (not a Jesuit) has assured me that it was "obvious" that Montini was gay, and that this "explained" his anxiety (fear of being discovered?), and also the concept of "self-mastery" found in *Humanae Vitae*. Having sublimated his own (possibly unavowed) sexual urges, he expected others to do the same. I find that all very speculative. For the moment, one could equally conclude, as some have held, that homosexuals have a special vocation to celibacy.

It certainly gives one furiously to think. There is a German proverb which says: *Wer verfolgt, folgt,* which roughly means that the persecutor is tempted by the very thing that one persecutes. It doesn't come off easily in English, but in French it works: *Qui poursuit, suit.*

Finally, a brief word about AIDS. We need to go on stressing that this is not a "gay disease," that it is not some divine punishment for immorality, and that it is caused by a virus, not by promiscuity. At the same time, it would be folly not to recognize that AIDS has changed the gay lifestyles and the whole sexual scene. The virtues of "prudence" and "justice" now have to enter into moral judgments about relationships, alongside the well-established duo of love and temperance. A gay friend of mine who lives in Britain but who has spent some time on the west coast of the United States now dreads receiving letters from there because they nearly all bring bad news; someone else he knows has AIDS or has just died of the disease.

Timothy Radcliffe, O.P., the prior of the Dominican house in Oxford, says that the ministry of gay people to gay people is one of the most important forms of lay ministry in the Church today. AIDS has done that. These words of Pope John Paul II, though spoken in another context, clearly apply to the crisis of AIDS: "Do not turn away from the handicapped and the dying. Do not push them to the margins of society. . . . Let us treasure them, and recognize with gratitude the debt we owe them. We begin by imagining we are giving to them; we end by realizing that they have enriched us."[16] I'll settle for that.

Yours fraternally in the Lord

Notes

1. C. R. A. Cunliffe, "Throwing Down the Gauntlet," *Quest Journal,* June 1986, p. 9.

2. A. Dulles, *A Church to Believe In* (New York: Crossroad, 1982).

3. C. R. A. Cunliffe, editorial commentary on the Vatican letter in *Quest Journal* Supplement, November 1986, p. 25.

4. D. Grippo, "The Vatican Can Slight Scripture for Its Purposes," *National Catholic Reporter,* 26 December 1986, pp. 9, 12; reprinted in this volume on pp. 33–39.

5. R. Calvert, letter to the editor, *National Catholic Reporter,* 23 January 1987, p. 10.

6. W. Kenkelen, "Gay Catholic Group Expelled from Three U.S. Dioceses," *National Catholic Reporter,* 23 January 1987, p. 2.

7. G. Moran, "Gays: The Rome Way," *National Catholic Reporter,* 26 December 1986, p. 12.

8. In A. Flannery, ed., *More Post-Conciliar Documents* (Dublin: Dominican Publications, 1982), vol. 2, p. 491.

9. Ibid.

10. Ibid.

11. Ibid.

12. Ibid.

13. Ibid.

14. Ibid.

15. Cunliffe, editorial commentary on the Vatican letter, *Quest Journal* Supplement, November 1986, p. 25.

16. These were the words of John Paul II at the anointing of the sick service at Southwark Cathedral, London, on 28 May 1982.

16

Homosexuality and the Incarcerated Woman

Margaret Traxler

The warden giving us a tour of the women's state prison was young and new at his job. His dedication to his new task was obvious. As we entered a closed-off unit with a special lock-up, he pointed to doors with a small see-through glass built into them. In each, we saw young girls, no more than eighteen or nineteen years old, isolated in a small six-by-eight-foot cell with an open toilet and a bunk fastened to the wall.

"Why are they in solitary?" I asked. The eager young warden raised his eyebrows and replied, "They were caught in the act." My further inquiry, "And what was the act?" was answered, "They were embracing with open blouses." For this single offense two young women were given twenty-nine days in solitary confinement!

This incident happened more than fifteen years ago when the Institute of Women Today, an ecumenical organization I founded to serve women's material and spiritual needs, began to care for women in prisons. Surely "embracing with open blouses" calls for pastoral understanding! In a penal system which isolates men with men and women with women only obtuse leaders would believe that somehow human sexual desires will automatically close down as soon as the prison gates close people into the prison compound.

An institution as influential as the Catholic Church has the potential to bring compassion and pastoral concern to an essentially immoral structure like the U.S. corrections system. More often than not, the rich, white-collar criminal goes to "safe" minimum security prisons and the poor, often minority offender gets sentenced to a maximum security prison where, in some instances, even the guards cannot protect the inmates.

When the Vatican's Congregation for the Doctrine of the Faith issued its document on homosexuality, once again the Church's dereliction of pastoral duty and abandonment of 550,000 residents of U.S. prisons was evident. Over the past fifteen years I have been asked by prison wardens and counselors questions related to homosexuality. Often they admit having asked similar questions of chaplains of many faiths and having rarely received a satisfactory response. One of the wardens remarked, "If society at large has approximately a 10 to 14 percent homosexuality rate, is there not something that the creator is trying to tell us? Are we hearing archaic ethics? Why can we not receive better and more satisfactory answers from our spiritual leaders?" One female warden observed that psychiatrists and medical personnel provided better answers in their respective professional fields than the chaplains provided about sexual ethics.

Prison rules governing sexual practices vary in women's prisons. In one state facility, if residents "get a ticket," which is a report of misconduct written by a guard, for alleged homosexual conduct, a council of prison staff hears the case to decide guilt or innocence. Being ticketed usually means automatic guilt for which there is no redress for the accused. Consequences can range from days added onto the sentence being served, to solitary confinement, to confinement to the dormitory.

When asked about the theological reasons for church sanctions on homosexual activity, I sadly report that my Church's teachings provide little compassion or pastoral understanding. Official church teaching, based on psychological and medical misinformation, remains unyielding and unchanged. The Vatican letter merely underscores the traditional stand of churchmen on the issue of homosexuality.

To prison administrators, residents, and counselors I recommend the book *Human Sexuality: New Directions in American Catholic Thought*, which includes a discussion of the impact of Scripture, anthropology, history, and the empirical sciences on a theology of human sexuality. This book contains helpful modern reflections which could well serve as a *vade mecum* for sexual ethics as we enter the twenty-first century. The authors warn that it would be unjust and unfair to those of homosexual orientation "to make moral judgments upon them and their behavior in the name of Christian morals without appreciating the complexity of the Christian attitude toward sexuality in general" (Kosnik, Carroll, Cunningham, Modras, and Schulte, 1977: 186–87). The prejudicial attitudes of discrimination against homosexuals lie deep within the Judeo-Christian traditions and can be attributed in no small measure to the Catholic Church. Outright condemnation of homosexuality in the Levitical Holiness Code must be seen in its historical context.

In the mid-sixties at a home for run-away teenage girls on Chicago's Westside, a committed and dedicated staff often reported what they called their "number one problem," the infatuation of the resident girls with individual staff members or with one another. Although this could be expected, some of their behavioral responses definitely worried the staff members. Through some traveling workshops for intergroup relations of the National Catholic Conference for Interracial Justice, I arranged for some clinical psychologists to meet with the staff. After an hour in which the staff voiced concerns about the young women involved in the many levels of emotional attachments, one of the clinical psychologists said quietly, "Never be afraid of love; only fear hatred." The mercy and understanding of this statement contrasts strikingly with the hostile tone of the Vatican letter.

There is a common practice in some prisons for the younger residents to choose a "prison mother" and for the older ones to choose "prison daughters." I can appreciate the value of such a custom. Many of the young women never experience love and affection from their biological mothers; similarly, many of the older women, if they had a daughter, were unable to spend much time with her. I heard protective language such as, "You are carrying contraband by having that shopping bag," or, "Your lights were on beyond curfew last night. Real trouble if you don't watch it. . . ." The prison mother-daughter bondings help develop closer emotional, female-female relationships and nourish friendships which are the crux of relational sisterhood. Again, "never be afraid of love; only fear hatred" serves well as a rule of thumb.

Women in prison know vaguely about God's will and have a deep wish to live according to what they perceive as God's law. Unfortunately, some of the preachers in their lives have given them a cold and distant impression of God and how God expects them to live their lives. On one occasion a woman confided to me that she was a victim of incest, rape, and domestic conflict. "I wake up at night," she said, "and find myself in a sweat. Then I lie awake afraid of the day to come." After listening with silence and love, I advised her to treat her "wrestling with the sheets" like a bad thought. "Get rid of them," I urged. She looked at me steadily and asked, "What is a bad thought?" While in my very Catholic training a "bad thought" was a very clearly defined concept, she had no idea at all what a "bad thought" meant.

Homosexuality is used by sadists in some prisons not only to confuse the residents but especially to punish and to shame them. In Texas a cruel penal system indicts the society which would tolerate homosexuality. In the book *Racehorse, Big Emma's Boy*, Race Sample gives a true account of the unreported murders of homosexual prisoners by guards and the secret burials of the prisoners. Racehorse, a black man who is still living, tells a tale of horror he witnessed as an inmate of a Texas prison. Two black male inmates were found in a compromising homosexual act. After the dinner in the mess hall, the sadistic warden called everyone to attention as he ordered the two "offenders" to strip naked and to stand on the table. A prisoner-chaplain was then instructed to conduct a "marriage ceremony" after another prisoner had been ordered to the carpenter shop to fetch a round washer to serve as a wedding ring. The two accused were told to embrace in various positions; the warden then remanded them to solitary confinement for two months in four-by-eight-foot rooms with no lights and no toilet facilities except a tiny hole in the middle of the floor (Sample, 1961).

Pronouncements by churches, such as the Vatican letter on homosexuality, only abet depraved guards in their harsh treatment of homosexual prisoners. The churches have a direct responsibility to minister and to serve, not to defeat or condemn. The Vatican letter is without grace or moral support for the more than half million incarcerated men and women in prisons and jails in the United States. Those imprisoned throughout the world deserve more compassion and concern from a professedly loving Church.

One warden said to me, "I have ordered copies of *Human Sexuality* for all our counselors. Where formerly the guards ticketed inmates for merely holding hands, we have now formed new guidelines for evaluating intimacy and friendship." He continued, "We feel we now have arrived at more humane vestiges of bonding and companionship."

God's love calls each person to live justly and purely according to one's individual conscience. To make mature, moral decisions, a person must exercise free will guided by an enlightened and educated conscience. Not all of the voices one hears in order to achieve a balanced and correctly formed conscience come solely or necessarily from the Vatican. Men and women in prisons deserve more compassion and concern regarding formation of conscience on the subject of homosexuality than the Vatican document provides. In an institution that professes to be profoundly loving and universal, the Vatican letter on homosexuality disgraces both words, Church and Catholic.

References

Kosnik, A., W. Carroll, A. Cunningham, R. Modras, and J. Schulte. *Human Sexuality: New Directions in American Catholic Thought*. New York: Paulist Press, 1977.

Sample, R. *Racehorse, Big Emma's Boy*. Austin, TX: Eakin Press, 1961.

17

A View from the Pews

Margaret Susan Thompson

In 1982 two students in my United States women's history course at Syracuse University—both bright, self-identified feminists—knocked nervously at my office door. "I don't know how to say this," stammered one of them, "but someone in the class is spreading the rumor that you're a lesbian." Both young women smiled tentatively, pleadingly. "Reassure us," they said with their eyes. "Tell us it isn't so!"

I looked at them and said calmly, "Oh?" At first they seemed taken aback, and then they looked even more imploringly than before. There was a moment of silence, until I asked, "Well, what do you expect me to say? [I knew what they *wanted* me to say.] Did you expect anger? Denial? [Yes!] Proud assertion of heterosexuality—of 'normalcy' [Yes, YES, *YES!*]"? Again there was silence—this time, mingled with signs of shock, even fear. Finally, when they realized that I was not going to say any more, the two students turned and left.

Later in that same term, after several class sessions in which lesbianism had figured prominently, I asked them if they could begin to understand why I had responded as I did on that earlier occasion? Why had I not acquiesced to their need for reassurance about my sexual identity? I think they did understand the points I had tried to make: that the label of "lesbian" should not be perceived as pejorative and that *any* negative response to their original plea would have been implicit endorsement of homophobia. I think they understood and left my office this second time with a little less homophobia than they had before. But the lesson was only half-learned, I discovered later, as word reached me through a third student, that the other two had interpreted my explanation as oblique evidence of my "straightness," and that they were spreading the news accordingly through the class.

The third student, the one who told me that affirmation of my "normality" was being circulated, was a close friend of the other two. She was also a lesbian—something of which the others were unaware. She had

149

never revealed this essential dimension of her identity with these supposed friends because she was afraid that their response would be rejection. I don't know if her assumption was justified; I'd like to think that it was not, but I can't do so with any confidence.

It's five years later now. Has anything changed? One thing that has changed is that, thanks to a couple of well-attended lectures in a subsequent course on religion and politics, as well as a 1986 arrest for civil disobedience at Griffiss Air Force Base under the auspices of our local chapter of Pax Christi, I am now known on campus not only as a feminist but also as a committed Roman Catholic. In a lot of ways, this makes me more unusual than my being a feminist; practically no one on the Syracuse faculty is explicitly "religious," and overt expressions of faith are hardly everyday events. But the upshot has been that quite a large number of students, not all of them Catholic by any means, have come to me to talk about matters of conscience and faith. They know I'll listen and won't laugh at them, and also that I won't view them as freaks for having such thoughts in the first place. Consequently, I think I've seen some aspects of my students that probably few of my colleagues have seen, and my understanding of my own role and responsibilities has been significantly deepened and altered. As a teacher, as a feminist, and as a person of faith, I now believe that my responsibilities to my students go well beyond the merely academic.

The implications of these responsibilities present a constant and difficult challenge. Specifically, I am forced almost daily to confront the substance of my own beliefs as well as those of my students; I am forced to ask questions of myself, even as I try to answer theirs. And the dilemma is particularly acute when the issues that get raised relate to institutional church teachings with which I cannot myself agree. How do I deal with students' doubts? How do I deal with my own? Can I present a vision of faith to those who come to me for help that is both personally honest and truly "Catholic"?

I have no definitive answers to any of these questions. But I think that they are important and probably not too unusual. I'm not a theologian, and I'm not in any way a church "professional." In fact, I have no specific training in counseling, psychology, or even sociology (not even a single course!). Thus the only "Catholic" or even human perspective I can offer is that of a "person from the pews," of one who is trying to live explicitly as a Christian in the walk of life in which I find myself. I am, in short, your basic lay person—the person to whom most institutional church teachings presumably are directed, the person for whom "scandal" is supposed to be avoided, the person whose voice is rarely heard in either official or unofficial ecclesial circles.

It's important, I think, to emphasize my typicality, rather than any distinctiveness to my insights or experiences. Like about 57 percent of the self-identified Catholic laity in the United States, I attend mass weekly in a local parish and I try to pray daily. Beyond that, I serve on my parish council, was in a Renew group, lector occasionally, and serve as a Eucharistic minister. After a few alterations in language, I have no problems reciting the Nicene Creed, and I even (if only occasionally) go to confession. I am *not*, in other words, some sort of aberrant radical!

Similarly, the Catholic students who come to talk with me are *not* those who have completely given up. These are the ones who *want* to believe, who think there is a God and who, if given the choice, want to feel comfortable worshiping in the tradition of their upbringing. They come to me, I think, rather than (or in addition to) a chaplain, because they want reassurance from the "ranks," and not simply from someone whose Catholic commitment is professional. They want to believe that it is possible to be a Catholic in the "real" world, to be a member of a Church that is demanding as well as inspirational. But they have doubts. And the more serious and thoughtful they are, the more doubts they are likely to have.

Within the past year or so, many things have happened to exacerbate those doubts. The censuring of the Vatican 24, Charles Curran and Archbishop Hunthausen, a synod on the laity whose delegates were all bishops, a celibate hierarchy that seems obsessed with matters of reproduction, and overrepresentation of Catholics among Iran-Contra operatives are all problems that concern and trouble my students. Individuals tend, of course, to care more about some of these matters than others. But almost without exception, every one of the young people who has approached me since Halloween of 1986 has raised the issue of the Vatican letter on homosexuality. For some, this has become the sort of catalytic question that birth control posed twenty years ago. For others, it is merely another example of institutional judgmentalism in the area of sexuality. For a few—the lesbian and gay—it has led to a pivotal religious crisis. The surprising thing is that practically no one, including the straight majority, has found herself or himself untouched. And, without exception, every one of these students has challenged the letter's teaching and has asked the sorts of difficult questions to which I can give no satisfactory answers.

What is somebody who thinks of herself as a *teacher* supposed to do? This sense of helplessness merely compounds my own incomprehension and anger at a document I do not understand and cannot accept. Perhaps the only good that has come from all this is an enhanced appreciation of the notion of faith as "mystery" and as an essence beyond reason and knowing. Yet that is a little too abstract for the young people before me, who want something both more and less than inchoate (and incompetent) philosophizing. So I listen, and speak only occasionally, and sometimes find myself drifting off into that fantasy land of the powerless: a dream world in which I can imagine that someone *else* has to struggle with my situation. What if that someone else were the pope, or Cardinal Ratzinger, or any of those nameless, faceless, male celibates in the bowels of the Vatican Congregation for the Doctrine of the Faith? In the unlikely event that any of them found themselves in the company of my students, how would *they*—how *could* they—respond?

I think of a serious would-be physician, who asked me why Roman officials seem bent upon ignoring both the entire body of scientific knowledge that suggests sexual orientation is inborn and not acquired *and* the theological implications of that knowledge. If sexuality is a factor of birth, he wonders, why would an omnipotent God deliberately create "disordered" people? And, assuming that they *are* "disordered," with inclinations that must not be realized, why would such a God not simultaneously also give them the gift of celibacy? Does this mean that God intentionally places people in impossible situations? Is this the God of the Gospels?

And how do I respond to the student who has never really thought much about gay and lesbian sexuality, and who is even willing to consider the idea that such activity may be "wrong," but who still can't deal with the harshly punitive tone of the Vatican letter? "I thought Jesus came *for* sinners," this one muses. "Wouldn't he then reach out to them with love?"

In walks a bright and deceptively quiet freshwoman. Enrolled in a research seminar intended for juniors and seniors, she is determined to prove herself. The general theme is religion in America; she wants to explore some dimension of modern Catholic dissent, and it's clearly more than an intellectual exercise. "My Italian grandmother would be horrified if she knew what I was doing but she'd be more horrified if she knew *why* I was doing it," the young woman confides. "I simply can't take things for granted anymore. I can't deny being a Catholic, but I want to *understand*. How can such a beautiful Church do such ridiculous things to its own body?" Ultimately she decides to focus on the Vatican 24, after rejecting her initial plan to examine homosexuality. "I can at least see merit, some validity, in the Church's opposition to abortion, if not to dialogue," she said. "But I simply can't get inside their heads on this other thing. *What,*"she demanded to know, "is their *problem?*"

A young woman who described herself to me as "aggressively hetero-sexual feminist," said the Vatican letter had accomplished something constructive. For the first time, she felt a kinship with lesbians and gays, common victims with her of patriarchal contempt. She *wants* to go to church, but how can she worship meaningfully in such an irrational milieu, where only celibate men are presumed to speak with authority? For her, this allegedly "pastoral" letter may be the straw that breaks the camel's back and may ultimately force her to pursue her spiritual search outside the Catholic tradition. "It's not what I want," she says. "Is it possible that God *wants* me to leave the Church and is just using this as the tool to kick me out?"

The telephone rings. It is a friend of mine, a mother of several children including a twenty-one-year-old daughter who is about to return home from the 1986 cross-country Peace Walk. This woman of tremendous faith, one of those who is always there for the homeless and the hungry and the other victims of the world, is agonizing over how to "be there" for her own daughter, a lesbian. "She's already so disillusioned with the institutional Church and now this. What can I say to her? Is there anyone around here she can *talk* to? Is it right for me to urge her to keep hanging in to an institution that seems determined to condemn her? Can *I* continue to hang in?" I give her a couple of names, promise to pray, and feel completely incompetent.

I think of my own parents. When I was growing up, they welcomed so many different kinds of people into our home that I could never figure out what "normal" was supposed to mean, unless it was supposed to mean everybody. Looking back, I realize that two of their closest friends were a lesbian couple and that the two men who shared a house and sometimes visited were probably gay. All I knew then was that they were friends, that they were nice people, and that my parents apparently enjoyed their company. I thank God for bringing these supremely normal and loving individuals into my life at an early age. I have never had to contend with the sorts of fears and speculations that result from isolation or ignorance. I'm sure my friend raised her children in exactly the same way. She has no regrets, I know, but she is angry.

When Christmas comes, I hear as always from one of my dearest college friends, not a Catholic. After years of insecurity and loneliness, she's now one of the most *complete* human beings I know. She writes of a new and exciting job, of renovations on the house, of a stepson at an Ivy League college and two other children doing well. She sends "greetings from Penny," her lover of nearly ten years and the natural mother of these children; they are off to spend the holidays with my friend's parents. I think of how unhappy this woman was before she fully understood and accepted her sexuality, and rejoice in the contentment she knows now. Her postscript reads, "Still can't understand you and your Church. Explain it to me sometime, okay?" I put the card aside, realizing how irrelevant Ratzinger's epistle is to her life. I find myself rejoicing in the fact that she's not Catholic.

The card from a gay friend is not so joyful. Born a Catholic, he and his lover of seven years find themselves "longing to go to midnight mass tomorrow, but probably won't; the 'Vatican Rat's zinger' leaves too bitter a taste, and Eucharist is impossible." He says they will gather with some close friends to welcome Christmas, but that "it just won't be the same. My head tells me that this is not of God, but my heart is broken. Can you see me as an Episcopalian?"

After the holidays classes resume. I read more and more articles about gay-bashing and accelerating open racism on college campuses. I remember the reaction of one among many Reagan supporters in my class on the American presidency in 1984. When asked how he (incidentally, a Catholic) could vote for the president's reelection in light of his appalling record on civil rights, the young man looked at me in astonishment and said, as if to someone completely obtuse, "What are you talking about? *I'm* not black!" Can I wonder at such arrogant self-righteousness when cardinals define AIDS as the "vengeance of God against queers," when the Vatican states that violence directed against gays is somehow "their own fault," and when those who *minister* to lesbians and gays are kicked out of their religious orders, lose their jobs, and/or have their priestly faculties revoked?

Meanwhile, one of our most compassionate diocesan priests responds to a reporter's question about the Vatican letter with respectful and obviously well-considered reservations. The newspaper reports his remarks accurately, along with his statement that he had attended a locally held workshop on gay and lesbian ministry in the fall *before* the letter was promulgated. Some, at least, do not regard this as indicative of priestly determination to minister effectively to all people. Within two weeks, a letter arrives in the Syracuse chancery from New York's Cardinal John J. O'Connor who, after acknowledging that he has no right to interfere in the internal affairs of another diocese, asks our bishop to "investigate" this priest's activities and to "set him straight." Upon investigation, it turns out that the letter was prompted by O'Connor's receipt of a "clipping sent anonymously in an envelope with a Syracuse postmark." And I wonder, doesn't a "prince of the Church" have better things to do with his time? Nothing came of this little incident insofar as that priest was concerned. But our now-retired ordinary has been replaced by the former vicar general of New York, while an auxiliary with lots of local support, and who had attended the same workshop as a means of expanding his own pastoral understanding, is today still an auxiliary.

* * *

If what I have written appears to be merely a collection of random reflections, it is probably a better representation of my own experience than something more organized might be. Neither my life nor my faith, apparently, are intended to fit into clearly explicable patterns. I try to cope, and try to respond to others, and find both those things very difficult.

I am left with the question of what to say to my students. With each one I encounter, I come away more and more convinced of the reality of their desire for faith—*Catholic* faith—and more and more frustrated by my inability to give them useful answers. Like them, I would like to be able to look to official leaders for actual leadership; like them, I come away unable to believe that their teachings reflect either incarnate reality or the will of God. I tell them, and believe, that "we are the Church," and that the Spirit speaks to us as truly and validly as it does to Vatican bureaucrats. I tell them to hang in, and that it is possible to be a practicing Catholic and still dissent from what is not part of the doctrinal core of the faith. I say all this as much to myself as to them, and wonder if any of us can buy it. I go home at the end of the day, increasingly convinced that what is *truly* disordered here is not the sexual orientation of about 10 percent of the People of God, but rather the pharisaic legalisms of the bunch of insular patriarchs who purport to represent a messiah of love and compassion.

If I and my students are to find an answer, we will find it in God and not in these men. My Bible opens to what has become for me a beacon of hope, the story of the Canaanite woman. She is an alien, a lay person, and a woman, and yet she dares to approach Jesus for help. The disciples— institutional ancestors, we are told, of the hierarchy of today—beg Jesus to tell her to shut up and go away. He ignores her and then calls her a dog. This beautiful woman, so marginal a figure that we are not even told her name, persists. She pleads not for herself but for her daughter. And ultimately Jesus sees the light. He calls her a "woman of great faith" and rids her daughter of the demon. The woman disappears; we never hear of her again. But she remains the only person in Scripture who does one extraordinary thing: she is the only one who changes Jesus' mind.

I tell my students that this is an easy story to miss. Despite its appearance in two of the four Gospels, it arises in the Sunday readings only once in three years (and in mid-August, when they're likely to be on vacation!). I refuse to allow my nascent paranoia to let me believe this is deliberate, and yet. . . . It is a revolutionary incident, and who could blame a defensive hierarchy from trying to keep it from us?

If the bishops can see themselves in "apostolic succession" to these disciples, then we powerless and nameless lay people can surely claim this anonymous and prophetic woman as one of us. Marked by faith, fearlessness in faith, persistence, and compassion, her determination changed not only Jesus' mind but salvation history. She tells those of us with nothing that we have nothing to lose, so we may as well take risks and confront religious authority, even God.

But she also holds out hope. While demanding of us the courage to ask each member of the institutional magisterium if he can honestly present himself to us as representing Christ if he is not open to personal conversion, she holds out the possibility that even radical change is both possible and legitimate. Her prayer, after all, *was* answered. And so we, her daughters and sons, can pray with her to be rid, once and forever, of the demon.

18

Lesbianism and the Vatican: Free to Be Ministers of the Gospel?

Sarah M. Sherman

In the fall of 1960 after high school graduation, at age eighteen, Sister Joanne (a composite of a number of persons whom I know or have known) entered the religious community which educated her in high school. There had been nothing extraordinary about Joanne's growing up. With the usual traumas, fears, and joys of most young girls of her time, she made grades in the slightly above average range, played with dolls, and played football and Red Rover with the kids down the block. When high school days rolled around, she had her share of dates: one or two with Mr. Dreamboat and the rest with the friend next door. Joanne had never become deeply sexually involved with a boy because of the Church's, her teachers', and her parents' stern warnings about the dangers and punishments of petting or "going too far." Although she was close to being engaged once, Joanne never really had the time, opportunity, or experience necessary to investigate or develop male relationships of much depth or maturity.

Although Joanne had a natural affinity for things religious, she never seriously considered religious life until her junior year in high school. At that time, her search for self-identity and for God became centered in the witness and example of several teachers and of one nun in particular. The mysterious and esoteric goodness which Joanne experienced in this woman attracted her as nothing else ever had. Driven by a desire to emulate this sister and to realize in her own life that same quality of goodness and care for others, Joanne entered one of the larger apostolic communities of women religious serving in the eastern United States. Inserted into the disciplined and regimented formation and lifestyle practiced at that time, Joanne questioned little because "everybody knew that this is what you had to do if you wanted to become a religious."

Because Joanne had learned a kind of phobia for sex as a teenager, she did not question, although she thought it strange, when rules and admonitions seemed so concerned with the discouragement of "particular friendships." Joanne barely knew the word *homosexual;* no one spoke of it in those days. Regardless, she could almost slice with a knife the fear of same-sex relationships she experienced in those early years. Of course the fear and anxiety had been present also in the environment during her adolescent years, but as she had exhibited signs of being "normal," along with her friends, the question was never raised. No one ever wanted to address the issue unless it was absolutely necessary. But, in the homosocial living situation of the convent, homophobia oozed out like oil, often without ever being named or spoken of.

Joanne learned to be a "good religious"; for the most part she lived religious life "according to the book." Rigid rules and community structure made it difficult to develop her own personal autonomy or to enter into mature relationships with either men or other women. As a result of the relational deprivation on that level, Joanne found much of her emotional satisfaction in the adulation and attention of her high school students. Joanne was a good teacher and she knew it, but something was definitely missing in her life. God was still there but was becoming more and more remote.

Change came rapidly into religious life in the late sixties and early seventies. Because cultural shifts and profound developments in theological understandings had been so long in making themselves felt in the Catholic Church in general and among women religious in particular, the external changes made their appearances much more rapidly than the deeper, slower human transformation and spiritual awakening that prompted the changes.

Over a period of years, though, Joanne and her friends, freed from those practices and restrictions that fit another cultural age, and called by renewed disciplines that built first of all on the maturity and wholeness of the person, developed a new freedom to be themselves and new freedom for gospel service. Through a sometimes painful process of unlearning old fears and behaviors, and learning to trust and cherish herself as a person and as a woman, Joanne discovered her God in a new and richer way. In learning to love herself, Joanne found the belief that she had clung to for years—that God loved her wildly, totally, unconditionally—had become her deepest and most sustaining conviction. The old discontents that had nagged her at times and had tempted her to want to leave religious life altogether had all but disappeared for now.

Celibacy took on a whole new meaning as she learned to develop friendships with both men and women in a new and fuller way. Friendship was fulfilling, and her service of the poor through education was an outflow of her happiness rather than a crutch to get her through the week. She was no longer dependent upon her students to help her feel important or worthwhile.

There was a disturbing element to all this: in the process of coming to know herself better and developing a more wholistic approach to the world and her own personal, spiritual development, Joanne was encountering many of the fears and the phobias that had held her bound in the past. She confronted and learned to let go of anxieties that had been repressed and lay dormant for many years. In this searching, her sexuality, that which makes her so much of who she is, came more into focus. Over a period of several years of fitting the pieces of her present feelings and desires together with long-buried feelings and patterns of the past, Joanne discovered what she could never have otherwise even intimated until this point in her personal development; she was a woman, a religious, who was also lesbian.

Why do I spend so much time in telling this fictitious story? I do so because, although the details vary from person to person, this story can be told, I believe, much more often in truth than we might imagine.

Are there many lesbian women in religious communities today? Probably not. Statistics indicate that approximately 7 percent of women in a general population have a homosexual orientation, meaning that they are predominantly or exclusively attracted to other women erotically and emotionally. It would seem reasonable that the percentage in religious life would generally reflect population trends. However, Carl Jung observes that homosexuals make a special contribution to the spiritual development of humanity. "They are endowed with a wealth of religious feelings which help them to bring the 'ecclesia spiritualis' into reality, and a spiritual receptivity which makes them responsive to revelation" (Jung, 1959: 87). Other commentators have noted that they seem drawn to nurturing professions such as teaching, nursing, and ministry, and that many show a real concern for future generations in ways other than biological reproduction. These observations lead to the conjecture that the spiritual and nurturing character of life and ministry in religious congregations would attract even a higher percentage of those with a homosexual orientation.

We do not know how many women in religious congregations are lesbian, but several observations should be made. Because of the restrictive and repressive nature of past disciplines governing personal practices and relationships, and because of our general lack of understanding of homosexuality in the past, few women religious arrived at a deepened understanding and awareness of sexual identity until recent years. Education regarding sexuality and much discussion in the printed and electronic media have brought facts and myths alike to light. Wholistic growth toward adult maturity among many women has helped them to develop a healthy self-awareness and emotional sensitivity.

Second, in the process of entering into a deepened awareness of themselves as sexual persons, one of the searching struggles is to integrate into this developing identity their celibate commitment. This integration inevitably must happen every time one undergoes an identity shift in the process of maturation. The questions of the how and why of celibacy must be dealt with again, as they were at age eighteen, twenty-five, thirty-five, and so on.

Third, lesbian women are some of the same women who have dedicated the last ten, twenty, forty years of their lives to healing wounds, counseling the doubtful, serving the poor, struggling with the oppressed. They have given their lives in the effort to make our Church and society places of healing, caring, and liberation.

Lastly, in addition to the women already within religious community, there is also considerable number of lesbian women who today experience a persistent call to the spirituality and ministry of religious community.

The homophobia which continues to grow and flourish in society and the congregational structure itself presents serious concerns and problems for these women within community and those considering entrance. "Do I make known my orientation? To whom? How will I be treated? Will I be able to continue ministering as I have in the past or in the way in which I feel called?"

Education does help over a period of time. As long as individuals are willing to be courageous in their honesty and integrity and are supported by others who hold firm in their beliefs in the face of misunderstanding, judgment, and injustice, understanding will eventually be reached. In the meantime, however, the suffering inflicted on individuals and groups is tremendous as all women struggle together for acceptance and liberation.

In a tenuous situation at best, for wholeness and survival, lesbians and gay people must of necessity be grounded in the fidelity of the God who loves them totally and in the deep conviction of their own inherent goodness and worth as persons. Without these basic beliefs in the depths of their being, the homophobia of society could easily destroy them.

In recent years, the U.S. Catholic Church has moved forward significantly in understanding and support of lesbian and gay persons. Sensitive pastoral letters of individual bishops and groups of bishops, courageous witness on the part of some church ministers, articles and treatises by theologians, and pastoral outreach by such groups as New Ways Ministry, Dignity, and SIGMA (Sisters in Gay Ministry, Associated) have helped to increase understanding, build support networks, and develop compassion, care, and mutuality in the true spirit of Jesus and the gospel.

A new concern has come, however, for these homosexually oriented women and men who struggle to remain in the Church and in the ministry of religious congregations. The Vatican letter on the pastoral care of homosexual persons severely restricts the mode and possibility of pastoral outreach to and among homosexuals. Probably of greater concern is the way in which the letter strikes at the sense of self-worth and goodness of the homosexual person: "Although the particular inclination of the homosexual person is not a sin, it is a more or less strong tendency ordered toward an intrinsic moral evil, and thus the inclination itself must be seen as an objective disorder" (no. 3). Later, this same letter discussed this "disordered sexual inclination which is essentially self indulgent" (no. 9).

What do these statements and pronouncements do to enhance one's belief in one's own goodness as a person? What joke did God play on persons such as Sister Joanne, first leading her to believe in her dignity, beauty, and lovability as a person and as a woman, then suggesting that she is emotionally disordered? How can persons, through this letter, be freed to believe in themselves as ministers of the gospel? Sadly, in this instance, the leaders of the Church have assumed the side of judgment rather than of understanding and acceptance.

Women in the Church are becoming more and more an endangered species in the face of unchanging attitudes regarding the admission of women to shared ministry and decision-making in the Church's various structures. A lesbian woman is a twice-endangered species. Treated in policy and practice as inferior and subordinate to men, she also, if homosexual, is now judged, according to the Vatican Congregation for the Doctrine of the Faith, to have an objective disorder and to possess a disordered sexual inclination which is essentially self-indulgent. Many women in the Church stand on the brink—questioning whether they can remain in fidelity and integrity, questioning whether if they remain, their very personhood can survive and be alive in the service of others. In honesty, compassion, and justice, the church community needs to answer their questioning together.

Although the Church needs at times to be strong and firm in its teaching, its strength must be born of the compassion and understanding that Jesus modeled and to which he calls each one of us. God called a people in Jesus, who spoke and acted care, compassion, and forgiveness. Jesus did not utter judgment of the individual, but invited her and him into dialogue so that the truth and goodness of the situation could be freely accepted and embraced. Jesus calls us in the Church to this same dialogue with all of our sisters and brothers. The more we judge and separate out groups and individuals who are different from us, the more difficult, if not impossible, that dialogue becomes.

The time and energy that was spent in composing a document which has already blocked or hindered many valid pastoral initiatives on behalf of homosexuals would have been much better spent listening to these persons, entering into their personal stories, their dreams, and their hopes. Judgment *can* be transformed into understanding, empathy, and support, but not until we walk together in one another's shoes. The journey of the lesbian religious minister has often been a lonely one—but it need not be. God asks so much more of us.

References

Jung, C. G., *The Collected Works*. Translated by R. F. C. Hull. New York: Pantheon, 1959.

Part III
THE FUTURE: DEBATE AND DEVELOPMENTS

19

Thoughts While Reading over the Bishops' Shoulders

Joan H. Timmerman

I want to make, quite simply, three points that cannot be completely developed here but will undoubtedly be considered at greater length elsewhere. The context is that of the Vatican letter on the pastoral care of homosexual persons. The outcome, I hope, will be increased energy and effort in addressing the important questions of the relationship between sexuality and faith in fully actualized human life.

To the Bishops, Not to the Faithful

In response to this letter from the Congregation for the Doctrine of the Faith, it is essential to reflect on the fact that it is written to *bishops*, not to the Catholic faithful, the theologians, the gay and lesbian Catholics, and certainly not to "the city and the world." This is of the greatest significance for its interpretation by persons who have occasion to read it, as it were, "over the bishops' shoulders" or, more likely, at the greater distance of notation and commentary in the media. By its title it should function as an internal administrative memo: a reminder of previously promulgated policy; an invitation to colleagues charged with the administration of the local churches to respond or react to the policy under question. It could be used as a manner of communication appropriate to the principle of collegiality and an opportunity of sorts for the bishop to increase his knowledge of his people.

The content of the letter and the advice that is put forward for the bishops is clearly not new teaching. It does not offer new argument or rationale for old teaching, nor does it change the teaching in the direction of a more rigorous conceptualization or enforcement. A pastoral, not a theological or moral response, is envisioned.

To keep this in mind is to set rightly the duties and obligations the letter may be taken to impose. The bishops must consider carefully and make decisions on how and if reaction to this letter is warranted. Why then has it precipitated so many theological and moral responses? I believe it is appropriate to take the fact that the letter is an open letter, made available to all, as a cue that there is an issue before the official Church. It is legitimate to see it as an opportunity for those who have experience or knowledge in the matter, or even those who function well to facilitate discussion, to come forward to assist the bishops in discerning the Spirit.

The whole Church is concerned to promote the pastoral care of the whole Church. It is important, at the same time, to be clear that while nonbishops are certainly in order when they recommend or urge specific responses to their local ordinaries, nonbishops ought not consider this letter or its implications as a direct mandate to them, much less an ecclesial judgment on themselves or their lifestyles. If, in effect, as it has turned out to be in so many cases,[1] I would argue that has been at least in part a failure of individuals to understand the appropriate level of authority with which to endow this communication.

As always in Catholic pastoral practice, the general principle, even when stated as a rule or guideline, is intended to be processed through a pastoral consciousness that discerns its application in a concrete life situation. To assume that it is directly applicable without such discernment may be an American tendency, but it need not and should not be considered required by faith or even reverence to the magisterium. When a direct application is recommended, for example, when a group such as Dignity has been denied use of the parish church as a direct application of the statement that the bishop must withdraw support from all organizations that do not accept the official teaching on the immorality of homosexual activity, that judgment should be able to be supported by a theological and pastoral rationale. It is not the good shepherd but the hireling who would seek the political solution of accommodating the authority on a few points so that it would be satisfied. The authority needs to be educated as well to be able to see how God is working in *this* particular situation, unfamiliar perhaps to him in Rome, but the daily responsibility of the local bishop.

What this means for the faithful is that letters like the one under discussion in this volume must in no way be construed by them or used against them to produce guilt, increase alienation from the community, or decrease self-esteem and the hope that comes from knowing that one is loved and accepted by God.

Restriction of Sexual Activity

If gay and lesbian persons are indicted by this letter, so are we all. In a number of ways, responses to the phenomenon of homosexual love stands as a test case of attitudes to sexual love. It is for this reason that I believe more (intellectual) good than evil is likely to come from the discussion it precipitates. Clarity is an intellectual good. I do not, of course, deny that practical and pastoral harm (e.g., loss of hope, of faith, increase of anger and doubt of the credibility of the Church) will and has already followed. What I mean to affirm here is that, somewhat similar to the Vatican letters on the ordination of women and on human life, this document shows the reasoning invoked to support official teaching to be so inadequate that it must be abandoned. The alternatives that remain for thinking individuals are to obey without reason, thus abandoning one of the glories of the Catholic theological tradition—the affirmation of the compatibility of faith and reason; to give up the search for a reconciliation between spirituality and sexuality; or to begin constructive work on a more promising intellectual approach. For some time, church leaders from American bishops to Roman moral theologians have been speaking of the need for a theology of sexuality. Since that call has coincided with the rejection of most attempts to provide prolegomena to such a theology,[2] the call has shown itself to be more rhetoric than reality. I believe that the letter which has been the catalyst for this volume of essays can and should be a catalyst for a more consistent and inclusive theology of human sexual relationship.

The letter's pastoral admonitions rest on an assumption of the "truth" of the official sexual ethic of the Roman Catholic Church, namely: all sexual activity by persons who are not in an officially sanctioned marriage and for whom each act of intercourse is not open to procreation is objectively evil. While this particular letter names homosexual activity, specifically, as morally disordered, it must be taken, if consistent, to lay the same judgment on the great majority of adult persons. Sexual activity is prohibited, even though it be within a context of freely given and accepted love and lifelong fidelity, because it "is not able to transmit life; and so it thwarts the call to a life of that form of self-giving which the Gospel says is the essence of Christian living."

This seems to me to be one of the most reductive statements ever written. Not only does it reduce sexuality to procreation in contradiction to the far more authoritative statements of Vatican II, but it reduces the "essence of Christian living" to biological reproduction. Such a formulation suggests, once again, that what has been dealt with in this document is not human sexuality, homosexual or heterosexual, but the obligation of "nature" to reproduce. Other expressions of sexuality are assumed to be unnatural, since human sexuality is assumed to be for the purpose of procreation, but nowhere is the critique of that interpretation of natural law, a critique that has been argued widely and well in the last decade, even recognized.[3]

The critique has identified, among other problems, two distinct interpretations of natural law. When used within the context attributed to the Roman jurist Ulpian, nature refers to biological forms and processes, and extrapolates from the organ to its biological purpose as the totality of its "natural" use, that is, in this extrapolation, its only *moral* use. This approach has been and continues to be used for sexual questions *only*. It has been shown to be inadequate to the richness of human experience, which is after all, a psychological, social, and spiritual transaction through the symbolism of the biological interaction.

A cursory reading of teachings on social issues and ethical questions relating to property, war and peace, and other issues show that they are assumed to be of historical, rather than simply biological significance. The appeal to natural law is still used in formulating and supporting these teachings, but here it is a completely different approach, one traced to origins in Ciceronian thought, which recognizes the variables of history, culture, intent, circumstances, and consequences as affecting the morality of human action. Joseph Fuchs, referring to natural law as the "human thing to do in a given situation," suggests the complexity that is presumed in this more recent interpretation of natural law. Social, political, and economic questions are recognized as complex for they affect many persons in their deepest freedom and dignity. Contrary to the simplistic approach to sexuality, this second approach to natural law does not allow itself the luxury of language such as "intrinsically disordered," but is far more modest in its pretensions at knowing what nature, that is, God, intends, and at presenting those as absolute moral norms.

Paraphrasing a line from the Vatican letter may demonstrate this point. There appears to be an attempt to define the orientation, not just the acting out of that orientation, as an objective disorder. This would go beyond the position of the 1975 "Declaration on Certain Questions Concerning Sexual Ethics" in identifying the condition itself as an obstacle to grace, or in the words of the Vatican letter, "a more or less strong tendency ordered toward an intrinsic moral evil" (no. 3). It goes on to warn that persons with such a "condition" must not "be led to believe that the living out of this orientation in homosexual activity is a morally acceptable option. It is not."

When language like that is used for the tendency of persons to accumulate money, power, instruments of war, one may hope for new credibility in using such language to influence sexual behavior. Is living out of an orientation to accumulate wealth, even and inevitably to the detriment of others, condemned anywhere as a disorder out of which it is morally unacceptable to act? The condemnation of greed and exploitation, when it appears at all, is couched in language that is exhortatory and respectful of intention, circumstance, and consequences, not the language that would dare to define persons in terms of intrinsic evil and thereupon feel justified in judging the moral potential of all their actions with regard to money.

Lust is certainly a vice, as is greed and envy, but it is an enormous gratuity to designate an orientation to express love to another of the same sex as a "disorder in the individual," depriving his or her acts "of their essential and indispensable finality, and able in no case to be approved of" (no. 3). When sexual questions are approached in the same way that the complexity of social questions are considered, then one will be able to respect the theological consistency and pastoral concern that purport to motivate this letter. Then it will be clear that to shame, shun, isolate, and deprive of their civil and religious rights the so-called disordered ones was not done in the name of good and evil so much as from fear and guilt regarding sexual existence.

The wisdom that is to be found in this letter, in my view, appears in number 12: "Christians who are homosexual are called, as all of us are, to a chaste life." Once again that sets the task: to become clear about what the virtue of chastity requires within the givens of one's history, culture, and individual life situation. As a virtue for all Christians, it has never been identified with abstinence from all sexual activity. Chastity is a matter of grace and conscience, not law.

A Problem for Sacramental Theology

The fear and distrust of nature as represented in official teaching on sexual issues remains an embarrassment for sacramental theology, which proceeds not from fear and suspicion of nature but from the presupposition that all of nature and human history share in the grace and redemption made present and active among us by the mystery of Christ's life, death, and resurrection. It presumes a mystery of grace entered into by faith and through the power of the Spirit by initiation into the community. This community is understood by faith to be sacramental, that is, empowered by the Spirit to proclaim, actualize, and celebrate the redemptive love of God in Christ. If this sort of a formulation is to make theological sense, it depends entirely upon a Christology that affirms that the whole of reality has been taken up into the mystery of God's love poured out on us. While Christian theology in the West has developed far more completely the understanding of redemption in history, it has never excluded nature from the mystery of grace. One of the tasks of sacramental theology in our time is to develop and formulate more precisely the workings of grace in nature so that the implications of the Incarnation come to be more fully appreciated.

There is also an understanding of ecclesiology which makes sense of the notion that the community continues to function in history as sacrament of the risen Christ. The community can hope to stand as an effective symbol of God's healing and reconciling grace, not by its own merits but through the Spirit of God poured out freely upon its members. A morality consistent with that identity and mission has always been part of the agenda of the community; however, any efforts to set up human moral superiority as the condition for grace or the cause of salvation have been opposed and condemned. The conundrum is that the doctrine that has been so able to explicate Christ as the Lord of history in the midst of war, revolution, hunger, and famine has been so unable to deal with grace in nature, including human nature as sexual. Perhaps it was because the emergence of Christology in the early Church coincided with the cultural alignment of the male with spirit and history and the female with body and nature. There was no urgency, perhaps not even possibility, to develop images of the Christ of faith in terms of sexual, female, or natural life.

For whatever reason, the early theologians did not construct a theology of redemption by way of the sacramental potential of body and nature. Their theology of redemption was rather based on an image of redemption by way of the control of and freedom from the bodily and the material. Spiritual growth was conceptualized as escape from the physical. That failure of imagination was in turn a failure of naming, and produced a long history of dualism in which good and evil were named, at least in the popular mind, as overcoming of the physical or "succumbing" to the physical.

The consequences have been disastrous for the spiritual lives of many. Sacramental ritual neglected the arena of the sexual and celebrated human action as specifically action of mind and will. The body was used in the celebration, but, by and large, even in matrimony, what was celebrated was the victory of spirit over body. But dualism no longer has dominance in philosophical or psychological systems and is losing ground in theological formulations. In our time it is well known that growth as a·human, spiritual being requires the integration and acceptance of all aspects of our being. We are now clear in affirming that it is human persons, not just bodies, who are sexual.

Sebastian Moore, in a recent book review (*Commonweal*, 7 November 1986, pp. 600–601), wrote in a particularly succinct and insightful way about the origins of the sense of shame that appears, nonetheless, to surround sexuality in some religious texts. He points out that the traditional interpretation of the fall sees the effect of disobedience to God to be the loss of harmony between "higher" and "lower" nature. But as he analyzes Pope John Paul II's consideration of that loss of harmony he identifies a distortion that has become part of the Christian tradition with regard to sex. The traditional interpretation considers the fault to be in the failure of the "lower" to obey the "higher," which produces lust (rebellion of the lower against the higher) which results in shame. In such considerations the shame is a legitimate response to lawless lust. But how does Genesis deal with the fall? Moore shows that the Genesis story also features the failure of the "higher" to befriend the "lower" as key to the loss of harmony within the person and between the sexes. The true connection between shame and the act of disobedience can then be named. It is the hubris of those who would pretend to be gods that would lead them to be ashamed and embarrassed at being sexual. In fact, rejection of the sexual and attempts to exclude it ("outlaw" it) are symptoms of the fallen condition. When outlawed in such fashion, the "lower" nature gets its own back by behaving lawlessly. This is lust. But lust is produced by shame, not vice versa. The disorder, that which leads to unacceptable acts, is not sexual orientation but contempt for the sexual.

The application of such an analysis to the present subject is obvious. It is appropriate to condemn lustful actions. But to generate shame at one's being as sexual is, in fact, to fall into the sin of the "human pretending to be god." The denigrating of sexuality is an immediate effect of such sinful arrogance, and the likely cause of lust. The trap into which Moore finds much of traditional Catholic thinking about sexuality to have fallen is that of identifying sin with sexuality and virtue with the hubris of denial of it. The downgrading of sex in the quest for God, contempt for the flesh, and failure to honor sexual union are the results of sin, not the restoration of order. The official teaching on sexuality, I believe, remains caught in that trap, which is to me an adequate but disturbing explanation of the many inconsistencies that plague sacramental theology. How else can one explain that in sacramental theology we have no problem saying that outside sacramental baptism there is certainly salvation and grace; outside sacramental reconciliation there is certainly forgiveness and grace; but outside sacramental marriage there is no possibility of morally acceptable, much less graced, sexual activity?

As these questions are looked at carefully and repeatedly I believe that reason will be able to overcome fear in thinking about sexual variation.

Notes

1. I am aware that some individuals have considered it necessary to separate themselves formally from the communities in which they worshiped and ministered prior to the publication of this document. Apparently it was their judgment that the letter was so alienating that it required a dramatic and radical act of protest. The harm in such a situation is as clearly to the community which will now lack their presence as it is to their sense of identity and mission as Christians.

2. See especially the response to Anthony Kosnik et al., *Human Sexuality: New Directions in American Catholic Thought,* Catholic Theological Society of America study (New York: Paulist, 1977); to Philip S. Keane, *Sexual Morality: A Catholic Perspective* (New York: Paulist, 1977); and to the work of others, including my own *The Mardi Gras Syndrome: Rethinking Christian Sexuality* (New York: Crossroad, 1984).

3. See especially Joseph T. Arntz, O.P., "Natural Law and Its History," in *Moral Problems and Christian Personalism, Concilium* 5 (New York: Paulist, 1965), pp. 39–57; and Charles E. Curran, "Sexuality and Sin: A Current Appraisal," in his *Contemporary Problems in Moral Theology* (Notre Dame: Fides, 1970), as well as Curran's *Catholic Moral Theology in Dialogue* (Notre Dame: Fides, 1972), pp. 111–49.

20

In Defense of Omnipotence: The Case against Dialogue

Mary Jo Weaver

Reading the Vatican letter on homosexuality as a historian, I am reminded of other decrees and other times. The vehemence of the language, for example, and the idea that the Church is under attack from deceitful enemies was a subtext of *Pascendi,* the encyclical issued by Pius X at the turn of the century to condemn modernism. The demand for sexual abstinence recalls a long tradition of fearfulness about sex and a belief that virginity is a superior means of communion with the divine. A refusal to discuss the issue or to listen to those with a different viewpoint is not surprising from an institution that condemned freedom of the press and freedom of speech as late as the pontificate of Gregory XVI in 1832. The idea that the Church can "transcend the horizons of science," brings many documents to mind: my personal favorite is *Humani Generis*. In 1950 Pope Pius XII responded to questions raised by scientists studying human evolution by saying, "original sin is the result of a sin committed in actual historical fact by an individual man named Adam" (Freemantle, 1956: 298). The claim that matters of faith are beyond the realms of science has often been used to mean that matters of faith are impervious to scientific discussion.

The Catholic Church, in attempting to protect its members from the dangers of unbridled passion, has always condemned unregulated sexual expression. In a world where reason, control, unchanging doctrine, clear lines of command, and good order are prized, the appetites must be constrained. To put it another way, human experience cannot be allowed to change what are perceived to be eternal truths.

With no attempt to deny authority, critics have decried authoritarianism. Mindful of the divine transcendence, prayerful people have witnessed to the reality of divine immanence. Fully responsive to the sacred character of divine revelation, theologians have recognized its dyna-

173

mism and continuance. Those condemned by the Vatican in the last century did not deny faith, religious authority, transcendence, or revelation; rather, they asked for dialogue about how these matters relate to human experience and scientific evidence.

Modernists and evolutionists were persuaded that eternal truths ought not be exempt from challenge when experience and experimentation brought forth new evidence. They suggested that a scientific investigation of the Bible would lead to conclusions at variance with traditional teaching and so were condemned or silenced. Scholars and pastors who longed to discuss serious questions of sexual morality were convinced that the modern world needed new approaches to vexing problems. Their dilemmas, which came from intellectual challenges and real pastoral situations, led them to say that old notions of eternal truth needed to be evaluated in light of human growth and new discoveries. They have been condemned or silenced by ecclesiastical authorities in order to protect the very faithful whose doubts and questions formed the basis of the inquiry in the first place.

Modern ethical questions arise because of new discoveries in the self or in the world of science. When old formulations or rules are challenged, therefore, ecclesiastical officials usually find it necessary to distinguish their position from that of modern science. According to church officials, scientists operate in a different world. As the authors of the Vatican decree against the ordination of women said, "human sciences, however valuable their contribution to their own domain, . . . cannot grasp the realities of faith" (Swidler, 1977: 46). Since scientific method is a process of discovery continually on the way to something else, whereas the deposit of faith is to be guarded from novelties, church officials believe science to be a dim light compared to the guidance of divine revelation. More to the point, scientists test their hypotheses against human experience; scientific discovery is, by its very nature, tentative. No wonder the Church believes that it can and sometimes must "transcend the horizons of science."

The position defended by the Church, which usually is presented as a matter of fidelity to divine teaching, is really a brief against dialogue. However much it may appear to be a reaction to the Enlightenment or to the scientific revolution, the Church's position is, at bottom, a defense of omnipotence, that is to say, it guards church teaching from the perils of potentially transforming conversation. As such, the Church's case against homosexuality (or women priests or changes in sexual morality or anything new) rests on the principle of unchangableness: revelation is closed; authority is fixed; faith is a deposit to be transmitted without alteration;

human beings, male and female, have God-given natures and destinies appropriate to those natures.

Since human experience and scientific evidence challenge these principles, human experience and scientific evidence are inadmissable in the court of religious appeal. Furthermore, the Church defends itself by means of a clear division between the sacred and the profane, a division which allows no dialogue on the theory that sacred matters are beyond discussion. Modernists, democrats, evolutionists, scientists, feminists, and now lesbians and gay men tend to blur the division between the secular and the sacred. They demand discussion as they witness to the modern belief that revelation is an event still occurring; that authority is to be shared; that faith is a personal relationship with a divine being which grows and changes, rather like friendship; that human nature, as Gregory Baum (1980) reminds us, is that "to which we are divinely summoned" (p. 23), an event rather than an eternal given.

Paradoxically, those who believe that they are the guardians of divine revelation fail to understand its dynamism. They stand guard over the good news without being able to believe how good it is, and so confuse their wills with God's will. The divine being who has been revealed in the Bible, in the traditions of the Christian Church and in the events of the suffering world is not afraid of ambiguity. The good news, as manifest in the Christian tradition, promises a partnership between humanity and divinity in which both develop as they are drawn forward into new concepts of mutuality.

Ecclesiastical officials are threatened by this kind of God. Like Marabel Morgan in *The Total Woman* their respect for their Master belies a rather profound contempt for "His" ability to deal with conflict. Morgan advised women to secure their place in their husband's favor by giving him anything he wanted anytime he wanted it. The wives were also told to surprise their husbands by meeting them at the front door dressed only in Saran Wrap and red ribbons. Such titillation was an attempt to placate a man who was presumed to be either fickle and restless or totally unable to deal with the vicissitudes of ordinary reality. Wives were not to "bother" their husbands with details of household problems. They were told not to ask questions or to contradict anything he said. The clear implication was that the husband was either totally uninterested in anything but himself or that he would crumble at the first sign of ambiguity or conflict.

Ecclesiastical officials defend a God who resembles Morgan's husband, a being who cannot be disturbed by the real agonies of our lives, who needs constant reassurance that nothing will ever change and that he need never bother himself with our lives. Yet if we are to believe the promises of biblical religion, the creator and sustainer of life is willing to enter the human process and is less troubled by human conflict than are those who guard the ancient deposits of divine self-disclosure.

The Vatican letter on homosexuality is one more case in point, partly because of the position it defends, but as much for the ways in which it denies any possibility of dialogue. While the American bishops tell us that nuclear war is a discussion topic, the pope tells us that sexual morality is a war in which to "refuse to sacrifice one's own will in obedience to the will of the Lord is effectively to prevent salvation." While the Church, mindful of the moral imperative to care for the poor and to overturn unjust structures of oppression, welcomes exploitive financiers into its midst, it interprets the Bible to exclude "from the people of God those who behave in a homosexual fashion."

These statements, which inflict violence on homosexual men and women, should be seen as part of a pattern of debilitating helplessness on the part of the Vatican. They are a series of agonized screams from authoritarian officials who by refusing to listen now find it increasingly difficult to be heard. Ever since the Reformation, the Church has been involved in a war against the modern world. Although it may seem ironic that papal language about warfare is calm while statements about sexual ethics are bellicose, it is virtually predictable. In the Vatican model, control *over* is seen as the highest good. The Church, before the Reformation, perceived itself as the guardian of the highest good; the Church was able to exercise control over the political, intellectual, and moral life of the world. Today, however, its authority is limited to the moral or spiritual order. In terms of moral theology, control over the passions is central, chastity is the highest virtue, and spirituality is described as a state of mastery. Those who threaten its spiritual hegemony, therfore, or whose lives show other ways of understanding fidelity or spiritual growth are perceived as having a special kind of enmity.

However painful this letter is for lesbians and gay men, it must be read in a historical context of repression and authoritarianism. In the nineteenth century, when the Church could still compel intellectual assent, it condemned the modernists in terms as violent and hostile as Catholics had seen since the sixteenth century. Yet, today, the findings and the work of many of the modernists are accepted by Catholic scholars with no qualms. The letter on homosexuality is another part of the same system promulgated by a Church refusing all invitations to dialogue and defending an outworn paradigm.

It is today a commonplace to interpret the events following the Second

Vatican Council as a battle between two paradigms. Interpreters identify the classical-conservative viewpoint on the one hand and posit the historical-progressive one on the other. Describing the *emergence* of this conflict in the eighteenth century, Frank E. Manual (1959) put it in terms of Wagnerian drama. *The Eighteenth Century Confronts the Gods,* he entitled his book, explaining the end of the classical era. Meriol Trevor (1969) assessing the nineteenth century named the struggle as that between the prophets and the guardians. Today we would probably discuss the two sides as hierarchical and egalitarian or, in terms borrowed from the women's movement, as patriarchal and feminist. Whatever we call these modes of operation, they are engaged in warfare rather than in dialogue.

The patriarchal paradigm does not welcome evidence from science or from human experience. Because it confuses its own wishes with God's wishes, it avoids and often condemns dialogue. The Roman Catholic Church could be diagnosed as suffering from an acute case of what William Lynch (1974) called the "absolutizing instinct" (pp. 105–25). If that is the case, then we probably should not expect change to come from ecclesiastical officials.

The Church, in its own self-understanding, does not make mistakes. Catholic homosexuals who desire to stay in communion with their Church, therefore, will have to make their decisions without benefit of official approval. Support for homosexual relationships will not come from the officials of the Catholic Church (or from most other churches) who are busy defending God from these unsettling questions. Understanding of homosexual relationships, invitations to dailogue, new ways of understanding fidelity and commitment will have to be found in one's own conscience, in decisions informed by evidence and sustained by a community of faith and intimacy existing either outside the present structures or, subversively, within them. Homosexual Catholics will have to seek guidance from those whose religious experience leads them to perceive other ways of understanding God's loving summons to full human life. It is not the first time divine blessing and compassion have been sought and found outside the walls of the institution.

References

Baum, G. "Catholic Homosexuals." In *Homosexuality and Ethics,* edited by E. Batchelor, Jr. New York: Pilgrim Press, 1980.

MARY JO WEAVER

Freemantle, A., ed. *The Papal Encyclicals in Their Historical Context*. New York: Mentor-Omega, 1956.
Lynch, W. *Images of Hope: Imagination as a Healer of the Hopeless*. Notre Dame: University of Notre Dame, Press, 1974.
Manual, F. *The Eighteenth Century Confronts the Gods*. Cambridge: Harvard University Press, 1959.
Swidler, L., and A. Swidler, eds. *Women Priests: A Catholic Commentary on the Vatican Declaration*. New York: Paulist, 1977.
Trevor, M. *Prophets and Guardians: Renewal and Tradition in the Church*. London: Hollis and Carter, 1969.

21

Teaching in Transition

James R. Pollock

In general, the twentieth century has seen a rich development in official Catholic teaching regarding human sexuality and marriage. The relatively few documents of the Church's universal magisterium which have specifically addressed these matters, though themselves unequal in weight, length, and depth, nevertheless illustrate a seriousness and concern about articulating the values concerning sexuality and marriage that the Church increasingly has striven to clarify and emphasize. In a century characterized at face value by growth in the breakdown of marriage and family life and the commercialization of human sexuality, the Catholic Church has patiently affirmed and reaffirmed the dignity of human sexuality, the sacred character of marriage, and the inviolability of family life.

Naturally one could suggest many explanations for the development of Catholic teaching in this century—and one could ask whether the development has been uninterruptedly or unidirectionally positive. But it would be difficult to gainsay the fact that the Church, in its universal magisterium, has consistently attempted to speak clearly the values related to human sexuality.[1] It must be stated in this context that the major magisterial pronouncements of this period in the Church's life have focused more on the nature of marriage and family life than they have specifically focused on the nature of human sexuality. Consider the list of principal documents: *Casti Connubii* (1930), *Gaudium et Spes* (1965), *Humanae Vitae* (1968), *Familiaris Consortio* (1981), and a host of lesser statements from Pope John Paul II, such as, in his audiences, commenting on the Book of Genesis and reaffirming and nuancing the teaching of *Humanae Vitae*.[2] Another much longer study would be necessary to plumb the depths of development in these official documents. Globally, however, it is noteworthy that there has been development and refinement of the teaching, and that some of the major lines of development have been a clearer statement of the priority of conjugal love as the context or ground for affirming the unequivocal inseparability of the procreative and unitive dimensions of the conjugal act and, by extension, of any meaningful act of sexual intercourse, which the Church sees as necessarily occurring within marriage.[3]

Finally, one should note the increasingly philosophical depth and penetration of John Paul II's statements concerning the nuptial meaning of the human body itself and the role of sexuality in coming to self-understanding, complementarity, and the presence of God as divulged in the intrinsic meaning of sexuality itself.[4] Although the Church's official teaching regarding human sexuality comes in for considerable attack from diverse quarters, these documents will reward careful readers with a sense of the extraordinary efforts the Church has made to revitalize and reformulate its teaching.

On a lesser, but nonetheless universal, level of official teaching, recent years have seen the issuance of three principal documents regarding human sexuality, documents that address moral, educational, and pastoral concerns. These are *Persona Humana* (1975) from the Congregation for the Doctrine of the Faith, "Educational Guidance in Human Love" (1983) from the Congregation for Catholic Education and the CDF letter on the pastoral care of homosexual persons (1986) addressed to the Catholic bishops throughout the world.

These documents, like the papal and conciliar documents mentioned earlier, are of unequal weight and significance. For example, one could note simply that the Congregation for The Doctrine of The Faith is generally considered a more influential congregation than the Congregation for Catholic Education. Similarly, the document on pastoral care (addressed only to bishops, lacking footnotes, entering into areas of considerable detail and specificity, etc.) is less substantive than *Persona Humana,* which is a formal declaration. These differences need to be carefully considered, but that is not the focus of this chapter. What is of more immediate interest to us at this point is an examination of the contributions of these last three documents mentioned with regard to homosexuality. Even this topic will be explored in a somewhat restricted sense, namely, the question of whether the congregations' teachings manifest any development or change. Even more precisely, it will be worthwhile to focus particularly on the distinction between the homosexual orientation and homosexual behavior, that is, genital expression. It cannot be stressed too much that this entire discussion must be read in light of the Church's ordinary approach which sees human sexuality as intrinsically ordered to marriage and of great significance in the life of faith. We will not be able to discuss all the ramifications of this reality in such a brief study, but it is essential that the context be at least stated and understood.

One clear area of development or change within the three documents on human sexuality is the statement from the CDF letter on homosexuality that "Although the particular inclination of the homosexual person is not a sin, it is a more or less strong tendency ordered toward an intrinsic moral evil and thus the inclination itself must be seen as an objective disorder" (no. 3). This statement is a further refinement or clarification of the evaluation given in *Persona Humana* which the Congregation sees as necessary because "an overly benign interpretation was given to the homosexual condition itself, some going so far as to call it neutral or even good" (no. 3) in unidentified commentaries that followed the publication of *Persona Humana*.

The way for this refinement or further precision regarding the nature of the homosexual inclination had already been paved in the little-studied "Educational Guidance in Human Love." In that document's fourth section, "Some Particular Problems," the Congregation for Catholic Education had said:

> Homosexuality, which impedes the person's acquisition of sexual maturity, whether from the individual point of view or the interpersonal, is a problem which must be faced in all objectivity by the pupil and the educator when the case presents itself.
>
> Pastorally, these homosexuals must be received with understanding and supported in the hope of overcoming their personal difficulties and their social mal-adaption. Their culpability will be judged with prudence; but no pastoral method can be used which, holding these acts conform to the condition of these persons, accord them a moral justification.
>
> According to the objective moral order, homosexual relations are acts deprived of their essential and indispensable rule.
>
> It will be the duty of the family and the teacher to seek first of all to identify the factors which drive towards homosexuality: to see if it is a question of physiological or psychological factors; if it be the result of a false education or of the lack of normal sexual evolution; if it comes from a contracted habit or from bad example or from other factors. More particularly, in seeking the causes of this disorder, the family and the teacher will have to take account of the elements of judgment proposed by the ecclesiastical Magisterium, and be served by the contribution which various disciplines can offer. One must in fact, investigate elements of diverse order: lack of affection, immaturity, obsessive impulses, seduction, social isolation and other types of frustration, depravation in dress, license in shows and publications. In greater profundity lies the innate fraility of man and woman, the consequence of original sin; it can run to the loss of the sense of God and of man and woman, and can have its repercussions in the sphere of sexuality. The causes having been sought and understood, the

family and the teacher will have an efficacious help in the process of integral growth: welcoming with understanding, creating a climate of hope, encouraging the emancipation of the individual and his or her growth in self-control, promoting an authentic moral force towards conversion to the love of God and neighbor, suggesting—if necessary—medical-psychological assistance from persons attentive to and respectful of the teaching of the Church.[5]

It is noteworthy that this document, which refers freely and frequently to *Persona Humana,* has already changed the language and discourse about homosexuality. Its citations are somewhat selective, evidenced, for example, by the fact that, although it repeats some of the categories of possible "causes" of homosexuality, it no longer makes the clear distinction between "homosexuals whose tendency comes from a false education, from a lack of normal sexual development, from habit, from bad example, or from other similar causes, and is transitory or at least not incurable; and homosexuals who are definitively such because of some kind of innate instinct or a pathological constitution judged to be incurable."[6] In the paragraph which reiterates *Persona Humana*'s judgment regarding the pastoral approach to "these homosexuals," it should be pointed out that "these homosexuals" are those that have been described as "definitively such": yet, "Educational Guidance in Human Love" uses this paragraph as a lead into a discussion that seems to be considering all homosexuality as of a transitory or perhaps "curable" type. This is a curious inversion of the teaching embodied in *Persona Humana* and it is surprising that it is not acknowledged in a straightforward manner and explained.

It is necessary to reflect at greater length on the significant transition in teaching regarding homosexuality that is apparent in these three documents. It would appear that the CDF letter is referring principally to those whom *Persona Humana* has judged to be definitive homosexuals, since it speaks of an inclination that is "a more or less strong tendency ordered toward an intrinsic moral evil" (no. 3). One would think that the transitory or at least not incurable homosexuals of *Persona Humana* could not have a tendency ordered toward an intrinsic moral evil, if in fact this tendency may somehow be "cured." Or, if the transitory inclination is cured simply by being held in check or reoriented to heterosexual objects, then it would appear to be part of a broader inclination, namely, the human sexual orientation itself. The "transitory" language of *Persona Humana* seems to be in accord in some ways with Kinsey's well-known concept of the human sexual continuum. It would be helpful, however, if the Congregation would attempt to clarify the exact nature of the transitory inclination mentioned earlier. In a sense, it would be especially important to clarify the nature or order of inclination or tendency that is being spoken of. In other words, is this psychological or biological? Is it in some way cultural or learned behavior (as the transitory type seems to suggest)? Does it exist in an emotional framework of the entire person or is it in some sense isolatable. Similarly, has the congregation itself abandoned its earlier careful distinction of types of homosexuals and their behavior in favor of the collapsed categories employed by the Congregation for Catholic Education?

When we focus specifically on *Persona Humana*'s description of the homosexuals who are definitely such, we must confront the fact that this is "because of some kind of innate instinct or a pathological constitution judged to be incurable."[7] It must be pointed out that *Persona Humana* prefaced this discussion with a tentative statement: "A distinction is drawn, and it seems with some reason."[8] Nonetheless, an innate instinct is not the same thing as a pathological constitution. The former implies no negative value judgments as such whereas the latter, by its very use of the word *pathological,* does. This, of course, is part of what led to the "overly benign" interpretation the CDF letter speaks of. Innate instincts, fuzzy and vague in their own way, are nonetheless not reprehensible: nor are they ordinarily ordered to what is intrinsically morally evil. Quite the reverse is true. Basic human appetites for such diverse goods as food, water, self preservation,and knowledge are at least analogously and arguably all innate instincts, as the sexual appetite is. Any of these may of course become disordered, but that would not seem to constitute an orientation to an intrinsic moral evil. The moral evil of the disorder could only be a result of the instinct's being satisfied, freely and knowingly, in some disordered way. Of course we also encounter here the ongoing dispute concerning just what an "intrinsic moral evil" is. We cannot enter into this debate here, though it is naturally germane to the overall discussion.

It is clear, in any event, that the three documents presently under discussion are not clear or consistent in their understanding of the nature of the homosexual inclination or tendency as such. This should not be surprising, since this is an extremely complex area, not susceptible of simple or unrefined discussion.[9] It is at this point, however, that one is forced to admit that the gradual refinement and clarification of the official teaching regarding homosexuality and homosexual behavior or activity are far from complete. *Persona Humana*'s helpful distinctions cannot simply be ignored or bypassed, as though they had not been made in the first place. The CDF letter represents a clear effort to clarify teaching, but it does so, in continuity with "Educational Guidance in Human Love," by backing away from or ignoring implications of *Persona Humana*'s teaching. This too should not be surprising. In earlier comments on this century's major papal and conciliar teachings on sexuality and marriage, I have already noted a gradual development and refinement in the teaching. While *Humanae Vitae,* for instance, upholds the teaching of *Casti Connubii* and is in continuity with it, it does so through a considerable rearrangement and reformulation of that teaching. This has always been the case as the Church officially develops its teaching in ways that are more or less coherent with the language and concerns of different ages.

The context of official development of church teaching regarding sexuality in general is a helpful one for understanding the ambiguities and transition noted in recent church teaching on homosexuality. Immediately following the distinction between curable and incurable homosexuals, *Persona Humana* went on to say that "In regard to this second category of subjects, some people conclude that their tendency is so natural that it justified in their case homosexual relations within a sincere communion of life and love analogous to marriage, in so far as such homosexuals feel incapable of enduring a solitary life."[10] The emphasis here on "relations" reinforces in some ways a common misunderstanding of the nature of homosexuality, one that leads in the direction of the "objective disorder" language of the CDF letter. When homosexuality is understood principally as an orientation to certain sexual or genital acts, justice is not done to homosexual persons. Their reality is circumscribed within very narrow limits that the CDF letter itself wisely rejects in a later section: "The human person, made in the image and likeness of God, can hardly be adequately described by a reductionist reference to his or her sexual orientation" (no. 16). One could add that this orientation itself is a manifestation of the capacity and need of human persons to grow in loving relationships that in some way mirror the life-giving love of the God in whose image and likeness we are all created. In other words, homosexuality, at least of the "definitive" variety (though it must be admitted that this designation needs considerable rethinking and nuancing), is not an orientation to sexual activity as such any more than definitive heterosexuality is. Any sexual activity must be seen in the context of the totality of the persons involved. A homosexual person is not driven in some compulsive manner, as the CDF letter rightly points out,[11] to sexual activity: that person is "driven" to experience love, fidelity, meaning, intimacy, in human terms, in terms of relationships that bond individuals to one another in ways that manifest the presence of the God whose love grounds our being.

The lives of human persons, whether homosexual or heterosexual, are not adequately described by the conclusion of a syllogism: "The Church, obedient to the Lord who founded her and gave her the sacramental life, celebrates the divine plan of the loving and life-giving union of men and women in the sacrament of marriage. It is only in the marital relationship that the use of the sexual faculty can be morally good. A person engaging in homosexual behavior therefore acts immorally. . . . Homosexual activity is not a complementary union able to transmit life: and so it thwarts the call to life of that form of self-giving which the Gospel says is the essence of Christian living" (no. 7). This may be true, as long as the discussion focuses around "homosexual activity." And it may be understandable that, in the still primitive level of understanding that we possess of both heterosexuality and homosexuality, or of human sexuality in general, the Church has labored strenuously to unveil and clarify the significance of human sexuality from a faith perspective. This perspective recognizes human sexuality to be a clear imprint in our humanity of God's call to us to become godlike, to enter into the process of bearing and sharing life-giving love. It appears, however, that the Church's pronouncements on homosexual activity, however one evaluates them, have yet to grapple with the reality of an inclination that points to a legitimately human way of being.

It will remain part of the Church's task to continue to deepen and clarify the mystery of human sexuality and the values contained therein. Homosexual activity may not be a complementary union able to transmit life. But that has not yet even asked the question whether a homosexual relationship may represent the conjugal love that Paul VI, for example, rightly pointed out as the context in which the inseparability of the procreative and unitive dimensions of human sexuality find their true meaning.[12]

Thus far the Church has tended to address a preliminary issue in her official teaching, namely, the moral quality of behavior abstracted from the persons engaged in it. To a large extent, recent documents have principally addressed persons who don't exist, that is, persons whose sexuality is discussed as though it were experienced solely or exclusively in terms of genital sexual activity.

The transition in teaching that is manifest in microcosm in the changes between *Persona Humana*, "Educational Guidance in Human Love," and the CDF letter reflects probably necessary stages of development in the Church's teaching as the Church continues to refine its thinking. It is important, however, that the Church begin to ask questions more directly related to the experience of homosexual persons. The Church rightly "is also aware that the view that homosexual activity is equivalent to or as acceptable as the sexual expression of conjugal love has a direct impact on society's understanding of the nature and rights of the family and puts them in jeopardy" (no. 9). Perhaps this is true of homosexual activity, as it is true of heterosexual activity abstractly or partially conceived. It does not yet, however, indicate any degree of truth about homosexual relationships. Issues such as the nuptial or spousal significance of the human body, the nature of complementarity itself, and the meaning of the procreative and unitive (life-giving) dimensions of human sexuality must be raised afresh in the light of a deeper and broader understanding of the nature of human sexuality as encompassing far more of the truth of human persons than their sexual activity as such may encompass.

In this all too brief study, it should be clear that the Church in official documents has said far from the last or final word about human sexuality. The Church as been, and rightly so perhaps, preoccupied principally with the nature of conjugal love and marriage and what they indicate to us, at least partially, about the nature of human sexuality. The general development that is manifest in many ways in official teaching during the course of this century should lead us to conclude that the Church will continue to reflect on the mystery of human sexuality in the light of faith. Specifically with regard to homosexuality we can hope and trust that church teaching will be more and more informed by the rich insights of the overall teaching of the Church and by the experience of homosexual persons. Naturally this task will not be easy and will require considerable goodwill and humility on the part of all those who help contribute to its gradual elucidation. We have only been able to touch very briefly and generally on some of the directions the continued transformation of church teaching may take.

That the Church has inceasingly struggled to attend to the radical values of human sexuality and of human persons, however, should leave us with a realistic measure of hope. Our hope for the Church must take profound nourishment from the same source that she has so bountifully recommended to homosexuals in this latest document, and to us all throughout the ages, namely, the final and ultimate source of our Christian life, the paschal mystery of the Lord.[13]

As the Church continues to struggle to provide insight and direction for herself and for us all, let us see this successive and continuing progress rooted in the call to daily participation in the process of dying and rising anew with the Lord. The life-giving love that is forever new and transformed, even as it transforms us, has no more fundamental source; and our hope needs no more profound warrant.

Notes

1. The values dimension of human sexuality has been a prominent concern of Pope John Paul II. "In the teaching of John Paul II, the positive consideration of *values*, which one ought to discover and appreciate, precedes the *norm* which one must not violate. This norm, nevertheless, interrupts and formulates the values for which people must strive" (Congregation for Catholic Education, "Educational Guidance in Human Love" [Rome: Polyglot Press, 1983], no. 19, p. 8).

2. Helpful translations of John Paul's audiences on these topics have been provided by St. Paul Editions. They are reprinted from the English edition of *L'Osservatore Romano* and are: *Original Unity of Man and Woman: Catechesis on the Book of Genesis* (1981) and *Reflections on Humanae Vitae, Conjugal Morality and Spirituality* (1984).

3. See, for example, *Gaudium et Spes*, nos. 48–51; also "On the Regulation on Birth, *Humanae Vitae*" (Washington, DC: Office of Publishing Services, United States Catholic Conference, publication no. VI-80), nos. 8-16, pp. 5–10.

4. See the documents cited above in note 2; also *Blessed Are the Pure of Heart*, another publication of St. Paul Editions.

5. "Educational Guidance in Human Love," nos. 101–3, pp. 32–33.

6. Congregation for the Doctrine of the Faith, "Declaration on Certain Questions Concerning Sexual Ethics" (Washington, DC: Publications Office, United States Catholic Conference, 1975), no. 8, p. 8. Hereafter referred to by its customary title, *Persona Humana*.

7. Ibid.

8. Ibid.

9. This complexity is manifest in the methodology of the CDF letter. For example, no. 2 stresses that church teaching finds support "in the more secure findings of the natural sciences, which have their own legitimate and proper methodology and field of inquiry." No. 17 calls for "the assistance of the psychological, sociological and medical sciences, in full accord with the teaching of the Church." The precise relationships between natural and, for example, sociological sciences are not indicated. This should not necessarily have been expected in a document of this type, but the differentiation of "tasks" assigned to these sciences is certainly germane to the overall question of causes and "treatments" of homosexuality. A deeper analysis of this set of differing methodologies would be rewarding.

10. *Persona Humana*, no. 8, pp. 8–9.

11. "What is at all costs to be avoided is the unfounded and demeaning assumption that the sexual behavior of homosexual persons is always and totally compulsive and therefore inculpable. What is essential is that the fundamental liberty which characterizes the human person and gives [him his] dignity be recognized as belonging to the homosexual person as well" (The Pastoral Care of Homosexual Persons," no. 11).

12. In *Humanae Vitae*, no. 9, Paul VI says: "[T]here clearly appear the characteristic marks and demands of conjugal love, and it is of supreme importance to have an exact idea of these. This love is first of all fully *human*. . . . Then, this love is *total*. . . . Again, this love is *fecund* for it is not exhausted by the communion between husband and wife." He goes on in no. 12 to speak of "that teaching, often set forth by the magisterium, [that] is founded upon the inseparable connection,

willed by God and unable to be broken by man on his own initiative, between the two meanings of the conjugal act: the unitive meaning and the procreative meaning." Thus the transition that is important to note here is that Paul VI moves from a discussion of conjugal love as the setting for discussing the nature of conjugal acts. It is important to reflect on the significance of the loving relationships of persons that provide a rubric for understanding the meaning of the procreative and unitive meaning that Paul here speaks about. Obviously, he is addressing marriage and conjugal love and then moving to a discussion of the meaning of conjugal acts. What might this mean if a similar progression occurred in the discussion of the relationship of homosexual persons and the intrinsic possibilities of meaning when the acts of these persons are considered?

13. This theme is developed regarding homosexual persons in "The Pastoral Care of Homosexual Persons," no. 12.

22

Two Different Worlds, Two Different Moralities

Robert Francoeur

To begin my response to the Congregation for the Doctrine of the Faith's letter, let me spotlight what I believe is the twin crux of the conflict between the way the Vatican sees human sexuality and the way most sex educators, counselors, sexologists, psychologists, and many of the faithful see this reality today.

The philosophical mainspring behind today's conflict is that the Vatican has never resolved its centuries-old tension between the Judaic biblical world vision in which time is linear, a developmental arrow, and the Platonic-Aristotelian world view in which time is cyclic. The Vatican remains trapped in what Mircea Eliade called "the myth of the eternal return."[1] In the linear time of the biblical vision, creation is an epigenetic evolutionary process in which the very nature and essence of things is in the process of being created. In the archetypal world of the Vatican, all change is a superficial illusion because the nature of everything was established "in the beginning" and creation itself is nothing more than the unfolding of eternal archetypes *(eidoi)* already preformed within a cosmic duration that is nothing more than a ceaseless repetition, an *anakyklēsis*, and a shadowy incarnation of eternal *eidos*.[2]

In addition to having a different view of the world and creation than the Vatican, many educated Catholics have also adopted a different approach in their moral thinking. This is the second mainspring of our conflicting views. The Vatican and the hierarchy speak as though God specifically revealed to them the answer to every moral dilemma or question humans might think of between now and the end of time. Since they have all the divinely revealed answers, there is no need to debate or seek insights and new answers. Catholics need only faithfully give both internal and eternal consent to the black-and-white answers the Vatican teaches. No issue could possibly arise for which the celibate Vatican clerics do not already

189

have the true and right answer. On the other hand, educated Catholics around the world believe we are facing radically new situations inconceivable to the authors of the New Testament, new situations that demand creative solutions that apply perennial principles in new ways and perhaps answers that would have been unthinkable to Christians in previous eras.

Two Worlds, Two Moral Systems

Critical to understanding the conflict between the Vatican's views and those of many Catholics—a conflict highlighted by but by no means limited to sexual issues—are two very different world views. The Vatican's world view is clearly rooted in a fixed Aristotelian philosophy of nature and a creator who has created from above and outside. The hierarchy thus become the custodians of divine creation, the curators awaiting the return of the Infinite Museum Owner. (Remember the careful servant who dug a hole and hid the master's money in Matthew 25.) On the other hand, many Catholics struggle to be good and faithful servants who risk in order to return more than they were entrusted with. They take their inspiration from the Spirit and Word who move through matter. They are the creators who through faith, human experience, and risk strive to make considered judgments and take responsible actions which contribute to the unfolding of the ultimate kingdom. While the curators make rules for behavior in the museum, the creators strive to bring forth the living art works which will decorate the kingdom.

The quite different conclusions that come from the conflict between finished and unfinished creations are the ultimate reason the Vatican was so quick to condemn the study commissioned by the Catholic Theological Society of America.[3] Despite the condemnation, repeated surveys indicate the study does reflect the thinking of American Catholics. The question of who constitutes the Church and reflects the vitality of God's revelation thus comes front stage.

Nowhere in recent Christian thought on Genesis and human sexuality is the contrast between world views and the understanding of creation more striking than in the contrast between the Vatican letter on homosexuality and other Vatican statements on sexuality, and the "Report of the Task Force on Changing Patterns of Sexuality and Family Life" prepared for study at the request of the 111th Convention of the Episcopal Diocese of Newark, New Jersey, in early 1987.

The Judaeo-Christian tradition is a tradition precisely because, in every historical and social circumstance, the thinking faithful have brought to bear the best interpretation of the current realities in correlation with their interpretation of tradition as they have inherited it. Thus, truth in the Judaeo-Christian tradition is a dynamic process to be discerned and formulated rather than a static structure to be received. The Bible is misunderstood and misused when approached as a book of moral prescriptions directly applicable to all moral dilemmas. Rather, the Bible is the record of the response to the word of God addressed to Israel and to the Church throughout centuries of changing social, historical, and cultural conditions. The faithful responded within the realities of their particular situation, guided by the direction of previous revelation, but not captive to it. [p. 3]

To define is to limit, to control. We exercise power over what we can define. Those who try to define life, human nature, and the human experience attempt to control or hold power over life, nature, and experience. The illusion of their power remains intact only as long as their definitions and their authority to define are widely accepted. At least from the finite human vantage, even God did not choose to define the creation, choosing rather to create through the evolutionary process and in the present age continuing to create with human collaboration. The only definition of life acceptable in Christian thought is the kingdom of God which is not yet fully come. Those who would define life maintain that they control the kingdom, and in the case of the Vatican, rule the kingdom rather than serving as custodians of its keys. Having thus usurped the prerogative of the divine, the Vatican defines creation, a position which implicitly denies the Incarnation and rejects the Word who is becoming flesh.

The Vatican attempts to define reality. Other Catholics, looking at the ever-changing horizon, believe that the very attempt to define, limit, or control life violates its divinely designed evolving nature by trying to confine the unbounded in finite human words and actions. They may seek to describe what they experience in their sexual natures and make moral judgments within its context, but they are not about to attempt idolatrous definitions. Those whose vision is not open to the possibilities on the horizon use their power to force others into denying the dynamism of an ongoing creation in which we are active participants, co-creators. To maintain their own power, they are willing to imprison both humanity and the epiphany of the New Adam in the narrow museum constructed out of their patriarchal cultural biases and their lack of human imagination, faith, and courage.

In terms of different moral approaches, Jean Piaget, Lawrence Kohlberg, and Carole Gilligan have described the human experience in terms of three levels or languages.[4] On level one, that of egocentric or preconventional morality, the child responds to cultural rules and labels (good and bad, right and wrong) imposed from outside by a higher authority. On this level, labels are interpreted in terms of physical and hedonistic consequences of actions (rewards and punishments), or in terms of power of those who enunciate the rules. On level two, that of heteronomous or conventional morality, definitions of "good boy/good girl" and law and order are rooted in respect for an outside authority and conformity to that authority. On level three, the autonomous or postconventional, there is a clear effort on the part of the individual to discern moral principles and values and their applications. This is done apart from the authority of the persons or groups which have in the past determined (and imposed) moral principles and values. It is also done apart from the individual's own identification with these persons and groups.

William Stayton has applied these moral languages to religious institutions.[5] As with fundamentalist Christian sects, the Vatican mandates preconventional moral responses from a well-educated, often postconventional faithful, demanding heteronomous responses as the absolute requirement and indisputable condition for being "faithful." Despite acknowledging the necessity for "outside authority" and the acceptance of "authorities," the autonomous individual will reject the rules when respect for the authority is weakened by its failure to consider or speak to the experience of those on whom it seeks to impose rules for life and faith. This apparently has been the case with the Vatican's pronouncements on sexual morality since Vatican II.

Among "third-level faithful," heterosexual, homosexual, and bisexual, there is a clear effort to discern and develop values and moral principles of human relationship which are at once consistent with their faith and life experience, as well as with the history and traditions of the Christian community. While this striving to become a responsible person who is also Christian is in some senses apart from the "higher authority" of the ruling hierarchy, it must draw on the judgments and teachings of that authority which it accepts as necessary and legitimate. Unfortunately, in the pervasive autocratic attitude of the recent letter on the pastoral care of homosexual persons, the encyclical *Humanae Vitae*, and other Vatican documents, the Vatican distances itself from inclusion in the serious dialogue of third-level Catholic faithful. While the Scriptures and the life and teachings of Jesus, to which the Vatican appeals for both the basis of its authority and the correctness of its definitions, are clearly about real life experiences and the struggles of people for wholeness, the Vatican continues to speak at people from above and outside their experience.

Let me illustrate this double dichotomy in world views and in moral thinking in another way with my experience on a radio talk show. A distinguished monsignor and I were discussing the ethics of using new reproductive technologies to treat infertility. In the process, the monsignor inadvertently gave me an invaluable insight into the heart of the matter.

The monsignor stated that the Catholic Church's condemnation of artificial insemination and surrogate mothers was clear and unchangeable. These possibilities, he stated, clearly violate the natural functions of human sexuality, the goals of marriage, and the divinely ordained exclusivity of marriage. He claimed that this condemnation was supported by the findings of modern psychology on bonding between parent and child and the vital importance of this bonding for normal development. I asked whether any of the many childless couples who had used these medical procedures had been consulted by the Vatican to find out just what their personal experiences had been. I wondered, for instance, about the childless wife whose sister had been artificially inseminated with her brother-in-law's semen and in Christian charity served as surrogate mother for the couple. Since the sisters and husband had talked openly about their experiences in terms of love, fidelity, marriage, bonding, and child-rearing, it seemed to me such personal experience would be vitally important in any serious attempt to evaluate surrogate motherhood.

The monsignor did not see this input as relevant since "the Church" already knew the truth about this experience. I reminded him of the religious and medical authorities who had condemned the use of anesthesia in childbirth around 1850. They were convinced that an infant would know its mother did not and could not love it if she did not suffer in the delivery as Genesis said mothers must suffer. When, around 1860, Queen Victoria used anesthesia during her labor and delivery, the male medical and church authorities changed their definition of maternal/infant bonding because the experience of the Church of England contradicted their earlier presumptive definition. The monsignor thought the comparison irrelevant.

Driving home after the taping, I remembered a marvelous picture from a physician's guide showing "the proper demeanor" for a Victorian doctor examining a female patient. Genuflecting before the patient, the physician looks away from her with his arms blindly probing her "private parts" beneath a floor-length skirt. Since medical texts told the doctor what he would find in his blind groping, talking with the patient was as irrelevant as the Vatican listening to childless couples and surrogate mothers—or to homosexual men and women about their personal experiences with sexual orientation and loving relations.

The refusal of the Vatican and many clergy to listen with respect and sensitivity to those who have a different experience stands in sharp contrast to the Newark Episcopal report.

> Changing patterns of sexuality and family life confront pastors and congregations with new challenges and opportunities for understanding and for ministry. Rather than arguing about these issues we need first to listen to the experience of those who are most directly involved. Where homosexuality is concerned, fear, rejection, and avoidance by the heterosexual community is common and entrenched. We believe that pastors and congregations must meet members of the homosexual community person to person. The first step toward understanding and ministry is listening. We need as much as is possible to bracket our judgments and listen to persons as they are. The Church needs to acknowledge that its historical tendency to view homosexual persons as homosexual rather than as persons has intensified the suffering of this 5%–10% of our population. [p.13]

Driving home after the talk show with the monsignor, I thought also of Pierre Teilhard de Chardin, the Jesuit evolutionist and paleontologist who sought to integrate Catholic theology, spirituality, and scientific evolution. In his encyclical *Humani Generis,* Pius XII had decided that monogenism, the descent of humankind from a single primal pair, was what might now be termed by some an "informally infallible" doctrine. Darwinian evolution, and by implication Teilhard's evolutionary synthesis, were therefore heresy. Rather than consider the evolutionary worldview, the Vatican exiled Teilhard to the wilderness of the Gobi desert in Outer Mongolia.

Forty years later, Teilhard's evolutionary spirit was quite visible in the deliberations of Vatican II. This influence included the majority report of the postconciliar commission on the moral acceptability of artificial contraception which Pope Paul VI rejected in his encyclical *Humanae Vitae.* Unfortunately, John Paul II and the magisterium continue to ignore the *sensus fidelium* expressed by the overwhelming majority of Catholic married couples who are convinced that artificial contraception can be morally acceptable within the context of married love as they experience it.

In the 1920s, Teilhard pictured the human race floating on a raft in the middle of an ocean. Some of the people on the raft are looking at their feet, telling everyone that "nothing is changing; everything is the way it always was." These immobilist doctrinaires have no problem defining the world as they know it must be. The others, however, see a very different world because they are constantly studying the ever-changing horizons. For Teilhard, the Vatican theologians and authorities were looking at their feet and ignoring the real world when they condemned Darwinian evolution as heresy. Today Vatican moralists are still looking at their feet, ignoring reality, in their statements about the "intrinsically disordered" and unnatural orientation of homosexuality. Like the Victorian physician protesting his reverence for human dignity by looking away from his female patient, and the Anglican divines turning a deaf ear to women who had delivered their babies under anesthesia, the Vatican is not listening, and seldom has ever listened to views on scientific and sexual issues that diverge from their "informally infallible" definitions. One can easily imagine the Church hierarchs of the 1600s proclaiming that the sun revolves around the earth, and that this definition of the world, in the words of the Vatican letter on homosexuality, "finds support in [the Bible and] the more secure findings of the natural sciences" (no. 2). One can also hear the claim that the Church's "more global vision does greater justice" to the dignity and rich reality of the human person because man is obviously created at the physical and spiritual center of the universe. Three hundred years later the hierarchical Church is still trying to decide how they might rehabilitate Galileo!

Despite this long history of deafness and myopia, the Vatican letter opens with the claim that the Catholic moral condemnation of homosexual behavior "finds support in the more secure findings of the natural sciences, which have their own legitimate and proper methodology and field of inquiry. The Church is thus in a position to learn from scientific discovery but also to transcend the horizons of science and to be confident that her more global vision does greater justice to the rich reality of the human person in his spiritual and physical dimensions, created by God and heir, by grace, to eternal life" (no. 2). Unfortunately, the Vatican document does not look honestly at the realities of human sexuality or modern sexology, but rather at its own self-defined world. The Vatican already has the final answer, and its definition is at least informally infallible and therefore unchangeable.

In essence, the Vatican has abandoned the Biblical concept of an ongoing creation in which all reality is subject to essential change and newness as it evolved toward the New Adam and has endorsed a world view of Platonic archetypes and "the myth of the eternal return" to Adam and Eden in the beginning.[6] In making this exchange, the Vatican has locked itself into and speaks from a pattern of moral thinking which many educated Catholics no longer understand or accept.

Four Statements

Having set the stage, let me comment briefly on four specifics in the Vatican letter.

1. The homosexual orientation "itself must be seen as an objective disorder" (no. 3). Throughout the document it is asserted that only a heterosexual orientation and only heterosexual marital procreative acts are natural and intrinsically ordered. If this is God's intention, then how explain the regular and common existence of homosexual and bisexual behaviors alongside the predominant heterosexual behaviors in many animal species created by God? Though they are always a minority, men and women created by God through the secondary causalities of genes and hormones and endowed by God with homosexual and bisexual orientations are found in almost every culture and society, past and contemporary. Homosexual and bisexual relations are openly accepted in many cultures, past and present. If we are to speak realistically of what is natural and what God intends, we must consider the predominant weight of contemporary sexological, neuro-hormonal, and psychosocial research. This supports the hypothesis that all orientations, whether heterosexual, homosexual, or bisexual, are the combined and irreversible result of prenatal genetic/neuro-hormonal conditioned tendencies laid down in the developing brain and of chance postnatal socializing or enculturation. That prenatal component makes all sexual orientations natural, and not a matter of choice. Still, the Vatican chooses to define what is "natural" in its own limited terms.

2. "Providing a basic plan for understanding this whole discussion of homosexuality is the theology of creation we find in Genesis" (no. 6). This, I believe, is a crucial admission. I am convinced that the Vatican theologians still see the creation of both the universe and the sexual human being as a single event, finished and completed in the Garden of Eden instead of at the end of time in the Pleroma, the Second Coming of Christ, the real Adam. They have yet to learn from Galileo, Darwin, and modern science that the world cannot be validly defined by those who refuse to look at the ever-changing horizon. The Vatican rejects the vision that creation is an ongoing process, a cosmogenesis and anthropogenesis. They still live in a pre-Galilean, pre-Darwinian cosmology. They do not see the ongoing creation revealed by modern biblical studies, a cos-

mogenesis in which we are co-creators of the fullness of the human potential that is coming to be in the image and likeness of the divine. They see interlocking genitals, not persons called to explore the rich potential and reality of human nature and sexuality in terms of love.

3. "The Church, in rejecting erroneous opinions regarding homosexuality, does not limit but rather defends personal freedom and dignity realistically and authentically understood" (no. 7). Again, the Vatican's static finished view of Genesis and creation is apparent. An enlightening contrast, and a view of Genesis and creation more in tune with the dynamic world view of the Hebrews, was offered five hundred years ago in the midst of the Renaissance. In his oration "On the Dignity of Man," Giovanni Pico della Mirandola describes God speaking to Adam in these words:

> We have given to thee, Adam, no fixed seat, no form of thy very own, no gift peculiarly thine, that thou mayest feel as thine own, have as thine own, possess as thine own seat, the form, the gifts which thou thyself shall desire. A limited nature in other creatures is confined within the laws written down by Us. In conformity with thy free judgment, in whose hands I have placed thee, thou art confined by no bounds; and thou wilt fix limits of nature for thyself. I have placed thee at the center of the world, that from there thou mayest more conveniently look around and see whatsoever is in the world. . . . Thou . . . art the molder and maker of thyself; thou, restrained by no narrow bonds, according to thy own free will . . . shall sculpt thy nature into whatever shape thou dost prefer.[7]

The Inquisition condemned Mirandola five hundred years ago, just as the Vatican today rejects the ongoing nature of creation.

At issue here and elsewhere is the Vatican's demand that we accept its limited definition of what is the realistic and authentic understanding of personal freedom and dignity. We are expected to ignore the fact that this definition was produced by a group of celibate heterosexual males whom, I suspect, have never conversed with gay men and lesbians. That kind of pontification may work with uneducated laity, but it is hardly convincing for educated Catholics, clerical or lay.

4. "Homosexual activity is not a complementary union" (no. 7). The mysterious dimensions of human sexuality permeate our whole personality and everything we do as sexual persons. Yet the Vatican reduces the essence of human sexuality to heterosexual genital intercourse for biological reproduction. But how do we know that the "complementary union" of two humans has to be thus so limited and defined in anatomical terms? Certainly homosexuals in long-term loving unions such as those docu-

mented by David McWhirter, Andrew Mattison, Mary Mendola, and others do not see or experience the anatomical limits the Vatican envisions.[8] We are left with the statement of a few celibate male clerics who, like the Victorian doctor, claim they have the authentic interpretation of reality and can define the disease they propose to treat without ever talking with the patient whom they propose to cure.

Compare this dogmatic genital-obsessed judgment of the Vatican with the assessment of the Episcopal task force report:

> From the perspective of Jesus' teaching regarding the Realm of God, all heterosexual and homosexual relationships are subject to the same criteria of ethical assessment—the degree to which persons and relationships reflect mutality, love and justice. . . . The commitment to mutuality, love and justice which marks our ideal picture of heterosexual unions is also the ideal for homosexual unions. Those who would say homosexuality by its very nature precludes such commitment must face the fact that such unions do in fact occur, have occurred and will continue to occur. The Church must decide how to respond to such unions. [p. 7]

A Concluding Thought

Pronouncements like the Vatican letter are typical of magisterial power politics and a teaching authority isolated from human experience. In such statements, the hierarchy defines this or that as THE REALITY. They can do this because they claim that revelation has ended and that they are the recipient and sole custodian of that revelation and know what reality is. Thus if you or I believe we experience something that does not match their definition, they know we are deluding ourselves.

Despite demeaning moral pronouncements like the Vatican letter, many Catholics, regardless of sexual orientation, remain firmly rooted in our Catholic faith. Our faith, however, is in an ongoing creation in which the discerning of right and wrong is no longer limited to magisterial definitions as it was in ages past when only the clergy were literate.

Unfortunately, American Catholics have transfered much of their sense of democracy and respect for democratic law to their relations with the hierarchical Curia. We might be much better off if we adopted the European custom of taking Vatican statements "with a very large grain of salt." We can then put mandates such as the pastoral guidelines on homosexuality in proper perspective within the whole framework of life and our divine calling to an ongoing epiphany, the Divine Diaphany!

Fortunately, both revelation and reality are always much larger than human definitions. Like creation, revelation is an ongoing process. It is the epiphany, the gradual unveiling or shining through of Christ the Second Adam in history. This is the reality we cannot and must not forget. Creation and revelation continue today and are more often in evidence outside the hierarchical clerical structure. This is why the experiences of gay men, lesbians, and gay and lesbian couples seeking to incarnate the divine love in their daily lives are revealing new dimensions in the divine mystery of love not encountered in past revelations as interpreted by the Vatican.

From the beginnings of the Christian faith to the present, God has seen fit to reveal himself to the powerless and the oppressed. Repeatedly, the Vatican and many clerics appear unwilling to listen with sensitivity and a sincere desire to understand views and experiences that differ from theirs. "Listening," the Newark Episcopal report warns,

> opens the door of hospitality, which has so long been firmly shut. Such words as ministry and hospitality, however, still suggest a relationship of inequality, we and they. As such they perpetuate the image of the Church as separate from the homosexual community. In fact, however, we believe that the Church should be as inclusive of homosexual persons as it is of heterosexual persons. In this light, all the normal avenues of inclusion should be available to homosexual persons. . . . Ideally, homosexual couples would find within the community of the congregation the same recognition and affirmation which nurtures and sustains heterosexual couples in their relationships, including, where appropriate, liturgies which recognize and bless such relationships. [p. 14]

I'm afraid it will be a long time before the Vatican will catch up with that prophetic Christian vision!

Notes

1. M. Eliade, *Cosmos and History: The Myth of the Eternal Return* (New York: Harper and Row, 1959), pp. 88–91.
2. H.-C. Puech, "La Gnose et le temps," *Eranos Jahrbuch* 20:60–61.
3. "It bears repeating that there is much that is uncertain and provisional about the subject of homosexuality. . . . It bears repeating, however, that where there is sincere affection, responsibility, and the germ of authentic human relationship—in other words, where there is love—God is surely present." (A. Kosnik et al., *Human Sexuality: New Directions in American Catholic Thought* [New York: Paulist, 1977], p. 218).
4. L. Kohlberg and C. Gilligan, "Moral Reasoning and Value Formation,"

in M. S. Calderone, ed., *Sexuality and Human Values* (New York: Association Press, 1974).

5. W. R. Stayton, "Religion and Adolescent Sexuality," *Seminars in Adolescent Medicine* 1, no. 2 (1985): 131–37.

6. R. T. Francoeur, *Perspectives in Evolution* (Baltimore: Helicon Press), pp. 9–38.

7. P. D. Mirandola, *On the Dignity of Man, One Being and the One, Heptaplus,* translated by C. G. Wallis, P. J. W. Miller, and D. Carmichael (Indianapolis: Bobbs-Merrill Educational Publishing, 1965), pp. 4–5.

8. D. McWhirter and A. Mattison, *The Male Couple* (Englewood Cliffs, NJ: Prentice-Hall, 1984).

23

Cultural Imperatives, Taboos, and the Gospel Alternative

Rosemary Haughton

An unexpected benefit of the Vatican letter on homosexuality may be a more conscious development of moral theology and spirituality as they relate to homosexual feelings, sympathies, or behavior. There is still a tendency for Christians to try to deal with homosexuality as an exceptional case and to talk about a "pastoral" approach—which means "How do we deal compassionately with these problem people?" It seems to me that what we need is a basis for a moral theology which will allow people not to be regarded as problems but to make difficult, painful, and ambiguous choices along with other Christians, whatever their sexual preferences. However, in this chapter I do not attempt that task; rather, the more modest but essential task of clearing away some of the mystification which has made it possible for quite intelligent and compassionate people to remain stuck in moral attitudes developed in religious and social situations quite unlike our own, but now carrying a strong emotional charge of unexplained fear, righteous repulsion, and even hate. I also suggest, but only briefly, where we must begin to look for alternatives.

Human beings are plagued by a need to justify their own behavior. They do so not just individually but communally. (Indeed, it is impossible for an individual to "behave" in any manner except in relationship to others. Even the recluse makes the choice of solitude in awareness of and in response to the communal life which is refused.) So the need to justify and explain behavior is a community task, and usually it is one developed in a religious mode because it is so important and basic to the "being" of the community. If we think of it this way, ethics, or in a certain context, moral theology, can be seen to be less a set of a priori statements, based on philosophical argument or religious revelation, about how human beings *ought* to behave and more a judgment by hindsight (and sometimes from bitter experience) on how it has proved to be appropriate to behave in

201

202 ·   ROSEMARY HAUGHTON

concrete circumstances for the sake of what is perceived to be needed communal survival. So judgment necessarily includes an interpretation of the value of certain kinds of behavior, but from a certain point of view— that of the cultural survival of a particular community which has to do its surviving in specific environmental and social circumstances. This is why moral absolutes are a natural development in a unified culture. If certain kinds of behavior are needed, or are dangerous, for cultural survival, they will take on the character of "good" and "evil" and be inextricably mixed up in the religious identity of the group. But at the same time this hindsight judgment, since it evolves from particular circumstances, varies from culture to culture and from subculture to subculture, and again it seeks religious justification.

A very small-scale example will illustrate this. I work in a house which provides shelter for homeless people, of whom the majority are single women with children, because that is their greatest need. As a community of hospitality we have been in existence for nearly six years; the philosophy of the house is a Christian one, based on a recognition of the gospel demand to serve the poor and liberate the oppressed. Among the "oppressed" of our society, resort to drink as a way of dulling the pain of rejection and despair is common and very understandable, and in our earliest years we operated on the principle that any homeless person was to be welcomed, which naturally included men, and sometimes women, who drank. This was a moral judgment and decision of Christian people who know that all human beings are precious and that the Church's survival *as Christian* depends on recognizing this in daily living. But after a while it became apparent that the survival of the household as a place for women and children was being placed at risk by this principle. Most of the women are survivors of abuse by husbands, fathers, brothers, or "boyfriends," many of whom drank. Some women were themselves struggling to overcome past drinking problems of their own. The presence in the house of men, or other women, with drinking problems, caused them a degree of fear and stress which made it impossible for them to begin to deal with the multiple problems facing them. So the decision had to be made to exclude anyone with a drinking problem from the house. Within the mini-culture of the household, drinking was "bad," that is, it threatened the survival of the culture. Interestingly, because of the work we did with abused women and the stories we heard, it became very easy to *feel* that drinking was "bad" and not just inappropriate, even though our religious beliefs committed us to acceptance of all and compassion toward victims of a system creating poverty and its attendant symptoms.

I hope it is not necessary for me to spell out the fact that, in using this illustration, I am not equating alcoholism, which is a disease, with homosexuality, which isn't. I simply looked around for a simple example of how exclusion for practical reasons can easily acquire moral force.

In this tiny instance it is comparatively easy to recognize the source of a decision to exclude from the house people who drink, and to keep it in perspective, as a practical necessity, without branding as "evil" people with a drinking problem. But also it is easy to see how, in a much larger community with a long history, judgments developed over a long period on the basis of survival can become moral absolutes, with a great deal of emotional content as well.

This is, of course, a serious simplification. The psychic roots of moral criteria are complex and hard, perhaps impossible, to understand. Yet it is evident, as a matter of observation, that particular communities do develop moral criteria for the sake of social survival, and these are often backed by deep, apparently irrational, feelings. But these feelings are probably based in a real fear of the consequences of breaches of the appropriate code and are not originally irrational, though their origins are buried somewhere deep in the folk memory of the people, only to be ambiguously discovered in old stories and rituals.

The fear of homosexuality has very deep roots, and these roots are the same as those which created the sexual "double standard" in relation to premarital virginity and marital fidelity in many cultures. The roots of the fear of feminine infidelity and of homosexuality are exactly the same. In a culture based on some version of the patriarchal system (as almost all have been and are) the one thing that can create lethal family hostilities, social confusion, and consequent political instability is lack of a clear line of inheritance of property. So if the paternity of a male child is in question, the whole clan can be in an uproar. Hence all kinds of precautions are taken to closely monitor women so that they may serve as guarantors of inheritance. In time, these precautions take on a strong emotional tone; losing touch with their practical purpose, they become moral absolutes, transgressions of which stir up extraordinary depths of anger, fear, and guilt.

By the same token, homosexual feeling is also a threat. For a young man to set aside his duty to provide heirs and endanger his patrimony by focusing his energies in a relationship which precludes children is an insult to the whole system. In her novel *The Handmaid's Tale,* Margaret Atwood depicts a future fundamentalist Christian theocracy. A major part of the motivation of this theocracy is shown to be the fear of human extinction due to a declining birthrate and a high incidence of defective babies because of environmental pollution. So women are reduced once more to possessions with purely reproductive and servile functions and closely guarded to ensure clear inheritance for wealthy dominant males, with infidelity punishable by death. Homosexuals also are publicly hanged, with labels attached: their crime is "gender betrayal"—that is, they failed to serve the sacred purpose of perpetuating the race. The novel shows very well the attempts made to build up in the people the correct psychic revulsion at such deviations which will ensure that the law against them functions for the purpose of the dominant class, but on a secure basis of popular acceptance.

In this fictional (but all too believable) "Republic of Gilead," female homosexuality is punished equally with that of males because for those in power it presents the same threat to racial survival. But it is interesting that, historically, the fear of female homosexuality has been a late development. For a long time, in European and American Culture, romantic relationships between women were either ignored or regarded as rather touching, and even beautiful, provided they did not interfere with the serious business of marriage or with the less respectable demands of men. Whether these relationships were genital was not even much discussed, sexuality being a male preserve. In the minds of men it was inconceivable that for a woman another woman could constitute a serious rival to the attentions of the male. Moralists (male, of course) were divided on whether sexual relations between women were even possible; they argued learnedly about whether sexual "sin" between women could occur, given that the poor things lacked the essential appendage for intercourse (as they understood it) to take place. In other words, female homosexuality was not a serious moral issue because it didn't seem to threaten male dominance. Some even held that it was useful, since mutual girlish passions kept young women occupied with each other and less in danger of losing their virginity to the wrong man before a suitable marriage could be arranged.

It was only the rise of Freudian psychoanalysis, developing at the same time as the early feminist movements, that relationships between women became a focus of attention. Because women were beginning to be public persons and present in the work force, they were becoming a threat to male dominance. The panic evident in the violence and hatred directed toward suffragettes shows how deeply this threat was felt. Strong relationships between strong women were a very different matter from what could be dismissed as the immature explorations of young girls or the pathetic consolations of "surplus" spinsters. But the Freudian interpretation of female sexuality supplied exactly what was needed to justify masculine fears. Independent women, but especially women showing indifference to male sexual advances, could be viewed as unfeminine, unnatural, and perverted. A whole new moral orthodoxy emerged to help preserve endangered patriarchy.

I have dwelt on this development at some length because it shows so well how a system morally justifies its own fears, explaining the rightness of the judgments made, basically for the preservation of a particular form of culture.

The Catholic Church through the centuries has developed its own form of patriarchal culture. It is clearly contrary to the antipatriarchal, prophetic values of the gospel community experience, but it grew like that because the patriarchal model, in one version or another, was the normal one, the *obvious* and available and inevitable one. The imaginative, social, political, and spiritual leap made by Jesus was quite beyond the power of his followers to sustain. Moreover, the patriarchal tradition preserved in the Hebrew Scriptures was there to reinforce the Christian version as it developed. The Christian churches have, almost without exception, preserved and sanctified the patriarchal model, though occasionally modified by the principles of justice and compassion also present in the Scriptures and not easy to dispose of entirely.

Fortunately that is not the whole story. The explosive power of the gospel message has never been totally suppressed; it has continued to break out in many forms throughout history, and the succession of men and women who lived by that vision and gathered others to share it is the real Catholic tradition. But the mainline history of the Catholic Church, and of other major churches with a strong hierarchical structure, shows how individuals shaped by a patriarchal mode of operation have taken over a cultural system based on the importance of clear lines of property inheritance and reinforced it by moral judgments based on the need to secure a spiritual and religious "inheritance." "Apostolic succession" is a power system also requiring strong emotional sanctions of fear and guilt for its preservation.

The threat that women pose to this culture is obvious, since the "right brain" values associated with the feminine are a direct challenge to "left brain" systems of control. Similarly, any strong emotional bonding which cannot be harnessed to serve the ends of the power system (e.g., by producing more obedient subjects!) is deeply feared. All strong sexual feeling, heterosexual or homosexual, is suspect in such a culture because the energy of affection detracts from the essential focus of "loyalty" and obedience. It does not serve the purposes of the dominant religious culture. Homosexual love is especially repugnant because there is no way it can be channeled into reproduction. It can only be subversive. Therefore all the old land property-patriarchal taboos are called up from the depths, invoking ancient fears and reinforcing them with scriptural quotations out of context and shorn of any historical sense but still carrying the tremendous power of sacred language.

That's how it happens. It is important to recognize how it happens because it is only when we can understand the why and how of the development of moral attitudes that we can distinguish between taboos and cultural imperatives. But if we clear away the mystification (no small task, even in our own conditioned minds), we still cannot simply conclude that moral judgments made from past cultural imperatives, hardened by time and mystified by religion though they may be, never had any justification at all. It is possible to understand imaginatively how homosexuality might appear to be a real threat to a small beleaguered nation such as ancient Israel, whose survival as a cultural and religious entity absolutely depended on strong ethnic identity which was secured by ensuring unquestioned inheritance through the male line and a high birthrate. With their religious and racial identity one and the same, religion gave force to these fears by attributing them to divine ordinance. In a sense, they could be if we assume that Israel's survival and growth was indeed God's will. But we do not need to carry over that fear into a culture where population growth, not decline, is the threat. If God's will is being sought in this matter, we cannot invoke the opinion, however sincere, of people whose cultural agenda was totally different.

It is my purpose here mainly to clear away some of the fog of half-admitted fears and guilt that haunt many people because of the long history of religious homophobia, not to enter into the much more rewarding task of exploring the basis for a moral theology appropriate to our culture and faithful to the vision of the gospel. However, it is possible to perceive where such an exploration must begin, for the words and acts of Jesus, as we can perceive them through the Synoptic Gospels, cut right through the cultural imperatives of his time and place. This is, after all, why in the end he proved impossible to tame or assimilate and had to be destroyed.

What he did was to dismantle the existing patriarchal structure, substituting for the God in the image of an hierarchical elite the Abba who cast down the mighty and chose the little ones. He gathered men and women of all backgrounds to share in the building of a new kind of community and explicitly bade them prefer the new bonds of the brotherhood and sisterhood of believers to the bonds of the patriarchal family, open to the reign of God breaking in upon us. In this context he showed no concern at all for the traditional roles of men and women, of ruler and ruled, and recklessly juggled the categories of sinner and righteous until even his friends were confused and not a little shocked. For all the various categories into which human beings divide each other for purposes of control and social survival he substituted a general category of discipleship, cutting across lines of gender, class, race, and public standing. The nature of the relationship which he proposed for those in this category was demonstrated by the very visible sign of shared meals. Companions, sharers of bread; the relationship was to be one of friendship with all the heights and depths of courage, practical support and caring, compassion and fidelity that that word implies. That's not a bad place to begin to discern the elements of a moral theology which can fittingly be called Christian.

24

Homosexual Acts or Gay Speech?

André Guindon

The Vatican letter on homosexuality admits that "a new exegesis of Sacred Scripture . . . claims variously that Scripture has nothing to say on the subject of homosexuality" (no. 4). The Congregation for the Doctrine of the Faith could have added that a new hermeneutic of Scripture claims, moreover, that the moral discernments of specific practices made by Jewish or Christian communities never definitively resolve our own moral perplexities. Since the Congregation does not indicate what methods *it* applies to discover what Scripture really says and what this could mean for us, the letter bears all the trappings of a fundamentalist approach. The text serves as pretext for upholding positions which are grounded on extrabiblical criteria.[1]

In 1969 Joseph Ratzinger wrote a scholarly commentary on article 10 of *Dei Verbum,* an article which is misleadingly quoted in the letter (no. 5). In this commentary, he states that Vatican II "expressly points out the subordination of the teaching office to the word, i.e. its function as a servant." He insists that "the point of view which sees only Scripture as what is unclear, but the teaching office as what is clear" is "a very limited one." He goes on to argue "that to reduce the task of theology to the proof of the presence of the statements of the teaching office in the sources is to threaten the primacy of the sources which, (were one to continue logically in this direction) would ultimately destroy the serving character of the teaching office."[2] If Ratzinger, the cardinal prefect of the Congregation, wanted to avoid the distortion that Ratzinger, the theologian, singled out in 1969, the letter he issued in 1986 should have employed acceptable exegetical and hermeneutical methods to prove that the positions it maintains are actually present in the sources. This, the letter does not do.

What, then, are the real bases of the claims made by the Vatican letter, specifically that homosexual acts are "intrinsically disordered" or "an intrinsic moral evil" and that "the inclination itself must be seen as an objective disorder" (no. 3; also nos. 7, 8, 10)? The clearest and most decisive basis for the letter's position is, in my view, the anthropological and ethical model which the Congregation uses to understand and appraise human sexuality.

From Vatican II on, synods, popes, and bishops have repeatedly invited Catholic theologians to deepen, in the words of the Congregation, "their reflection on the true meaning of human sexuality" (no. 17). Many of us have spent most of our teaching and researching careers trying to do precisely that. Prompted by the great renewals in the human sciences, ethics, and theology, we have reconsidered the sexual experience of contemporary men and women and offered new models of sexual ethics.

All to no avail. This letter totally disregards the work of contemporary ethicists as it does that of contemporary biblical scholars. It once again takes up a pre-Vatican II discourse on human activity understood as a biopsychical function directed toward a "complementary union, able to transmit life" (no. 7) and endowed with immutable "intrinsic" and "objective" laws of operation.

In 1976 I proposed that sexual activity should be understood as language.[3] A number of well-known ethicists have picked up the idea.[4] Sex among human beings is a human gesture. A human gesture is a bodily movement whereby an addressor expresses herself and communicates meaning to an addressee. When sexual activity is not animal but human, it does more than "produce" things such as sensorial reaction, heat, tumescence, orgasm, ejaculation, or insemination. Human sex expresses and communicates emotions and meanings.

Linguists define "language" as a function expressing and communicating thought between human beings. They define "speech" as the oral, written, or gestural expression and communication of an individual's thought. Since Roman Jakobson's famous "closing statement" at the University of Indiana's interdisciplinary symposium on stylistics in 1960, most linguists also acknowledge that one of language's six functions is the emotive or expressive function. In every genuine human communication, the addressor's interiority is revealed.[5] If a human person who is interacting sexually with another person is not expressing and communicating something about himself to another, what exactly is going on between them that can be labeled specifically human?

If sex as specifically human is a gestural language of sorts, it should be understood with the help of adequate conceptual tools. Contemporary linguistics has drastically changed our way of comprehending the relationship between human speech and thought. The classical, Aristotelian view was semantic. It saw the child as enjoying both thinking and the linguistic ability from birth. She lacked only a native language. To communicate her thoughts to others, she had to learn the words and sentences of one specific linguistic system, for instance the English language. We think, today, that this is not what the child is really doing. From the daily language being spoken around him, he is extracting, at incredible speed, a whole system of extremely complex and abstract rules concerning the formation of words (morphology) and the construction of sentences (syntax).[6] The contemporary view of language holds that a child who starts speaking is doing much more than repeating what others are saying about the world around him. He is learning a grammar, that is, rules that enable him to make sense of his world and to share his understanding with others. Learning to speak is learning to think and, eventually, to think for oneself.[7]

The human world began to exist as meaningful when *Homo sapiens* began to speak as we do, probably sometime between 300,000 and 400,000 years ago.[8] Human beings transmitted this slow cultural construction to their progeny. Yet the vocabulary and linguistic rules received by each child are nothing more than possibilities made available to her for expressing the world as she sees it and appraises it. She inserts herself in it by "speaking up" in her turn. The linguistic baggage she inherits is but a sedimentary layer which is at her disposal for creating her own original version.[9] As long as a language is not being used by an individual speaker, it is no more than a formal structure. Realities of the world are not structured as meaningful human realities until a user makes the language her own and speaks her world. Belgian philosopher Jean-François Malherbe rightly observes that the "objectivity" of language is much less stable than a certain realistic and mythical notion has understood it to be. The consistency of a word hinges on the consistency of contexts. Since contexts are unstable, a word or gesture never has a once-and-for-all acquired consistency.[10] American linguist S. I. Hayakawa is right: "No word ever has the same meaning twice."[11]

Applied to sexual language—this distinctive expression and communication of shared intimacy—the contemporary, syntaxic understanding of speaking substantially modifies the nature of ethical consideration. I will suggest three such major modifications.

First, the use of the expression "homosexual acts" should be dropped. Not that this expression is unjustifiable. Its misuse, however, has made it unfit to adequately denote the referent, that about which a statement says something. The letter's use of the expression "homosexual acts" is a case in point. Coherent with its practice of giving no explanation for anything it states, the Congregation makes no effort to tell the bishops what it means by "homosexual acts." The Congregation seems to take for granted that

there are specific instances of "physical behavior" or "material perform-
ances" which, independently of any user's meaning-making operation,
have an evil meaning. Meanings would exist in the world before a community of speaking persons has structured them. Since they would be in
the things themselves, "intrinsically," and not in the sayings of those who
constitute their human world by speaking, such meanings, true or false,
good or bad, never change. Human persons would not be free to create
their world of meanings. They would find the world all figured out. Their
task would consist merely in forming a mental replica of what is out there.
Like computers—and unsophisticated ones at that!

In terms of a contemporary understanding of language, this interpretation of sexual gestures makes no sense. The creative possibilities of each
person wishing to express and to communicate himself to another are real
since nobody else has ever lived and expressed this exact situation before.
Each person does not need to reinvent the language. Much is available in
the experience of the community of users. Nevertheless, each person will
say something new when he uses the language of his community. Thus a
gay person who is acting as a genuine human being, and not as a mere
sensory machine, will use gayspeak as it is found in a given community of
users. I will come back to this precise aspect of the problem in my third
point. Here, I wish to stress the fact that the individual person molds this
communal gayspeak to say himself in the given context in which he finds
himself. He does not stumble upon "objective homosexual acts" in the
world which he must duplicate, as it were. The slightest changes in his
facial expressions, bodily postures and movements, vocal modulations,
and so on,[12] become, when they are intended to say his own self tenderly
and sensuously to a same-sex partner, gay speech. Each modulation of
self-expression and communication is a "homosexual act." Hence the
problem: Is it possible for a person who has a homosexual orientation to
remain speechless? If not, is every aspect of this ongoing gay speech
"intrinsically" evil? If this is not the case, what are the criteria for
distinguishing permissible homosexual language from its forbidden expressions? Do we have to fall back on a nomenclature of "physical acts"
which represent an inadequate understanding of what sexual expression
and communication are between human beings? These questions cannot
be answered satisfactorily before we shift the focus of our discourse from
"homosexual acts" to "gay speech."

Second, the understanding of sexual interaction as speech gives ethicists
the conceptual tool needed to develop a criteriology which is specifically
human instead of merely animal. At long last, ethicists are able to look at
human sex as a moral rather than as a merely biological event. When will

we finally acknowledge the simple, obvious fact that to transmit biological life is not a specifically human criterion for sex? Animals, when they "perform" sexually with a heterosexual partner for the reproduction of the species are not more moral than when they use sex, as they often do, for satisfying other individual or collective needs.[13] Open to the transmission of life or not, animal sex is amoral because it is not meaning-creating speech. Animal sex produces nothing in terms of the historical meaningfulness of the relationship. The moral stake resides in the expression and communication of a caring meaning which makes better people and communities. Human criteria for evaluating the moral quality of sex are things like the following: whether their use of sexual language makes people whole in their embodied and spiritual selves; whether their use of sexual language structures identities which are autonomous yet outreaching; whether their use of sexual language is generous enough to call forth what is best in others; whether their use of sexual language has the responsible quality needed to adjust well to the authentic story of each other's lives. I recently elaborated these criteria in more detail, and I examined some of the implications for a gay lifestyle.[14] Such implications are utterly meaningless, I fear, for those who focus on "homosexual acts" rather than on "gay speech."

Third, we should revisit the dualistic-minded debate in sexual ethics over "objectivity" and "subjectivity." As mentioned earlier, a gay person who wishes to communicate her intimate self necessarily uses gayspeak as it is spoken in a given community of users. Should she try to invent a totally new language from scratch she would be misunderstood at best. A homosexual linguistic instrument already exists in her community. Each new user finds an objective language, filled with a whole history of human precomprehension of homosexual realities.

We are, to a great extent, the inheritors of Western European culture. Throughout long periods of its history—though not during all of it, as John Boswell reminds us[15]—Western European communities became overpreoccupied with social conformity. They yielded to the temptation of setting up a paragon of human perfection: the Mediterranean, Christian, and heterosexual male. Those who did not measure up to this yardstick were seen as defective at best, more often than not as vicious and heretical. So it was that gayspeak was filled with negative meanings, as was Turkspeak, Jewspeak, and womanspeak. It was thought that those who pursued a practice contrary to the heterosexual makeup of all living beings had acquired a dispositon to act sexually against their "nature." This was called a "vicious homosexual inclination," which was so vicious, in fact, that the vice became "unmentionable," as though it did not exist.[16] Anyone using gayspeak during certain periods of Western European history found this pre-comprehension built into sexual language. Some might have sensed that this was an incorrect understanding. They were powerless, however, to influence the language.

Nevertheless, the "objectivity" of the meaning of a language, gestural or otherwise, is not such that it never changes. If this "objectivity" is that given by a community of users, this community may eventually reappraise its evaluation when it discovers unknown aspects of its human world. As long as some aspects of our internal or external world remain unnamed, they do not function in the vision, understanding, and valorization of the world. Exceptional users of the langauge eventually come along and name them. Kepler, Newton, Kant, Einstein came along and respectively named the elliptic orbit of planets around the sun, universal attraction, transcendental consciousness, relativity. By the same token, the objective meaning of the language evolved, contrary to what Cardinal Richelieu thought when he founded the *Académie française* in 1634 and gave it the mandate to produce a *Dictionnaire de la langue française*. He thought that, by royal authority and decree, the *Dictionnaire* would rule on the good use of the French language once and for all. Lo and behold, a second edition of the *Dictionnaire* was soon necessary and many others were to follow suit. Why? Because as long as a community keeps on using the French language to name its world, the objective meaning of the language will keep on changing.

When the time was ripe for a new understanding, sexologists like Sigmund Freud came along and named an unnamed reality: the "homosexual orientation." This has nothing in common with the former "vicious homosexual inclination." Homosexual orientation or preference is seen as the result of still not clearly identified interactions between a human organism and its human environment. This newly named reality has drastically changed the objective meaning of the homosexual language. The Vatican letter ignores this new reality and deals exclusively with the former meaning. It is not addressing the reality of homosexual orientation at all. The outcome is sure to be as successful as Cardinal Richelieu's efforts to regulate the objective meaning of the French language by decree. To keep on "declaring" all forms of homosexual identity "intrinsically disordered" will not make them disordered any more than the repeated sixteenth- and seventeenth-century church declarations concerning the nonroundness of the earth succeeded in making it flat or square. Had the Congregation really been attentive to "the more secure findings of the natural sciences" (no. 2), it would have realized that the community of users has named totally new realities. Congregation "officers" are now the ones who stand as foreigners who do not understand the language they claim to judge. Before judging anything, one must first look up the definition. Recognizing the existence of this new meaning does not result in a general blessing of all uses of gayspeak. Each speaker does make a subjective use of the language in the given circumstances of his life and, in so doing, may speak correctly or incorrectly. We are back to the issue of enouncing moral criteria for a fruitful homosexual use of the sexual langauge as I indicated in my second point.

Until the Congregation substantially modifies its anthropological and ethical model for dealing with human sexual gestures, its chances of having any kind of impact on the Christian community's sexual discernments will continue to decrease. The language of the letter is like classical Greek or Latin: a dead language which expresses another cultural world. It cannot adequately express ours because no living community of users actually understands our world with this language. As long as the Congregation focuses on mechanically regulating the use of "homosexual acts" rather than on discerning the humanizing and dehumanizing uses of "gay speech," it will be talking for "outsiders," for people who are not actively engaged in making sense of the world as we know it today.

Notes

1. J. Barr, *Fundamentalism* (London: SCM Press, 1977).

2. "The Transmission of Divine Revelation," in H. Vorgrimler, ed., *Commentary on the Documents of Vatican II* (New York: Herder and Herder, 1969), vol. 3, p. 197.

3. *The Sexual Langauge: An Essay in Moral Theology* (Ottawa: The University of Ottawa Press, 1976).

4. See, e.g., B. Häring, *Free and Faithful in Christ* (New York: Seabury, 1979), vol. 2, pp. 492–571; J. B. Nelson, *Between Two Gardens: Reflections on Sexuality and Religious Experience* (New York: Pilgrim, 1983), pp. 32–34.

5. "Closing Statement: Linguistic and Poetics," in *Style in Language* (Cambridge: MIT Press, 1960), pp. 350–77. See also, on the issue of the validity claims of genuine communication, J. Habermas, *Communication and the Evolution of Society* (Boston: Beacon Press, 1979), pp. 1–68.

6. See the summary presentation in R. Brown and R. J. Herrnstein, *Psychology* (Boston: Little, Brown, 1975), pp. 441–81. See the pioneering work of Noam Chomsky on "generative-transformation grammar," particularly in *Syntactic Structures* (The Hague: Mouton, 1957) and *Aspects of the Theory of Syntax* (Cambridge: MIT Press, 1965).

7. See L. Dewart, *Religions, Language and Truth* (New York: Herder and Herder, 1970), especially pp. 37–44.

8. See P. Lieberman, *The Biology and Evolution of Language* (Cambridge: Harvard University Press, 1984).

9. J. Ladrière, *L'Articulation du sens*, vol. 2, *Les Langages de la foi* (Paris: Cerf, 1984), pp. 94–100, talks about a "structuring horizon."

10. *Le Langage théologique à l'âge de la science* (Paris: Cerf, 1985), p. 84. See, on the mythical notion of a creator-word prenaming all human realities and leaving no linguistic initiative to the creature-word, G. Gusdorf, *Speaking* (Evanston: Northwestern University Press, 1965).

11. *Language in Thought and Action* (New York: Harcourt, Brace and World, 1978), p. 54.

12. See, e.g., D. Morris, *Manwatching: A Field Guide to Human Behavior* (New York: H. N. Abrams, 1977); P. Ekman, ed., *Emotions in the Human Face* (New York: Cambridge University Press, 1982).

13. See, W. Wickler, *The Sexual Code: The Social Behavior of Animals and Men* (Garden City: Doubleday, 1972);

14. *The Sexual Creators: An Ethical Proposal for Concerned Christians* (Lanham: University Press of America, 1986). Chapter 7 examines some aspects of gay speech, pp. 159–204.

15. *Christianity, Social Tolerance, and Homosexuality: Gay People in Western Europe from the Beginning of the Christian Era to the Fourteenth Century* (Chicago: University of Chicago Press, 1980).

16. M. Goodich, *The Unmentionable Vice: Homosexuality in the Later Medieval Period* (Santa Barbara: ABC-Clio, 1979).

25

How the Church Can Learn from Gay and Lesbian Experience

J. Giles Milhaven

The Catholic Church has at present no sexual ethics. The recent Vatican letter on the pastoral care of homosexual persons illustrates the confusion. On the homosexual issue, as on many other issues of sexual morality, the Vatican teaches and commands the opposite of what a large proportion of pastors encourage, theologians teach, and ordinary Catholics in good conscience do.

Catholics who agree with the Vatican on one issue are likely to deliberately ignore it on another (e.g., contraceptives or masturbation). Liberals for whom pope and bishops have lost all credibility on sexual issues divide among themselves, for example, on the "goodness" of homosexual love or on the value of celibacy and "sexuality without sex." There is scarcely a single moral issue involving sex on which there is a consensus among Catholics.

The confusion in the Church on practically any particular moral question of sex has a cause. There is no consensus on what sex in general is about. The Catholic people of God have no communal answer to the question, "Why is sex important?"[1] They have no answer because for fifty years a massive battle has raged undecided in the Church. We live in an epoch when new moral stances steadily replace old ones as experience gets scrutinized more honestly. Witness new, accepted positions in principle on racial equality and equality of gender. On sexual morality, the issue has been joined in the Church for half a century now. Will the official teaching of the Church become true to the sexual experience of Catholics? Will the statements of pope and bishops correspond to what people feel and know in making love?

Experience gained ground for a while. *Casti Connubii,* for example, and, more amply, Vatican II, affirmed what the supreme magisterium of the Church had never before affirmed: the experience of sex could and

216

should be in itself an awareness of love. The fathers of the Council had listened to the testimony of married people and chose their words accordingly. Pope and bishops have chosen, since that time, not to listen further to the sexual experience of Catholics.

The Vatican letter on homosexuality is a tragically perfect example. The Vatican does not misinterpret sexual experience. It ignores it. It makes its judgments on the nature and value of sex without a single reasoned appeal to the experience of sex. The magisterium's reluctance to learn from experience is curious, for pope and bishops continue to follow Vatican II in breaking with millennial Catholic tradition and affirming stoutly the interpersonal quality and high intrinsic value of what happens consciously in loving sex. To evaluate something conscious, why not consult people conscious of it? Why not listen to married people, for example, on their experience of sex with and without contraceptives? If sex is by nature and intrinsic worth a consciously interpersonal happening, why not consult Catholics, married or unmarried, on what happens when they have sex that they judge to be good and worthwhile?

*   *   *

We theologians have listened more than pope and bishops have to the real experience of sex. But not much more. We need to.[2] As a theologian, therefore, I have a question for Catholic lesbians and gays. I ask it respectfully, hopefully. They can help me and other Catholic theologians to forge a sexual ethics true to Catholic faith and human experience. By answering the question they could help the Vatican issue sounder pastoral guidelines than it has done and continues to do. The present chapter is an attempt to make my question as clear as I can.[3]

The question I ask Catholic lesbians and gays is: Why is sex important for you? I ask it, in fact, not only of Catholics but of any Christian who is both actively Christian and actively lesbian or gay. I ask it of any who declare themselves and conduct themselves as members of a Christian Church, yet live a sexual life condemned by their Church. These people stay active in their Church. They stay actively lesbian or gay. A tension persists in their lives. For some the tension is great. For others the tension is much less, but real and unrelenting. Despite the tension, these men and women experience it worthwhile to maintain both their life in their Church and their homosexual life.

Other gays and lesbians find the tension too much. Some choose an actively homosexual life and leave the Church. They leave the Church either by explicit intent or by gradually ceasing to participate in the activities of the Church. Others choose to stay active in the Church, and refrain, or keep trying to refrain, from homosexual behavior.

I ask my question of gays and lesbians who choose to stay both active Christians and active homosexuals. They experience their sexual activity to be worth disobeying their Church. They experience their sexual activity to be worth having to endure over and over being condemned by their Church for this activity. They must experience the sexual dimension of their life to be very important.

Another theologian might be caught by their loyalty to the Church. What can they see in the Church worth staying in it despite its contempt for their sexual lives? Why is the Church so important in their experience? A valid, promising question. I, however, am drawn to the other pole of their tension. What can they see in their sexual lives to be worth carrying on in the face of the mortal accusations made against them by the Church they respect and love? Why is this sexual life so important to them?

One can, of course, turn the question onto the accusing Church. Having seen again Pasolini's film *The Gospel according to Saint Matthew*, I feel like crying out in anger to the Catholic hierarchy as Jesus to the Pharisees: "You, Pope, cardinals, bishops, pastors who repeatedly condemn homosexual behavior, why do you bind heavy burdens and lay them on people's shoulders? Why will you not lift a finger to remove them? Why is their sexual life so important to you?

"Accepted principles of moral theology and of scriptural exegesis provide no decisive argument against homosexual living. This is shown by the fact that the condemning theologians disagree among themselves on the grounds for condemning. Why then do you lay the burden on sincere Catholics to keep trying to avoid any homosexual act? Why is it so important to you to prohibit and condemn, when you cannot be sure the act is wrong? Why is sex so important you?"

I have on other occasions urged this question on Catholics who condemn homosexual behavior and might be listening to or reading my words.[4] The hopeless mental torture undergone by some Catholic gays and lesbians because of their respect for church authority haunts me like images of Buchenwald and Dachau.

*   *   *

I ask my question now, not of the condemners, but of actively lesbian or gay Christians. Somehow I sense I can learn from them. I have noted a curious fact of my work as Christian ethicist. When I write or speak about matters other than homosexuality, I often invoke or appeal to homosexual experience. I use gay or lesbian experience to illustrate a point as I work into some problem of heterosexual morality, for example, divorce and remarriage, or some question concerning sexuality in general. More curious: I use gay or lesbian experience to illustrate a point concerning some problem of human values that does not involve sexuality at all; for example, what intrinsic value anger can have, or what characterizes an interpersonal relation.[5]

My turning to gay or lesbian experience to help me with ethical problems that have nothing to do with homosexuality as such is unplanned, unreflective, spontaneous. I am not clear why I do it. One thing that draws my intellect instinctively is the gaiety, the happiness, of certain Catholic homosexuals I know. These men and women are happy in their sex life as in their church life. The peace and joy of their lives as a whole suggest to me that the basic lines of their life must be moved by a spirit of goodness and be humanly worthy and worthwhile.[6] The homosexual current of their life radiates peace and joy to the rest of their life. This is all the more evident in long relationships. A well-known peculiarity of sex is that, as the sexual relationship goes on over the years, having sex is less important in itself and more in its coloring and suffusing the whole relationship.

Pervasive peace and joy here betokens wisdom. The great Greek and Christian philosophers claimed that only the wise and virtuous lead happy lives. Happiness is a sign of wisdom. Surely a Christian ethicist can learn from these people. So I put my question to them.

I know well a mature, well-developed, serene person. She is an extraordinarily active Catholic. She is at the moment looking for a loving, committed lesbian relationship, like ones she has had in the past. I want to ask her: Why is it so important that the relationshiap be sexual? You take the official teaching of your Church seriously. Why not follow it? The hierarchy, the official teachers of your Church, declare that your "homosexual orientation" is not sinful as long as you do not act on it. It encourages you to look for a loving committed relationship as long as it is without sex. I know you have warm friendships with a number of women and men. Why is it important that you have one that is also sexual?

I sense that my friend is right. I believe that a fully sexual relationship would not only be good for her. It is *important* that she have it. Why? I want to learn from her. But what I want to learn from her is not something particularly about homosexuality. Her wisdom seems broader and deeper than that. The roots of her wisdom go far enough down that insight can move up from them into other places.

I ask a parallel question of another gay friend. My sense here is similar, but not as strong. He, too, is Catholic and takes seriously his Church. The sexual relationships he has or looks for are simultaneously multiple, relatively uncommitted. I have no inclination to criticize morally such relationships nor even to inquire ethically about them. Neither am I convinced that he is right in having them. I just feel ignorant. But I know my friend well enough to sense there must be some genuine human good in these promiscuous experiences. I don't see clearly what that good is. It is out of ignorance, and out of this obscure hope to learn from his experience something that will illuminate heterosexual and nonsexual issues, that I ask him: Why is it important for you to have these relationships? You, too, have good relationships with a number of women and men. Why is it important that you have some that are sexual?

*　*　*

Understand my question. I am not asking my two friends or other Catholic gays and lesbians to justify their sexual activity. It is none of my business. I see no sign that I could help them in doing so. Nor that they need help. Nor that they would help me by justifying their homosexual living. The kind of question I am wrestling with when their experience comes to my mind is not a question of justifying anything. It is a question of "importance."

Of course the fact that something is important to someone does not justify it. To find out what the chair of my department really thinks of me may be important to me. But if the only way of finding out is to break into his office and read carbons of his private memos and correspondence, I am not justified in doing so.

On the other hand, it is only after I learnt how important it is for certain groups to be treated in this or that particular way that I was able to reason to particular rights of theirs. By this route I came to recognize the right of blacks at my university to make up a certain proportion of the faculty, administration, and student body. I came similarly to see the right of single parents in my city to have larger welfare checks and child care assistance.

Catholic theologians are only beginning to recognize that there is a number of different kinds of couples who out of their personal lives make the same point to the teaching Church. They say to the Church: sex is important for the two of us. You do not take its importance into account in your teaching. You must not know of it.

Even if we consider only couples who love each other, live together, and are committed to loving and living with each other, we can think of six different, commonplace situations where the importance of sex for the couple challenges the traditional prohibition of sex: couples of the same sex; couples of different sex where one is married to someone else; where one is bound by vows of celibacy; where both are completely free to marry but are not yet ready for a lifelong commitment; where they are married to each other but should not have more children and rhythm does not work; where they are married to each other but because of a physical condition of one of them can have sex only by mutual masturbation.

Because sex became important for these couples, they raise the question: Is it justified though the Church prohibits it? Theologians cannot reason to an answer without first understanding the experience of importance that raises and urges the question. I use, without defining, the word *importance* because I believe most of the couples would or could easily use it. The word fits their experience. It fits their experience better, I submit, than words favored by ethicists like good or beautiful or meaningful or necessary.

I repeat: that sex is important for someone does not automatically justify it. If it did, rape could be justified. Or sex entered into simply to gain power over someone. I personally cannot imagine circumstances where a well-married person, like myself, would be justified in having a sexual relationship outside marriage, however important that relationship might be to him or her. On the other hand, I imagine easily circumstances where a divorced person is justified in entering a sexual relationship because the relationship is so important to her or him and the likely harm and hurt to others are minor.

The word *important*, I submit, expresses well the experience, the starting point, that leads active Christians to go on and, with further reasoning and reflection, justify and adopt sexual behavior condemned officially by their Church. These Christians may not need to articulate in explicit concepts why sex is important for them. Nor how they reason from its importance to its being justified. Their personal maturity, urgent love, intuitive intelligence, and good sense may suffice for sound judgment. Aristotle, Thomas Aquinas, and other seasoned moralists trust the spontaneous, intuitive judgment of the engaged, virtuous person.

But we theologians, before any ethical reasoning, need to articulate conceptually why these persons experience sex as important in leading the good lives they lead. The task of the moral theologian is to help the

J. GILES MILHAVEN

rest of the Church by drawing with broad conceptual strokes a model of the moral life. Gay and lesbian Catholics could help the theologian by doing what they themselves (unless they are also theologians) don't need to do: put into general terms why sex is important for them. Perhaps because our culture still massively disapproves of lesbian and gay sex, homosexual couples, more squarely than the five other kinds of couples I listed, face the importance of sex for them.

Notes

1. Cf. my "Sex and Love and Marriage and Love and Sex," *National Catholic Reporter*, 13 and 20 January 1978. This title is the editor's; mine was and is: "How Important is Sex?" In this article I started an answer to the question, but the truest words are the final ones: "I have tried to say something to this question. Much more needs to be said."

2. André Guindon says it well in his *The Sexual Creators: An Ethical Proposal for Concerned Christians* (Washington, DC: University Press of America, 1986), pp. 12–13:

> The ethicist is one who reflects on the experience of those men and women who seek to make sense of their sexual life. Ethics can be neither taught nor learned like mathematics or physics. It presupposes a lived experience, immediate and eventful grasp of moral values, without which all ethical discourse is meaningless and ineffective. It is against the very nature of the good to be known without being experienced. No one knows the good and values it if one does not "live" it. Listening attentively and with empathy to the community of purposeful men and women living sexual lives, the ethicist articulates the meaning inherent in the experience, proposes a sexual anthropology which, while passing the test of scientific knowledge, is in line with this meaning, and, from these premises, works out, without ever losing touch with the sexual experience and its scientific analysis, a coherent sexual ethic.

Welcome advances in methodically drawing on experience of sex in forming a Christian sexual ethics are this book of Guindon and Lisa Sowle Cahill's *Between the Sexes: Foundations for a Christian Ethics of Sexuality* (Philadelphia: Fortress, 1985). It is surely no coincidence that both works are more open to positive values in homosexual love than most previous Catholic moral theologies. Guindon is more affirmative of homosexual relationships in his chapter, "Gay Fecundity or Liberating Sexuality," than he was in his earlier *The Sexual Language: An Essay in Moral Theology* (University of Ottawa Press, 1976).

3. I formulated the question first for gay and lesbian Catholics of the Consultation on Homosexuality, Social Justice, and Roman Catholic Theology. Their responses challenged and aided me to work my question out further in the present essay.

4. Cf. my reviews of John J. McNeill, S.J., *The Church and the Homosexual*, in *National Catholic Reporter*, 8 October 1976, p. 12, and *Washington Post World*,

12 September 1976, p. H3, and of *Human Sexuality: New Directions in American Catholic Thought* by Anthony Kosnik et al., in *National Catholic Reporter*, 17 June 1977, pp. 7–9.

5. Influencing me on heterosexual and nonsexual issues have been erotic lesbian poems of Adrienne Rich, Susan Griffin, Judy Grahn, and Audre Lorde. Nothing recently has expanded and intensified my sense of interpersonal values as much as S. Griffin, *Pornography and Silence* (New York: Harper and Row, 1981) and the superb essay of A. Lorde, "Uses of the Erotic; the Erotic as Power," *Sister Outsider* (Trumansburg, NY: Crossing Press, 1984), pp. 53–59.

6. Charles Curran has invoked the "traditionally accepted notion that joy and peace mark the good conscience which is the adequate criterion of good moral judgment and decision" (*Themes in Fundamental Moral Theology* [University of Notre Dame Press, 1977], p. 220; similarly P. S. Keane, "Discernment of Spirits: A Theological Reflection," *American Ecclesiastical Review* 168 [1974]: 43–61). To my knowledge, no such tradition has existed in the public moral theology of the Roman Catholic Church. Let us start the tradition now, though I would change "the adequate criterion" to "one strong indication."

Ignatius of Loyola never applied his rules of discernment of spirits to help determine the goodness of behavior condemned by church authority. But the logic and psychology of his rules support such an application, as I argued in an essay that the four readers of *Theological Studies* advised strongly against publishing there. Cf. Ignatius of Loyola, *Spiritual Exercises,* nos. 169–88, 328–36; K. Rahner, "The Logic of Concrete Individual Knowledge," *The Dynamic Element in the Church* (New York: Herder and Herder, 1964), pp. 84–170.

Contributors

Benedict M. Ashley is Professor of Moral Theology and Spirituality at the Aquinas Institute of Theology in St. Louis, Missouri.

John Coleman is Professor of Religion and Society at the Jesuit School of Theology and the Graduate Union in Berkeley, California.

Robert Francoeur is Professor of Biological and Allied Health Sciences at Fairleigh Dickinson University in Madison, New Jersey.

Pat Furey is a Catholic educator who for professional reasons has chosen to employ a pseudonym.

Jeannine Gramick is co-founder of New Ways Ministry and an advocate for lesbian and gay Catholics.

Dan Grippo is director of marketing and advertising for the *National Catholic Reporter*.

André Guindon is Professor of Moral Theology at St. Paul's University in Ottawa.

Peter E. B. Harris is an educator and former chair of Quest, a British organization for homosexual Catholics.

Rosemary Haughton is an extensive lecturer and author of thirty-five books.

Peter Hebblethwaite is a Vaticanologist, biographer, and correspondent for Catholic journals and newspapers.

Lillanna Kopp is a sociologist-anthropologist who lectures and writes about Catholic Church structures.

225

J. Giles Milhaven is Professor of Religious Studies at Brown University in Providence, Rhode Island.

Ronald Modras is an Associate Professor of Theological Studies at St. Louis University.

Robert Nugent is a lecturer and author on homosexuality and Catholicism and co-founder of New Ways Ministry.

Carolyn Osiek is Professor of New Testament at Catholic Theological Union in Chicago.

James R. Pollock is an Associate Professor of Theological Studies at St. Louis University.

John R. Quinn is Archbishop of San Francisco.

Mary C. Segers is an Associate Professor of Political Science at Rutgers University.

William H. Shannon is Professor Emeritus at Nazareth College in Rochester, New York.

Sarah M. Sherman is a former Executive Director of the National Sisters Vocation Conference.

Margaret Susan Thompson is an Associate Professor of History at Syracuse University.

Joan H. Timmerman is Professor of Theology at the College of St. Catherine in St. Paul, Minnesota.

Margaret Ellen Traxler is Director of the Institute of Women Today.

P. A. van Gennip is General Secretary of the Catholic Council for Church and Society, an agency of the Roman Catholic hierarchy of the Netherlands.

Ann Patrick Ware works in justice and peace areas for Church Women United.

Mary Jo Weaver is Professor of Religious Studies at Indiana University.